Exploring Future Opportunities of Brain-Inspired Artificial Intelligence

Madhulika Bhatia
Amity University, India

Tanupriya Choudhury
University of Petroleum and Energy Studies, India

Bhupesh Kumar Dewangan
School of Engineering, Department of Computer Science and Engineering, O.P. Jindal University, India

A volume in the Advances in
Computational Intelligence and
Robotics (ACIR) Book Series

Published in the United States of America by
    IGI Global
    Engineering Science Reference (an imprint of IGI Global)
    701 E. Chocolate Avenue
    Hershey PA, USA 17033
    Tel: 717-533-8845
    Fax: 717-533-8661
    E-mail: cust@igi-global.com
    Web site: http://www.igi-global.com

Library of Congress Cataloging-in-Publication Data

Names: Choudhury, Tanupriya, editor. | Bhatia, Madhulika, 1984- editor. |
  Dewangan, Bhupesh, 1983- editor.
Title: Exploring future opportunities of brain-inspired artificial
  intelligence / edited by Tanupriya Choudhury, Madhulika Bhatia, Bhupesh
  Dewangan.
Description: Hershey, PA : Engineering Science Reference, [2023] | Includes
  bibliographical references and index. | Summary: "Our Book mainly focus
  on convergence of artificial intelligence with Brain inspired
  intelligence. Applications of Artificial Intelligence in Brain
  simulation are countless. Brain simulation , recording and analysis of
  Brain signals and applying AI in it will be accommodating all domain of
  Artificial Intelligence and Brain Intelligence and how it can be related
  and utilized for many applications. The book will provide rich content
  for researchers and Scholars to explore new dimensions that can be
  implemented"-- Provided by publisher.
Identifiers: LCCN 2022049364 (print) | LCCN 2022049365 (ebook) | ISBN
  9781668469804 (hardcover) | ISBN 9781668469811 (paperback) | ISBN
  9781668469828 (ebook)
Subjects: LCSH: Neurosciences--Data processing. | Computational
  neuroscience. | Artificial intelligence. | Soft computing.
Classification: LCC QP357.5 .E97 2023 (print) | LCC QP357.5 (ebook) | DDC
  612.80285/63--dc23/eng/20221215
LC record available at https://lccn.loc.gov/2022049364
LC ebook record available at https://lccn.loc.gov/2022049365

This book is published in the IGI Global book series Advances in Computational Intelligence and Robotics (ACIR) (ISSN: 2327-0411; eISSN: 2327-042X)

British Cataloguing in Publication Data
A Cataloguing in Publication record for this book is available from the British Library.

For electronic access to this publication, please contact: eresources@igi-global.com.

Advances in Computational Intelligence and Robotics (ACIR) Book Series

ISSN:2327-0411
EISSN:2327-042X

Editor-in-Chief: Ivan Giannoccaro University of Salento, Italy

MISSION

While intelligence is traditionally a term applied to humans and human cognition, technology has progressed in such a way to allow for the development of intelligent systems able to simulate many human traits. With this new era of simulated and artificial intelligence, much research is needed in order to continue to advance the field and also to evaluate the ethical and societal concerns of the existence of artificial life and machine learning.

The **Advances in Computational Intelligence and Robotics (ACIR) Book Series** encourages scholarly discourse on all topics pertaining to evolutionary computing, artificial life, computational intelligence, machine learning, and robotics. ACIR presents the latest research being conducted on diverse topics in intelligence technologies with the goal of advancing knowledge and applications in this rapidly evolving field.

COVERAGE

- Adaptive and Complex Systems
- Pattern Recognition
- Intelligent Control
- Computational Intelligence
- Evolutionary Computing
- Artificial Intelligence
- Fuzzy Systems
- Brain Simulation
- Natural Language Processing
- Synthetic Emotions

IGI Global is currently accepting manuscripts for publication within this series. To submit a proposal for a volume in this series, please contact our Acquisition Editors at Acquisitions@igi-global.com or visit: http://www.igi-global.com/publish/.

Titles in this Series

For a list of additional titles in this series, please visit:
www.igi-global.com/book-series/advances-computational-intelligence-robotics/73674

Developments in Artificial Intelligence Creativity and Innovation
Ziska Fields (University of Johannesburg, South Africa)
Engineering Science Reference • © 2023 • 300pp • H/C (ISBN: 9781668462706) • US $270.00

Applying AI-Based IoT Systems to Simulation-Based Information Retrieval
Bhatia Madhulika (Amity University, India) Bhatia Surabhi (King Faisal University, Saudi Arabia) Poonam Tanwar (Manav Rachna International Institute of Research and Studies, India) and Kuljeet Kaur (Université du Québec, Canada)
Engineering Science Reference • © 2023 • 300pp • H/C (ISBN: 9781668452554) • US $270.00

Handbook of Research on Applications of AI, Digital Twin, and Internet of Things for Sustainable Development
Brojo Kishore Mishra (GIET University, India)
Engineering Science Reference • © 2023 • 538pp • H/C (ISBN: 9781668468210) • US $325.00

Applied AI and Multimedia Technologies for Smart Manufacturing and CPS Applications
Emmanuel Oyekanlu (Drexel University, USA)
Engineering Science Reference • © 2023 • 300pp • H/C (ISBN: 9781799878520) • US $270.00

Constraint Decision-Making Systems in Engineering
Santosh Kumar Das (Sarala Birla University, Ranchi, India) and Nilanjan Dey (Techno International New Town, Kolkata, India)
Engineering Science Reference • © 2023 • 312pp • H/C (ISBN: 9781668473436) • US $270.00

For an entire list of titles in this series, please visit:
www.igi-global.com/book-series/advances-computational-intelligence-robotics/73674

701 East Chocolate Avenue, Hershey, PA 17033, USA
Tel: 717-533-8845 x100 • Fax: 717-533-8661
E-Mail: cust@igi-global.com • www.igi-global.com

Table of Contents

Detailed Table of Contents

    Princy Diwan, Department of Computer Science and Engineering, O.P.
        Jindal University, India
    Bhupesh Kumar Dewangan, Department of Computer Science and
        Engineering, O.P. Jindal University, India

The domains of artificial intelligence and machine learning continue to advance at a rapid speed in terms of algorithms, models, applications, and hardware thanks to an exponential increase in the amount of data collected on a daily basis. Deep neural networks have transformed these domains by achieving extraordinary human-like performance in various real-world challenges, such as picture or speech recognition. There is also a lot of effort going on to figure out the principles of computation in extensive biological neural networks, especially biologically plausible spiking neural networks. Neural-inspired algorithms (e.g., deep ANNs and deep RL) and brain intelligent systems have revolutionized the fields of machine learning and cognitive computing in the last decade, assisting in a variety of real-world learning tasks ranging from robot monitoring and interaction at home to complex decision-making about emotions and behaviors in humans and animals. While these brain-inspired algorithms and systems have made significant progress, they still require large data sets to train, and their outcomes lack the flexibility to adapt to a variety of learning tasks and provide long-term performance. To solve these issues, an analytical understanding of the concepts that allow brain-inspired intelligent systems to develop information, as well as how they might be translated to hardware for everyday help and practical applications, is required. This chapter focuses upon the applications, challenges, and solutions of brain-inspired computing for daily assistance.

The field of neuroscience explains how the neural networks in the brain work together to perform a variety of tasks, including pattern recognition, relative memory, object recognition, and more. The mental activity that makes different jobs possible is difficult to understand. Understanding the various patterns present in natural neural networks requires a combination of artificial intelligence and neuroscience, which requires less computation. As a result, it is possible to understand a large number of brain reactions in relation to the activity that each person is engaged in. Human brain neurons need to be trained by experience in order to perform activities like moving the hands, arms, and legs while also considering how to respond to each activity. In the past 10 years, artificial intelligence (AI), with its potential to uncover patterns in vast, complex data sets, has made amazing strides, in part by emulating how the brain does particular computations. This chapter reviews the replication of neuroscience via AI in a real-time scenario.

Deep learning is becoming increasingly important in our everyday lives. It has already made a big difference in industries like cancer diagnosis, precision medicine, self-driving cars, predictive forecasting, and speech recognition, to name a few. Traditional learning, classification, and pattern recognition methods necessitate feature extractors that aren't scalable for large datasets. Depending on the issue complexity, deep learning can often overcome the limitations of past shallow networks that hampered fast training and abstractions of hierarchical representations of multi-dimensional training data. Deep learning techniques have been applied successfully to vegetable infection by plant disease, demonstrating their suitability for the agriculture sector. The chapter looks at a few optimization approaches for increasing training accuracy and decreasing training time. The authors delve into the mathematics that underpin recent deep network training methods. Current faults, improvements, and implementations are discussed. The authors explore various popular deep learning architecture and their real-world uses in this chapter. Deep learning algorithms are increasingly being used in place of traditional techniques in many machine vision applications. Benefits include avoiding the requirement for specific handcrafted feature extractors and maintaining the integrity of the output. Additionally, they frequently grow better. The review discusses deep convolutional networks, deep residual networks, recurrent neural networks, reinforcement learning, variational autoencoders, and other deep architectures.

Chapter 4
Madhulika Bhadauria, Amity University, India
Rishita Khurana, Amity University, India
Supavadee Aramvith, Chulalongkorn University, Thailand

Super-resolution reconstruction creates one or more high-resolution images from a collection of low-resolution frames. This chapter examines a number of super-resolution methods proposed over the last two decades and provides an overview of the contributions made recently to the broad super-resolution problem. During the procedure, a thorough examination of numerous crucial elements of super-resolution is presented, which are frequently overlooked in the literature. The authors have also outlined various advancements and studies that have been done in the particular domain. The prime focus of this chapter is to highlight the importance and application of super resolution in brain MRI and explore all the work that has been done in the field so far. The experiments on simulated and actual data are used to support novel strategies for tackling the difficulties faced while implementing the technique. Finally, several prospective super-resolution difficulties are identified, and methodologies are presented.

Chapter 5
Vania Karami, University of Camerino, Italy
Giulio Nittari, University of Camerino, Italy
Sara Karami, New York Institute of Technology, Canada
Seyed Massood Nabavi, Royan Institute, Iran

Dementia is one of the major issues in public health all over the world. Alzheimer's disease (AD) is its most common and famous form. Late detection of AD has irreparable effects for the people suffering from it. Cognitive assessment tests are the conventional approach to detect AD. They are quick to do, and not costly. However, they have low predictive values. Therefore, other ways such as magnetic resonance imaging (MRI) are used. Recently, advances in computer-aided diagnosis system (CADS) using MRI have provided useful information in the quantitative evaluation of AD at an early stage. Although it cannot be substituted with the doctors, but it helps. Many algorithms for CADS were presented, which means CADS is one of the growing techniques in this field. Because there is no standardized approach to determine the best one, it is essential to be familiar with general approaches to design a CADS. This chapter deals with a general approach for design and develop a reliable CADS using biomarkers extracted from MRI. The advancement of using CAS and MRI for AD are discussed.

There is significant interest in the development and implementation of smart and intelligent ambient assisted living (AAL) systems that can give daily support to help older people live independently in their homes. Additionally, such systems will lower the expense of healthcare that governments must bear in order to provide support for this group of residents. It also relieves families of the burden of constant and often tedious round-the-clock surveillance of these individuals, allowing them to focus on their own lives and commitments. As a result, recognition, classification, and decision-making for such people's daily activities are critical for the development of appropriate and successful intelligent support systems capable of providing the essential assistance in the correct manner and at the right time.

Brain-based artificial intelligence has been a popular topic. Applications include military and defense, intelligent manufacturing, business intelligence and management, medical service and healthcare, and others. In order to strengthen their national interests and capacities in the global marketplace, many countries have started national brain-related projects. Numerous difficulties in brain-inspired computing and computation based on spiking-neural-networks, as well as various concepts, principles, and emerging technologies in brain science and brain-inspired artificial intelligence, are discussed in this chapter (SNNs). The advances and trends section covers topics such as brain-inspired computing, neuromorphic computing systems, and multi-scale brain simulation, as well as the brain association graph, brainnetome, connectome, brain imaging, brain-inspired chips and devices, brain-computer interface (BCI) and brain-machine interface (BMI), brain-inspired robotics and applications, quantum robots, and cyborgs (human-machine hybrids).

Chapter 8

  Bikram Pratim Bhuyan, University of Petroleum and Energy Studies, India

Knowledge is an essential ingredient for the development of the majority of human cognitive skills. The subject of how to define knowledge is a challenging one. Knowledge is an organised collection of information that may be acquired by learning, perception, or the application of reasoning. This chapter focuses on human brains and computer knowledge models. Concepts and categories are offered as a paradigm for storing information, followed by semantic networks and a description of how individuals store and interpret information. The authors also explore artificial methods to store and retrieve information and make quick judgments, as well as biological features. After studying how information is stored and accessed in artificial and human systems, they analyse hemisphere specialisation. This chapter reviews trials that have advanced research in this area and examines if they interpret information differently.

Chapter 9

  Shiddarth Srivastava, Ajay Kumar Garg Engineering College, India
  Rashmi Sharma, Ajay Kumar Garg Engineering College, India

The ability to draw conclusions and take action from data hasn't altered all that much despite significant technological developments in recent years. Applications are still typically created to carry out predefined tasks or automate business procedures; therefore, the logic must be coded to account for all possible usage scenarios. They do not grow from their mistakes or adjust to changes in the data. Although they are cheaper and faster, computers aren't substantially smarter. Of course, people now aren't all that much brighter than they were in the past. For both humans and machines, that is about to change. The old notion of computing as process automation is being replaced by a new generation of information systems that offer a collaborative platform for discovery. These systems' initial wave has already improved human cognition in a number of areas.

Chapter 10

  Rishabh Chauhan, Amity University, India
  Garima Aggarwal, Amity University, India

Brain tumor is a common tumor and is damaging depending upon the type of tumor and the stage at which it is diagnosed. It is revealed by a doctor using magnetic resonance imaging of the brain. Analyzing these images is an exacting task, and human intervention might be a scope of error. Therefore, applying deep learning-based image classification systems can play a crucial role in classifying several tumors. This chapter aims to implement, analyze, and compare pre-trained convolutional neural network models and a proposed neural architecture to classify brain tumors. The dataset includes 7000 images classified into four classes of tumors: glioma, meningioma, no tumor, and pituitary. The proposed methodology involves cautious analysis of data and the development of a deep learning model. This has produced testing results with high accuracy of 99.0% and an error rate of 6.8%. According to the experimental findings, the proposed method for classifying brain tumors has a respectable level of accuracy and a low error rate, making it an appropriate tool for use in real-time applications.

Preface

In the field of machine learning and cognitive computing have been in the last decade revolutionized with neural-inspired algorithms (e.g., deep ANNs and deep RL) and brain-intelligent systems that assist in many real-world learning tasks from robot monitoring and interaction at home to complex decision-making about emotions and behaviors in humans and animals. While there are remarkable advances in these brain-inspired algorithms and systems, they need to be trained with huge data sets, and their results lack ñexibility to adapt to diverse learning tasks and sustainable performance over long periods of time. To address these challenges, it is essential to gain an analytical understanding of the principles that allow biological inspired intelligent systems to leverage knowledge and how they can be translated to hardware for daily assistance and practical applications.

Brain-inspired intelligence is an effort of the cognitive brain modelling is to simulate the cognitive brain at various difference scales to understand know how of the brain working as well as developing brain-inspired intelligent systems. Applying mechanisms and principles of human intelligence and converging brain and AI is now a days in research trend. Decoding brain simulation efforts and applying principles of human intelligence and developing brain-inspired intelligent systems with the application of AI. The information processing system Brain-inspired intelligent systems will prove next generation information processing by applying theories, techniques, and applications inspired by the information processing principles from the brain. The purpose of this book is to provide readers a brain inspired cognitive machine with vision, audition, language processing, thinking capabilities. It has great potentials in the field of large-scale, multi-modal data and information processing and can be used for daily assistance. The book will include introducing science of brain. Moreover will give introduction to readers to the theory and algorithms of brain inspired intelligence, neural cognitive computing mechanisms. Accordingly, it will appeal to university researchers, R&D engineers, undergraduate and graduate students to anyone interested in neural network robots, brain cognition or computer vision; and to all those wishing to learn about the core theory, principles, methods, algorithms involved in applications of Brain Inspired convergence with AI.

A DESCRIPTION OF THE TARGET AUDIENCE

Our book mainly focuses on convergence of artificial intelligent with brain inspired intelligence. Applications of Artificial Intelligence in brain simulation are countless. Brain simulation, recording and analysis of brain signals and applying AI in it will be accommodating all domain of artificial intelligence and brain intelligence and how it can be related and utilised for many applications. The book will provide rich content for researchers and Scholars to explore new dimensions that can be implemented.

Target Audience

Primary Audience: Undergraduate, post graduate students; Ph.D and research scholars as well as faculty of various universities.

Secondary Audience: Any one part of scientific community or general readers who want to explore this topic.

OVERVIEW OF THE CHAPTERS

Application of Brain-Inspired Computing for Daily Assistance

The domains of artificial intelligence and machine learning continue to advance at a rapid speed in terms of algorithms, models, applications, and hardware, thanks to an exponential increase in the amount of data collected in daily basis. Deep neural networks have transformed these domains by achieving extraordinary human-like performance in a variety of real-world challenges, such as picture or speech recognition. There is also a lot of effort going on to figure out the principles of computation in big biological neural networks, especially biologically plausible spiking neural networks.

Visualizing Neuroscience Through AI: A Systematic Review

The field of neuroscience explains how the neural networks in the brain work together to perform a variety of tasks, including pattern recognition, relative memory, object recognition, and more. The mental activity that makes different jobs possible is difficult to understand. Understanding the various patterns present in natural neural networks requires a combination of artificial intelligence and neuroscience, which requires less computation. As a result, it is possible to understand a large number of brain reactions in relation to the activity that each person is engaged in. Human brain neurons need to be trained by experience in order to perform activities like moving the hands, arms, and legs while also considering how to respond to each activity. In the past ten years, artificial intelligence (AI), with its potential to uncover patterns in vast, complex data sets, has made amazing strides, in part by emulating how the brain does particular computations. This chapter reviews the replication of neuroscience via AI in real time scenario.

Study and Innovative Approach of Deep Learning Algorithms and Architecture

Deep learning is becoming increasingly important in our everyday lives. It has already made a big difference in industries like cancer diagnosis, precision medicine, self-driving cars, predictive forecasting, and speech recognition, to name a few. Traditional learning, classification, and pattern recognition methods necessitate feature extractors that aren't scalable for large datasets. Depending on the issue complexity, deep learning can often overcome the limitations of past shallow networks that hampered fast training and abstractions of hierarchical representations of multi-dimensional training data. Deep learning techniques have been applied successfully to vegetable infection by plant disease, demonstrating their suitability for the agriculture sector. The chapter looks at a few optimization approaches for increasing training accuracy and decreasing training time. We delve into the mathematics that underpins recent deep network training methods.

Enhancing Brain Imaging Using Super Resolution: Challenges and Benefits

Super-Resolution reconstruction creates one or more high-resolution images from a collection of low-resolution frames. This book chapter examines a number of Super-Resolution methods proposed over the last two decades and provides an overview of the contributions made recently to the broad Super-Resolution problem. During the procedure, a thorough examination of numerous crucial elements of Super-Resolution is presented, which are frequently overlooked in the literature. The authors have also outlined various advancements and researches that have been done in the particular domain. The prime focus of this chapter is to highlight the importance and application of Super Resolution in brain MRI and explore all the work that has been done in the field so far. The Experiments on simulated and actual data are used to support novel strategies for tackling the difficulties faced while implementing the technique. Finally, several prospective Super-Resolution difficulties are identified, and methodologies are presented.

Overview on Incorporating a Computer-Aided System for Dementia: Early Detection of Alzheimer's Disease

Dementia is one of the major issues in public health all over the world. Alzheimer's disease (AD) is its most common and famous form. Late detection of AD has irreparable effects for the people suffering from it. Cognitive assessment tests are the conventional approach to detect AD. They are quick to do, not costly. However, they have low predictive value. Therefore, other ways such as magnetic resonance imaging (MRI) are used. Recently, advances in computer aided system (CAS) using MRI have provided useful potential in the quantitative evaluation of AD at early stage. Although it cannot be substituted with the doctors but it helps to decide better. Many algorithms for CAS were presented that means CAS is one of the growing techniques in this field. Because there is no standardized approach to determine the best one, it is essential to be familiar with general approaches to design a CAS. This chapter deals with a general approach for design and develop a reliable CAS using biomarkers extracted from MRI. The advancement of using CAS and MRI for AD are discussed.

Ambient Assisted Living (AAL) Systems to Help Older People

There is significant interest in the development and implementation of smart and intelligent Ambient Assisted Living (AAL) systems that can give daily support to help older people live independently in their homes. Additionally, such systems will lower the expense of health care that governments must bear in order to provide support for this group of residents. It also relieves families of the burden of constant and often tedious round-the-clock surveillance of these individuals, allowing them to focus on their own lives and commitments. As a result, recognition, classification, and decision-making for such people's daily activities are critical for the development of appropriate and successful intelligent support systems capable of providing the essential assistance in the correct manner and at the right time.

Brain-Inspired AI to a Symbiosis of Human Intelligence and Artificial Intelligence

Brain-based artificial intelligence has been a popular topic. Among the applications include military and defense, intelligent manufacturing, business intelligence and management, medical service and healthcare, and others. In order to strengthen their national interests and capacities in the global marketplace, many countries have started national brain-related projects. Numerous difficulties in brain-inspired computing and computation based on spiking-neural-networks, as well as various concepts, principles, and emerging technologies in brain science and brain-inspired artificial intelligence, are discussed in this paper (SNNs). The advances and trends section covers topics such as brain-inspired computing, neuromorphic computing systems, and multi-scale brain simulation, as well as the brain association graph, brainnetome, and connectome, brain imaging, brain-inspired chips and devices, brain-computer interface (BCI) and brain-machine interface (BMI), brain-inspired robotics and applications, quantum robots, and cyborgs (human-machine hybrids).

Knowledge Representation-Based Hemispheric Specialization of the Brain

Knowledge is an essential ingredient for the development of the majority of human cognitive skills. The subject of how to define knowledge is a challenging one. Knowledge is an organised collection of information that may be acquired by learning, perception, or the application of reasoning. This chapter focuses on human brains and computer knowledge models. Concepts and categories are offered as a paradigm for storing information, followed by semantic networks and a description of how individuals store and interpret information. We'll also explore artificial methods to store and retrieve information and make quick judgments, as well as biological features. After studying how information is stored and accessed in artificial and human systems, we'll analyse hemisphere specialisation. This article reviews trials that have advanced research in this area and examines if they interpret information differently.

Data Analysis Tools for Neural Data Cognitive Computing: Neural-Inspired Algorithms

The ability to draw conclusions and take action from data hasn't altered all that much despite significant technological developments in recent years. Applications are still typically created to carry out predefined tasks or automate business procedures, therefore the logic must be coded to account for all possible usage scenarios. They do not grow from their mistakes or adjust to changes in the data. Although they are cheaper and faster, computers aren't substantially smarter.Of course, people now aren't all that brighter than they were in the past. For both humans and machines, that is about to change. The old notion of computing as process automation is being replaced by a new generation of information systems that offer a collaborative platform for discovery. These systems' initial wave has already improved human cognition in a number of areas.

Performance Analysis of Pre-Trained Convolutional Models for Brain Tumor Classification

Brain tumor is a common tumor and is damaging depending upon the type of tumor and the stage at which it is diagnosed. It is revealed by a doctor using Magnetic Resonance Imaging of the brain. Analyzing these images is an exacting task and human intervention might be a scope of error. Therefore, applying deep learning-based image classification systems can play a crucial role in classifying several tumors. This paper aims to implement, analyze, and compare pre-trained convolutional neural network models and a proposed neural architecture, to classify brain tumors. The dataset includes 7000 images classified into four classes of tumors: glioma, meningioma, no tumor, and pituitary. The proposed methodology involves cautious analysis of data and the development of a deep learning model. This has produced testing results with high accuracy of 99.0% and an error rate of 6.8%. According to the experimental findings, the proposed method for classifying brain tumors has a respectable level of accuracy and a low error rate, making it an appropriate tool for use in real-time applications.

CONCLUSION

The book will prove a great help for reference about various contribution done by authors. The subject of the book is really challenging and lot of research going on. This will help the scholars, students, and industry people to really get an idea of what are the various application and scientific work going on in this area of brain intelligence in confluence of AI.

1. Grip of the latest technology
2. A plot that is engaging.
3. Contribution about research done by scientific community

This book can also be useful for those who needs reference about various contribution done by many experts. The content of the book is really challenging and lot of research going on which will help readers to increase their knowledge about the topic. This will help the scholars, students, and industry people to really get an idea of what are the various application and scientific work going on in this area of driving how AI is deriving health sector and helping health practitioners to predict disease intensity and which in turn gives grip of the latest technology and give a wide plot which keeps the readers engaged.

Preface

Madhulika Bhatia
Amity University, India

Tanupriya Choudhury
University of Petroleum and Energy Studies, India

Bhupesh Kumar Dewangan
School of Engineering, Department of Computer Science and Engineering, O.P.
Jindal University, India

Introduction

INTRODUCTION

Investigating the workings of the individual mind is shaping up to be one of the biggest difficult and interesting technical problems of the 21st era. It will make the growth of many facets of civilization, such as the economy, academia, medical services, nationwide security, and day-to- day living, easier (Yang, S. *et al.*, 2018)

The concept of Artificial Intelligence (AI) refers to the process of recreating human intellect in computers by teaching them the same way in which human beings think and learn. It includes the construction of algorithms and computer programs that are able to execute activities that traditionally need human perception. A few examples of these functions are visual perception, voice recognition, decision-making, and language translation. There are diverse varieties of artificial intelligence, the most common of which being Regulation networks, professional structures, and network learning. Artificial intelligence has the ability to automate numerous processes and enhance productivity in a broad variety of sectors, including universal medical and finance to shipping and production, which may benefit from the increased efficiency and automation.

Brain-inspired artificial intelligence, also called neural computing, is a field of artificial intelligence research that tries to make systems and algorithms that look and work like the human brain (Wang, L. and Alexander, C.A., 2019)

The research of the brain, as well as the development of artificial intelligence, which is modeled after the human brain, have both emerged as more significant topics in recent years. Brain-inspired artificial intelligence (AI) has the potential to revolutionize a wide range of industries, by providing new and more powerful tools for solving complex problems and improving efficiency and effectiveness.

Table 1. Some of the keyways in which different industries can benefit from brain-inspired AI include

S.No.	Industry name	Description
1.	Healthcare	AI that is based on the brain can be used to look at a lot of medical data, like brain scans and patient records, to find patterns and correlations that can be used to better diagnose and treat diseases. It can also be used to develop new therapies, such as deep brain stimulation (DBS) and transcranial magnetic stimulation (TMS), for the treatment of conditions such as Parkinson's disease, depression, and chronic pain.
2.	Robotics	By replicating the way in which the human brain processes visual information, artificial intelligence (AI) that is inspired by the brain may be utilized to give robots the ability to navigate and interact with their surroundings in a more logical and time-saving manner. This may pave the way for the creation of more sophisticated and adaptable robots that are capable of tackling complicated and dynamic jobs such as manufacturing, transportation, and search and rescue operations.
3.	Autonomous vehicles	In order to make autonomous cars safer, more efficient, and more adaptive to changing situations, artificial intelligence that is persuaded by the brain may be employed to give them the ability to navigate and make choices based on the information they see. This might pave the way for the creation of vehicles that are more technologically sophisticated and flexible, such as robots, drones, and automobiles that drive themselves.
4.	Image and video processing	It is possible to increase the accuracy and detail of image and video analysis by using brain inspired AI. This makes it possible to extract more information from photos and videos and to analyze them in a manner that is more efficient and effective. This has a number of potential applications, including in the areas of surveillance, security, and even entertainment.
5.	Financial services	Large volumes of financial data, such as stock prices, may be analyzed using artificial intelligence systems that are influenced by the human brain in order to uncover patterns and correlations that can then be utilized to make more educated investment choices.
6.	Manufacturing	AI that is based on the brain can be used to speed up production, improve quality control, and cut down on downtime. This can make manufacturing more efficient and save money, which can lead to higher productivity and lower costs.
7.	Human-computer interfaces	AI that is based on how the brain works can be used to improve how people interact with machines, which could lead to more efficient and effective workflows. For example, brain-computer interfaces (BCIs) allow direct communication between the brain and computers. This lets people with paralysis or other neurological disorders control devices with their thoughts and also lets humans directly interact with AI.

HISTORY

The progress that has been made in artificial intelligence (AI) over the course of period makes it abundantly evident that there are connections between AI and studies on the neuroscience. A significant number of the early developers of AI have also made significant contributions to the field of brain research. Through the use of microscopes, researchers were able to discover pathways between neurons in the human brain, which acted as fuel for the construction of artificial neural networks (ANN) (Fan, J. *et al.,* 2019)

The origins of artificial intelligence (AI) that is inspired by the workings of the brain may be traced back to the first days of AI research, when scientists first began investigating neural networks as a means of emulating the manner in which the brain processes information.

The perceptron, a type of neural network created in the 1950s by psychologist Frank Rosenblatt, was one of the first examples of AI that was based on how the brain works. The perceptron was a simple model of a single neuron that could learn to recognize patterns in data like images and speech. But the perceptron's abilities were limited, and it could only solve very simple problems (Kussul, E. *et al.,* 2001)

The building of artificial neural networks that were capable of computing complex operations marked the beginning of research into neurological processing in the 1940s (Hassabis, D. *et al.*, 2017) Researchers first began exploring the use of neural networks as a model for AI, but in the 1970s, there was the first AI winter. So now the question comes: what is AI Winter? The answer is that it is a time when people aren't interested in or willing to spend money on artificial intelligence.

The main reason for this was that the first AI systems weren't as good as they were made out to be. They couldn't do much more than simple things like recognize objects or follow simple instructions. This made a lot of people lose faith in AI and think that it would never be able to do anything more than these simple tasks. In the late 1970s and early 1980s, the second AI winter started. This happened because more and more people saw that AI hadn't lived up to its promises and that the technology wasn't as far along as had been hoped. This caused fewer people to be interested in AI and less money to be spent on it. But, in recent years, there has been a resurgence of interest in neural networks and other AI methods that are based on the brain. This is because computers are getting faster and there is more data available. This has led to a lot of progress in areas like speech and image recognition, natural language processing, and self-driving systems (Lutkevich, B, 2023)

In recent years, there has been a growing interest in using AI that is based on the brain to make machines that are smarter and can do more. For example, researchers have been looking into the use of "deep learning," a type of neural network that can learn to recognize patterns in data without being explicitly programmed. Also, scientists are working on making new types of neural networks that look more like the brain. For example, spiking neural networks look like the way neurons talk to each other by sending electrical spikes.

Overall, the history of AI that is based on the brain has been marked by a steady rise in more advanced and complex models, as researchers have kept looking for new ways to mimic the brain's

Figure 1. Evolution of Brain inspired AI

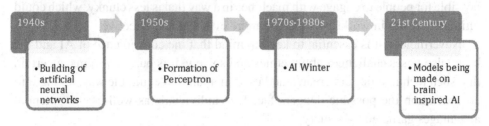

abilities. Even though there is still a lot to learn about the brain and a lot to solve, brain-inspired AI has a huge chance to change how we interact with machines and the world around us.

Human Intelligence and Converging the BRAIN and ARTIFICIAL INTELLIGENCE (AI)

The ability to think, learn, and adjust one's behavior in response to novel circumstances is what constitutes human intelligence. It is a phenomenon that is both complicated and multidimensional, and scientists do not yet have a complete understanding of it. However, new developments in neuroscience and artificial intelligence (AI) have started to shed light on the fundamental processes of human intellect, as well as how it may be copied or increased by AI. This is a significant step forward in the field of AI research.

The study of the human brain and the ways in which it might be utilized to guide the creation of artificial intelligence systems is one field of research that shows a great deal of promise. For example, researchers have been looking into how the brain processes information in the areas of perception, memory, and decision-making to learn how the brain works and how this information could be used to help build artificial intelligence (AI) systems.

Making brain-computer interfaces, or BCIs, is another area of study that is getting more and more attention. These interfaces make it possible for the brain and a computer to talk to each other directly. BCIs have the potential to enable persons with paralysis or other neurological problems to operate machines with their thoughts. They also have the potential to allow humans to directly interact with AI, therefore forming a connection that is mutually beneficial to both parties.

The idea that the human brain and artificial intelligence may one day converge is an intriguing one since it could one day lead to the creation of brand new technologies that can improve human intellect and capacities. Brain implants that are driven by AI might be used, for instance, to increase memory, attention, or decision-making; they could also be used to restore lost capabilities in those who suffer from neurological illnesses. In addition, by enhancing human-computer interfaces, it might make it possible for people to engage with machines in a way that is less clunky, which could ultimately result in workflows that are more efficient and effective.

Nevertheless, it is essential to keep in mind that the convergence of AI and the brain also poses challenges about ethics and society. It is our duty to make certain that such technologies are created and used in a fair and equitable way, taking into consideration the possible dangers faced by individuals as well as the potential advantages garnered by society.

In general, the combination of human intellect with AI has the potential to result in significant breakthroughs in a variety of fields, including technology, medicine, and society. On the other

hand, it is essential for researchers and politicians to consider the ethical implications of these breakthroughs and to make certain that they are used for the advantage of everyone.

Application of Artificial intelligence in Brain Stimulation is Countless

The use of artificial intelligence (AI) might provide novel approaches to the treatment of neurological conditions, which would escort in a new era of innovation in the area of brain stimulation. Deep brain stimulation (DBS) (Miocinovic, S. *et al.,* 2013) and transcranial magnetic stimulation (TMS) (Siebner, H.R., 2022) are two types of brain stimulation methods that have shown promise in the treatment of a wide range of medical disorders, including Parkinson's disease, depression, and chronic pain. However, these procedures have several drawbacks, such as the fact that they are not very specific and that they are expensive.

Types of Brain Stimulation

Deep Brain Stimulation (DBS) - It is an effective surgical treatment for movement disorders that cannot be controlled by medicine, including hypokinetic (slow) and hyperkinetic (unwanted) movement . In addition, it is now being researched as a possible therapy for a broad variety of other neurological and psychiatric problems .

Transactional Magnetic Stimulation - It induces brain neuronal activity non-invasively. TMS affects impulsive and suppressive neuron axons. Peripheral neural systems co-stimulation is also significant with TMS. Peripheral coexcitation perpetuates internally in auditory networks creating brain retaliates in other channels to support holistic fusion, focusing, and excitement.

By giving stimulation that is more specifically focused and individually tailored, AI may assist in overcoming these limits. For instance, methods for machine learning

Figure 2. Applications of AI in Brain Stimulation

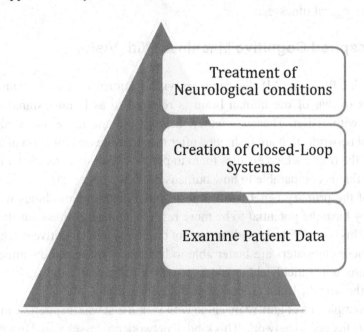

may be used for the analysis of brain imaging data, such as that obtained from MRI or PET scans, in order to locate certain areas of the brain that are related with a particular condition. This information may then be used to guide the placement of electrodes or the transmission of magnetic pulses, guaranteeing that the stimulation is aimed to the brain areas that have the greatest need for it particularly.

The creation of closed-loop systems is another domain in which artificial intelligence is being used in the field of brain stimulation. In these types of systems, a sensor is used to monitor the activity of the brain, and an algorithm is utilized to make real-time adjustments to the stimulation depending on the information that the sensor provides. This makes it possible to adapt the stimulation to the specific requirements of the person, which might reduce the risk of adverse effects or excessive stimulation.

In addition, AI can assist in the development of stimulation regimens that are both more efficient and effective. For instance, machine learning algorithms may be used to examine patient data in order to identify patterns that are correlated with a positive response to therapy. After gathering this information, the stimulation parameters, which include pulse amplitude, frequency, and duration, may be optimized based on the results.

In general, there is an almost infinite number of ways that AI might be used to stimulate the brain. It is reasonable to anticipate that, as technological progress continues, we will witness an increase in the number of creative and useful applications of AI that may be utilized to ameliorate the lives of those who suffer from neurological illnesses.

Brain-Inspired Cognitive Machines With Vision

Artificial intelligence (AI) that analyzes visual information in a manner that is analogous to that of the human brain is referred to as brain-inspired cognitive machines with vision. These computers have vision and make use of algorithms and neural networks that are fashioned after the structure and function of the visual system in the brain, which enables them to perceive and interpret visual images in a manner that is comparable to how humans do so.

One of the primary benefits of brain-inspired cognitive machines with vision is that they have the potential to be more resilient and adaptable than standard AI systems. This is one of the key advantages of brain-inspired cognitive machines with vision. These computers are better able to handle complex and dynamic images, and they are more quickly able to adapt to new settings and activities because they replicate the way the brain processes visual information.

One example of a cognitive machine with vision that was inspired by the brain is a deep learning neural network. This kind of network processes visual input by using convolutional layers. These convolutional layers are designed after the manner in which the visual system in the brain is structured. Within the visual system, distinct layers are responsible for detecting different elements, such as edges, textures, and forms. The computer may learn to identify things and situations in a manner that is comparable to how the human brain accomplishes it with the use of these layers.

One further example of this would be a model that learns the visual representations of things via the use of unsupervised learning techniques, in a manner that is analogous to how the human brain constructs an object representation. The computer is able to identify and distinguish items in pictures and videos with the assistance of these representations, despite the fact that it has never seen these objects before.

In addition to the processing of images and videos, brain-inspired cognitive machines with vision have also been used in other applications, such as autonomous robotics, where they can be used to enable robots to navigate and interact with their environment based on visual information. These machines can also be used to enable robots to learn from their mistakes and improve their performance.

However, it is essential to keep in mind that the study of brain-inspired cognitive machines equipped with vision is still in its infancy, and there is still a significant amount of investigation that needs to be carried out in order to fully comprehend and replicate the complexities of the human visual system. However, there is a significant possibility that these robots may revolutionize the field of artificial intelligence (AI) and make it possible for new applications to be developed in fields such as medical, transportation, and entertainment.

In general, brain-inspired cognitive machines with vision are a promising new area in the field of artificial intelligence research. These machines have the potential to revolutionize the way people interact with technologies as well as the environment around us.

Data Analysis Tools, Knowledge Representation, and Super-Resolution

The components of artificial intelligence (AI) systems that are inspired by the brain that are most important are data analysis tools, knowledge representation, and super-resolution. These technologies make it possible for artificial intelligence systems to derive meaningful insights from enormous and complicated datasets, to represent information and reason about it, and to reach high levels of precision and detail in the processing of images and videos.

In order to glean useful insights from extensive and complicated datasets, data analysis methods are used. These techniques may be used to recognize patterns and correlations within the data, as well as to construct predictive models that can be used to generate predictions about future occurrences or outcomes. For instance, machine learning methods such as neural networks may be used for the analysis of brain imaging data obtained from MRI or PET scans in order to locate certain areas of the brain that are linked to a specific condition. This information may then be used to guide the placement of electrodes or the transmission of magnetic pulses, guaranteeing that the stimulation is aimed to the brain areas that have the greatest need for it particularly.

The act of conveying information to a computer in a format that can be read, comprehended, and processed by the machine is referred to as "knowledge representation." It entails describing the links and connections between various pieces of information in a fashion that can be readily understood and queried by the AI system. This is done in order to make the system as efficient as possible. For instance, in the field of cognitive computing, knowledge representation is used to represent the knowledge that a machine has acquired about a particular domain, such as the human body, for the machine to comprehend and reason about the information that it is processing. This allows the machine to better serve its purpose.

The process of using super-resolution to boost the resolution of photos and videos is a technology that makes it possible to conduct analysis that is more precise and detailed. This may be of utility in the area of brain-inspired artificial intelligence, which requires high-resolution pictures of the brain for proper analysis and diagnosis. This can be of great use. For instance, super-resolution may be used to improve the

Figure 3.

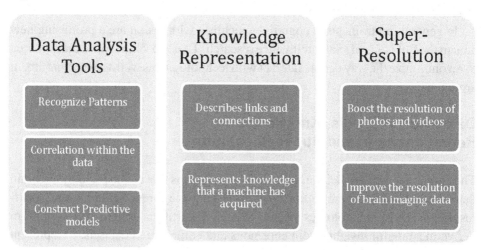

resolution of brain imaging data, such as that obtained from magnetic resonance imaging (MRI) or positron emission tomography (PET) scans. This paves the way for a more in-depth investigation of the structure and function of the brain.

In conclusion, the tools for data processing, knowledge representation, and super-resolution are essential components of AI systems that are inspired by the brain. They enable artificial intelligence systems to extract meaningful insights from large and complex datasets, to represent and reason about knowledge, and to achieve high levels of accuracy and detail in the processing of images and videos. This makes it possible to gain a better understanding of the brain and the functions it carries out.

Devyanshi Bansal
Amity University, India

Sachin Sharma
Amity University, India

Madhulika Bhatia
Amity University, India

Tanupriya Choudhury
University of Petroleum and Energy Studies, India

Bhupesh Kumar Dewangan
O.P. Jindal University, India

REFERENCES

Fan, J., Fang, L., Wu, J., Guo, Y., & Dai, Q. (2020). From brain science to artificial intelligence. *Engineering*, *6*(3), 248–252. doi:10.1016/j.eng.2019.11.012

Hassabis, D., Kumaran, D., Summerfield, C., & Botvinick, M. (2017). Neuroscience-inspired artificial intelligence. *Neuron*, *95*(2), 245–258. doi:10.1016/j.neuron.2017.06.011 PMID:28728020

Kussul, E., Baidyk, T., Kasatkina, L., & Lukovich, V. (2001, July). Rosenblatt perceptrons for handwritten digit recognition. *International Joint Conference on Neural Networks. Proceedings, 2*, 1516-1520. IEEE. 10.1109/IJCNN.2001.939589

Lutkevich, B. (n.d.). What is AI Winter? Definition, History and Timeline. *Enterprise AI*. https://www.techtarget.com/searchenterpriseai/definition/AI-winter

Miocinovic, S., Somayajula, S., Chitnis, S., & Vitek, J. L. (2013). History, applications, and mechanisms of deep brain stimulation. *JAMA Neurology*, *70*(2), 163–171. doi:10.1001/2013.jamaneurol.45 PMID:23407652

Siebner, H. R., Funke, K., Aberra, A. S., Antal, A., Bestmann, S., Chen, R., Classen, J., Davare, M., Di Lazzaro, V., Fox, P. T., Hallett, M., Karabanov, A. N., Kesselheim, J., Beck, M. M., Koch, G., Liebetanz, D., Meunier, S., Miniussi, C., Paulus, W., ... Ugawa, Y. (2022). Transcranial magnetic stimulation of the brain: What is stimulated? A consensus and critical position paper. *Clinical Neurophysiology*, *140*, 59–97. doi:10.1016/j.clinph.2022.04.022

Wang, L., & Alexander, C. A. (2019). Brain science and brain-inspired artificial intelligence: Advances and trends. *Journal of Computer Sciences and Applications*, *7*(1), 56–61.

Yang, S., Hao, X., Deng, B., Wei, X., Li, H., & Wang, J. (2018). A survey of brain-inspired artificial intelligence and its engineering. *Life Research*, *1*(1), 23–29. doi:10.53388/life2018-0711-005

Chapter 1
Application of Brain– Inspired Computing for Daily Assistance

Princy Diwan
Department of Computer Science and Engineering, O.P. Jindal University, India

Bhupesh Kumar Dewangan
iD https://orcid.org/0000-0001-8116-7563
Department of Computer Science and Engineering, O.P. Jindal University, India

ABSTRACT

The domains of artificial intelligence and machine learning continue to advance at a rapid speed in terms of algorithms, models, applications, and hardware thanks to an exponential increase in the amount of data collected on a daily basis. Deep neural networks have transformed these domains by achieving extraordinary human-like performance in various real-world challenges, such as picture or speech recognition. There is also a lot of effort going on to figure out the principles of computation in extensive biological neural networks, especially biologically plausible spiking neural networks. Neural-inspired algorithms (e.g., deep ANNs and deep RL) and brain intelligent systems have revolutionized the fields of machine learning and cognitive computing in the last decade, assisting in a variety of real-world learning tasks ranging from robot monitoring and interaction at home to complex decision-making about emotions and behaviors in humans and animals. While these brain-inspired algorithms and systems have made significant progress, they still require large data sets to train, and their outcomes lack the flexibility to adapt to a variety of learning tasks and provide long-term performance. To solve these issues, an analytical understanding of the concepts that allow brain-inspired intelligent systems to develop information, as well as how they might be translated to hardware for everyday help

DOI: 10.4018/978-1-6684-6980-4.ch001

and practical applications, is required. This chapter focuses upon the applications, challenges, and solutions of brain-inspired computing for daily assistance.

INTRODUCTION

Cognitive computing and artificial intelligence (AI) are about to undergo a revolution. The computing systems that power today's AI algorithms are based on the von Neumann architecture, which necessitates the rapid transfer of massive volumes of data back and forth during processing. As a result, there is a performance bottleneck and substantial space and power waste. Thus, it is increasingly evident that we need to switch to innovative architectures where memory and computation are better combined in order to develop effective cognitive computers. The von Neumann system's separation of memory and processing units necessitates frequent data transfers between storage and processing sections, which will result in high energy expenditures and performance degradation (Wang, Z. et al.,2020). According to studies, the brain's memory and learning processes are carried out by a network of around 1015 neurons that are linked together by a large number of synapses. These synapses contain a lot of functional connections between neuronal systems and internal relationships that are complicated with information flow. In fact, the Neural network representation of the human brain exhibits remarkable precision and processing information efficiently (Wang, W. et al.,2018). The brain accomplishes this feat by executing computational operations inside the memory and approximating them in the analogue domain, preventing data migration between the storage and the memory (Wang, P. et al.,2019). Therefore, the replication of brain function introduces a new computational methodology, called "neuromorphic computing" (Xia, Q., & Yang, J. J., 2019). Because of the structural resemblance between synaptic structures and memristive devices, neuromorphic computing is seen to be a promising field. Figure 1 depicts a brain synapse and memristor. The progression of the synaptic devices-based neuromorphic computing may create a route for very quick, energy-efficient computers (Zhang, X. Y. et al.,2020). In the past ten years, neural-inspired algorithms (such as deep ANNs and deep RL) and brain-intelligent systems have revolutionized the fields of machine learning and cognitive computing. These systems support a wide range of real-world learning tasks, from robot monitoring and interaction at home to complex decision-making about emotions and behaviors in humans and animals. The vast evolutionary history of living things has given them structures and abilities that allow them to survive in their surroundings. Emulation of these characteristics of living things is the aim of biomimetic technology. The development of electronic sensors and motor systems that resemble biological sensory organs is a goal of research in bioinspired electronics. In bioinspired applications such humanoid robots, exoskeletons, and other devices with motor systems, gadgets that mix an

Figure 1. Flow of chapter

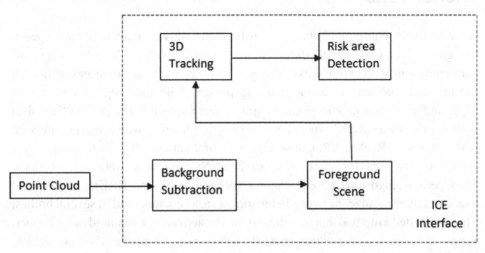

electrical item with a live body. Researchers must create biomimetic electronic sensors, motor systems, brains, and nerves in order to create bioinspired robotic and electronic devices that are compatible with the live body at the neuronal level and that are run by processes like those in a real body (Zhang, X. et al.,2020). Artificial organic synapses have mimicked the plasticity of the brain with considerably simpler architectures, cheaper production than neurons based on silicon circuits, and with less energy usage than conventional von Neumann computing techniques. Future neuromorphic systems may benefit from the incorporation of organic synapses. Due to their high level of parallelism, neuromorphic computing enables memory and computation to run simultaneously in the same computer core. Synaptic memory junctions, which encode the information, are the means by which artificial neurons receive inputs that are regulated (Park, T. J. et al.,2022). Since this kind of neural networks uses "spikes" for computation and communication, they are commonly referred to as Spiking Neural Networks (SNNs). SNNs are very effective because of their spike-driven event-driven architecture. In fact, it has been demonstrated that SNNs can consume an order of magnitude less power than an iso-network ANN when implemented on low power asynchronous neuromorphic hardware (Sengupta, A. et al.,2019). These networks should expand to their maximum capacity and approach the brain's efficiency when larger, more bio-realistic systems are created. Flow of the chapter is shown in below figure:

BACKGROUND

By effectively combining object identification, activity detection, and speech recognition, E. Cruz et al. demonstrate a robotic system for observing and communicating with individuals with cognitive illnesses. localization and navigation techniques to aid and recall the assisting patients with their regular duties. Our suggested approach entails implementing an Object Recognition Engine (ORE) tasked with identifying a specific object based on a well-known convolutional architecture is the Inception ResNet V2. Convolutional neural network (CNN) technique over region-based designs for neural networks (R-CNNs) to prevent erroneous detections. The OpenPose algorithm-based Behavior Recognition Engine (BRE) is then utilized to accurately recognize the user's behaviors in various rooms and in several homes. They suggested a method that was successfully tested on the humanoid robot Pepper, Pepper, where extra information about the robot, such as how the robot moved, was localized, adjusts to different circumstances (for instance, when a room's furnishings has been on a semantic localization system (SLS) and reorganized) depends on how the robot moves from one chamber to another specialized software that determines the route from the present room to the object. Hintzman's proposal for MINERVA 2, a simulation, is one of the most notable works in computer science that attempts to encode a human-inspired memory model. a simulation of human memory, where each event is kept in a memory table as a high-dimensional vector. In MINERVA 2, the retrieval process is a reconstruction rather than a table look-up, where each row of episodes "resonates" with the provided cue (Hintzman, D. L., 1984). For Robots in Assisted Living (RAL) navigation systems, H. Ponce et al. describe an approach based on nature-control systems. based on convolutional neural networks and Hermite optical flow (OF) networks (CNNs). Hermite OF is used in the integrated system. for obstacle motion detection and CNN for obstacle distance estimation. Instead of employing RGB-D sensors that produce depth maps of the scene, the authors estimate the distance to moving and stationary objects using a monocular camera. This technique has the benefit of requiring less training data for the distance estimator and none for computing the OF field. The robot simulator V-REP, which faithfully reproduces the circumstances of the physical environment, was employed by the authors for experimental reasons. To identify multiclass motor imagery, Tresp, V. et al. first present a subject-specific decision tree (SSDT) classification framework and then a data reduction technique. Electroencephalogram (EEG) signals for the measurement of the Using a brain-computer interface (BCI) that is based on the many Riemannian analysis of covariance matrices (Tresp, V. et al.,2015). To identify multiclass motor imagery, Wang, W. et al. first present a subject-specific decision tree (SSDT) classification framework and then a data reduction technique. electroencephalogram (EEG) signals for the measurement of the Using a brain-computer interface (BCI) that is based on the many Riemannian analysis of covariance matrices (Wang, W. et al., 2010). The SSDT classification framework's objective is to distinguish between the two MI tasks with the maximum recognition rate while simultaneously improving classification precision. this is accomplished by decreasing the classification error by computing a filter geodesic minimum distance to Riemannian mean (FGMDRM) in the tree. An embedded learning-based memory model was presented by (Chang, P. H., & Tan, A. H., 2017). The fundamental idea behind the model is to employ a latent representation of generalized items in order to accurately imitate the sensory memory, working memory, semantic memory, and episodic memory. In their research, some theories on human memory have been developed using their computational model to emphasize several crucial concepts to support the creation of future models of memory.

A generalized neural network-based memory model was developed for certain further investigations. An example of this is the neural episodic memory model (Tan, A. H. et al., 2007) proposed. episodic traces in response to an ongoing flow of sensory information feedback and suggestions from the environment. Chang and Tan created a memory model that gathered data about things, actions, times, and locations using a modified version of the adaptive resonance theory (ART) (Park, G. M., & Kim, J. H., 2016). Both of which were utilized to encrypt surveillance events. predetermined data gleaned from CCTV footage at a lobby entry. A hierarchical network of fusion ART in various levels formed the basis of the deep adaptive resonance theory (Deep ART) model developed by (Encarnação, P., 2013). The simulation may learn from the characteristics of occurrences and encode data from low-level to high-level meanings with a considerable degree of flexibility. (Saez-Pons, J. et al., 2015) 's scenario for a home-care robot suggested that users use the robot's memory as a memory rather than examining accumulated memories through direct interactions. prosthesis, using a visual interface to view historical events. An assistive robot and a smart home system were coupled by (Wieser, I. et al., 2016) to help elderly people who live independently deal with memory loss. The authors' episodic A post stream that looked like Twitter was used to illustrate events. A robotic system called IRMA was introduced by (Wu, C. et al., 2016) to assist individuals in looking for lost items in a model home setting. It included various components that made it possible for the robot to comprehend the user's request, investigate the surroundings, discover, and identify return the user's desired item from the target. A Kinect-based robotic system called Watch-Bot was introduced by (Gomez-Donoso et al., 2019) that could assess whether a user had forgotten anything while engaging in an activity and would subsequently prompt a reminder, device is also pointing out the misplaced object using a laser pointer.

APPLICATIONS OF BRAIN INSPIRED COMPUTING IN DAILY ASSISTANCE

Ambient Assisted Living with a Portable Robot

Currently, a major area of interest in the possibility of assisting and monitoring handicapped and elderly people is ambient assisted living (AAL) surroundings. senior citizens. By sensing events like entering a certain area, these devices can increase their quality of life and level of personal autonomy. Possible risk zones, probable mishaps like falls, or protracted stays in the same location. However, several issues still need to be addressed. There are still some regions, owing to the positioning of the cameras, outside the scope of AAL systems. There are other dangers within the camera's field of view. It is undetectable by the AAL system. These threats are no static, obscured, or relatively modest in size.

To address this challenge, a system is offered that incorporates a robot that explores such uncharted territory in search of fresh, possibly hazardous locations that escape the attention of the AAL. The AAL system then receives this data from the robot in order to perform better. Any robot equipped with color cameras, a moving base, and a laser or depth camera can be applied.

Based on each person's position and temporal trajectory, this AAL may identify a number of unsafe situations (Hou, Y., & Chen, S., 2019):

- **Dangerous Areas:** The monitored area may contain certain sites that have a risky designation. Any time a human is detected sufficiently close to one of these places, the AAL system will sound an alert. When there is a balcony or an exit door nearby, for example, is handy.
- **Fall:** If a person falls in an area that is under supervision, the system can identify that. After the issue has been identified, the system can either immediately sound an alert or wait a little while to determine whether a harmful situation genuinely exists.
- **Room Entry or Exit:** The number of persons in each location is known to AAL. This can be helpful to spot access into places that are off-limits, such as the cleaning or a nursing home's medication room.
- **Absence:** A person leaving a room alone for an extended amount of time might be another dangerous circumstance.
- **Extended Stay:** Any sensor used to monitor a toilet might cause controversy. The AAL system identifies a person entering a room without an exit in order to avoid installing a sensor in this type of room. If the individual leaves the main room after a certain amount of time, the system can sound an alert.

Figure 2. Block diagram of the AAL system

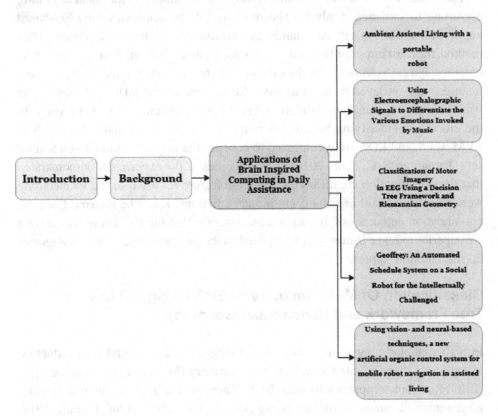

USING ELECTROENCEPHALOGRAPHIC SIGNALS TO DIFFERENTIATE THE VARIOUS EMOTIONS INVOKED BY MUSIC

Various emotions can be evoked by music and may show up as different electroencephalogram signals (EEG). Numerous earlier investigations investigated the relationships between particular elements of music, such as the underlying emotions evoked, and EEG signal characteristics. Nevertheless, no study has thoroughly studied musical EEG properties and chosen those with the most potential for distinguishing between emotions. From each of the 12 electrode sites, we can extract 27-dimensional features (Shon, D. et al., 2018). We can next apply a correlation-based feature selection strategy to find the feature set that is least redundant while still being most closely connected to the original features. The recognition accuracy of the original and chosen feature sets was then tested using a number of classifiers, including Support Vector Machine (SVM), C4.5, LDA, and BPNN.

Electrodes T3, T4, and Pz were most likely to be connected to the musical stimuli, according to statistical analysis. The most useful characteristics for EEG-based emotion identification without redundancy were found using the CFS approach. In this method, the most important EEG signal feature set for classifying human emotions is obtained. For each electrode, 18-dimension linear features and 9-dimension nonlinear features were retrieved in order to meet this objective. The influential feature set was then chosen using the correlation-based feature selection (CFS) approach. In the process of classifying human emotions, the classification algorithms BPNN, SVM, C4.5, and LDA were employed to confirm the impact of the chosen feature set (Diamantas, S. C. et al., 2010). The outcomes of the experiment demonstrated that the classification algorithm C4.5 and the feature set used for the Pz electrode were more successful in identifying human emotions. It can be inferred from the classification outcomes of 10 random assessments that the Pz feature sets chosen are superior to other feature sets when used as the primary feature set to categories human emotion statues.

Classification Of Motor Imagery in EEG Using a Decision Tree Framework and Riemannian Geometry

In a Riemannian viewpoint, it is a classification framework and data reduction technique to discriminate multiclass motor imagery (MI) electroencephalography (EEG) for brain computer interface (BCI). There is now growing interest in using Riemannian geometry in BCI decoding (He H. et al., 2018; Julin, J. et al., 2016; Popov, A. et al., 2017; Liu, F. et al., 2015; Guan, S. et al., 2019). For the purpose of keeping an eye on and engaging with elderly individuals and those with cognitive problems, a robotic system has been developed. The system will assist, direct, and motivate the patient as they go about their daily activities so that they can adhere to a predetermined plan. The ultimate objective of the suggested approach is to increase the independence and self-worth of those who are dependent (Cruz, E. et al.,2018). A contextual timetable and a programmable schedule make up the system. The patient must do a number of chores on the programmed schedule at specific times. If the patient has permission to delay certain duties, they may be done. The contextual schedule, on the other hand, is made up of a list of chores that the patient is permitted to do whenever necessary and is dependent on the room in which the user is situated. The patient has the option of attempting to do a job from the programmed timetable right away or delaying it. The robot will direct the patient to the proper room if they wish to do so, and then it will give them instructions on how to carry out the necessary task. The computer will prompt the patient to do a job later if he put it off. Each job, whether it comes from the contextual or programmed schedule, has a list of steps that the patient must take in order to finish it. The therapist in charge of the patient or approved family members set up and allocate the duties.

The four primary sorts of actions that our system now understands are object identification, behavior recognition, QR recognition, and spend time action. As indicated before, the caregiver for the patient might combine these operations to create complex jobs. For instance, "pour a glass of water" would require three distinct actions to complete.

The robot would first request that the patient obtain a glass and display It would then want to see the water bottle. Both The object recognition engine would be used in activities to a glass and a bottle can be found. Finally, the behavior recognition engine would be configured to recognize the real pouring movement.

Geoffrey: An Automated Schedule System on a Social Robot for the Intellectually Challenged

One of the key concerns of industrialized nations is the rapid rise in the proportion of elderly people, those with brain injury-related disorders, and cognitively challenged people. These people frequently need specialized care, sometimes even virtually constant overseers who assist them in managing their diaries. An automated scheduling system that is implemented on a social robot is suggested in order to address this problem (Cruz, E. et al.,2018). The robot maintains a journal of the tasks the patient needs to complete. The robot assists the patient in completing tasks when they are activated. The system can also determine if the procedures are being followed correctly or not, and it may send out alarms if it does. To achieve this, a collection of deep learning methods is applied. The caregivers and approved family members can change the timetable (Rangel, J. C. et al., 2018). The patients' self-autonomy and quality of life might both be improved by this solution. Today, brain-related injuries impact thousands of individuals globally. These illnesses can be brought on by a variety of events, including trauma, accidents, and even hereditary predispositions. With advancing years, changes that might result from an acquired brain injury can include varying degrees of intellectual ability loss.

These impairments affect social or vocational performance, memory or abstract thinking issues, the inability to distinguish between related words, trouble doing everyday household duties, among other things. The failure to follow the normal course of events when performing a task is specifically one of the most prevalent problems (Pollack, M. E. et al., 2003). Elderly and cognitively disabled adults frequently need the extra aid of a therapist to complete daily chores like tying their shoes, taking a shower, or eating meals. We suggest putting into place a social robot with an automatic timekeeping system that would help the patients with their routine household duties. The program will alert the patients about the scheduled duties on an arranged time and will also aid in completing the tasks by the patient through them step by step. It can determine whether a person is if things are going well, provide comments (Zhou, B. et al., 2018).

The suggested system's implementation would increase one's own independence and the standard of aged and cognitively disabled people's daily lives. Consequently, this work's primary contributions are (Cao, Z. et al., 2017):

- Installing a programmable scheduling system on a sociable machine.
- The combination of many techniques to observe if the patient is carrying out the actions he is designed to accomplish.
- A navigation system made up of a variety of the conventional and semantic localization SLAM.

The system is constrained in various ways. First, the creation of the map and training of the models is a necessary step that must be completed by professionals. In addition, the ORE and BRE models must be rebuilt if new items are needed because we want to add previously unplanned chores to the patient's calendar. By developing a suitable strategy that puts the patient's long-term evolution first, this problem might be lessened.

Using Vision- And Neural-Based Techniques, A New Artificial Organic Control System for Mobile Robot Navigation in Assisted Living (Ponce, H. et al.,2018)

An alternative to provide families and professional careers with a variety of options for caring for older persons is robotic assisted living (RAL). Due of the ambiguity and changing nature of settings present in senior housing situations, mobile robot navigation is a difficult task. In order to do this, the navigation system makes an effort to mimic the intricate process that human vision and judgement use. Using an artificial organic controller supplemented with vision-based techniques like Hermite optical flow (OF) and convolutional neural networks, we present a new, nature-inspired control system for mobile RAL navigation in this study (CNNs) (Shahraray, B., & Brown, M. K,1988). In particular, CNNs are used for estimating obstacle distance, whereas the Hermite OF is used for obstacle motion detection. In a 3D environment, we train the CNN using OF visual characteristics supported by ultrasonic sensor-based measurements. Our program uses a monocular camera and a simulated environment to avoid both moving and stationary objects. We employ the distributed control architecture's integrated development environment and robot simulator V-REP for the experiments (Mancini, M. et al.,2016; Bauer, Z. et al.,2018). The computation and analysis of quantitative evaluation, security, and smoothness metrics. Results indicated that the suggested. Using a unique hybrid fuzzy logic and artificial hydrocarbon networks controller system, this methodology effectively integrates a bioinspired OF method, a CNN technique for distance inference, and these three different approaches. This integration replicates a high cognitive vision technique that enables analysis of holistic data from the mobile robot's egocentric point of view (Shahraray, B., & Brown, M. K, 1988).

CONCLUSION

This chapter successfully covers the most crucial approaches, applications, and various techniques for the recognition of brain inspired computing. In a way to make this more impactful, various research papers have been reviewed in the background section. The main focus of this chapter is the application of brain inspired computing, for covering the applications of brain inspired computing the contribution of brain inspired computing in daily assistance has been discussed. Aid with memory in order to give a service to its customers, who are mostly the elderly, robots have tended to focus on a single goal. every day These robots are able to recall tasks and review events. and store this information for future usage. The participants' mean recall percentage of the events improves 19.63 percent after getting memory support from the robot, providing further proof that the robot is capable of providing powerful memory assistance based on information gleaned from prior observations.

ACKNOWLEDGMENT

This research received no specific grant from any funding agency in the public, commercial, or not-for-profit sectors.

Conflicts of Interest: The authors declare that they have no conflicts of interest.

REFERENCES

Bauer, Z., Escalona, F., Cruz, E., Cazorla, M., & Gomez-Donoso, F. (2018, November). Improving the 3D perception of the pepper robot using depth prediction from monocular frames. In *Workshop of Physical Agents* (pp. 132–146). Springer.

Cao, Z., Simon, T., Wei, S. E., & Sheikh, Y. (2017). Realtime multi-person 2d pose estimation using part affinity fields. In *Proceedings of the IEEE conference on computer vision and pattern recognition* (pp. 7291-7299). IEEE.

Chang, P. H., & Tan, A. H. (2017). *Encoding and recall of spatio-temporal episodic memory in real time*. Academic Press.

Cruz, E., Escalona, F., Bauer, Z., Cazorla, M., Garcia-Rodriguez, J., Martinez-Martin, E., ... Gomez-Donoso, F. (2018). Geoffrey: An automated schedule system on a social robot for the intellectually challenged. *Computational Intelligence and Neuroscience*.

Diamantas, S. C., Oikonomidis, A., & Crowder, R. M. (2010, July). Depth estimation for autonomous robot navigation: A comparative approach. In *2010 IEEE International Conference on Imaging Systems and Techniques* (pp. 426-430). IEEE.

Encarnação, P. (2013). Episodic memory visualization in robot companions providing a memory prosthesis for elderly users. *Assistive Technology: From Research to Practice, 33*, 120.

Gomez-Donoso, F., Escalona, F., Rivas, F. M., Cañas, J. M., & Cazorla, M. (2019). Enhancing the ambient assisted living capabilities with a mobile robot. *Computational Intelligence and Neuroscience*.

Guan, S., Zhao, K., & Yang, S. (2019). Motor imagery EEG classification based on decision tree framework and Riemannian geometry. *Computational Intelligence and Neuroscience*.

He, H., Li, Y., & Tan, J. (2018). Relative motion estimation using visual–inertial optical flow. *Autonomous Robots, 42*(3), 615–629.

Hintzman, D. L. (1984). MINERVA 2: A simulation model of human memory. *Behavior Research Methods, Instruments, & Computers, 16*(2), 96–101.

Hou, Y., & Chen, S. (2019). Distinguishing different emotions evoked by music via electroencephalographic signals. *Computational Intelligence and Neuroscience*.

Julin, J., Kumar, K. R., & Mahendran, S. (2016). Optical flow-based velocity estimation for vision-based navigation of aircraft. *International Journal of Applied Engineering Research, 11*(6), 4402–4405.

Liu, F., Shen, C., Lin, G., & Reid, I. (2015). Learning depth from single monocular images using deep convolutional neural fields. *IEEE Transactions on Pattern Analysis and Machine Intelligence, 38*(10), 2024–2039.

Mancini, M., Costante, G., Valigi, P., & Ciarfuglia, T. A. (2016, October). Fast robust monocular depth estimation for obstacle detection with fully convolutional networks. In *2016 IEEE/RSJ International Conference on Intelligent Robots and Systems (IROS)* (pp. 4296-4303). IEEE.

Park, G. M., & Kim, J. H. (2016, July). Deep adaptive resonance theory for learning biologically inspired episodic memory. In 2016 international joint conference on neural networks (IJCNN) (pp. 5174-5180). IEEE.

Park, T. J., Deng, S., Manna, S., Islam, A. N., Yu, H., Yuan, Y., ... Ramanathan, S. (2022). Complex oxides for brain-inspired computing: A review. *Advanced Materials*, 2203352.

Pollack, M. E., Brown, L., Colbry, D., McCarthy, C. E., Orosz, C., Peintner, B., ... Tsamardinos, I. (2003). Autominder: An intelligent cognitive orthotic system for people with memory impairment. *Robotics and Autonomous Systems*, 44(3-4), 273–282.

Ponce, H., Moya-Albor, E., & Brieva, J. (2018). A novel artificial organic control system for mobile robot navigation in assisted living using vision-and neural-based strategies. *Computational Intelligence and Neuroscience*.

Popov, A., Miller, A., Miller, B., & Stepanyan, K. (2017, February). Estimation of velocities via optical flow. In *2016 International Conference on Robotics and Machine Vision* (Vol. 10253, pp. 6-10). SPIE.

Rangel, J. C., Cruz, E., Escalona, F., Bauer, Z., Cazorla, M., García Rodríguez, J., ... Gomez Donoso, F. (2018). *Geoffrey: An Automated Schedule System on a Social Robot for the Intellectually Challenged*. Academic Press.

Saez-Pons, J., Syrdal, D. S., & Dautenhahn, K. (2015). What has happened today? Memory visualisation of a robot companion to assist user's memory. *Journal of Assistive Technologies*.

Sengupta, A., Ye, Y., Wang, R., Liu, C., & Roy, K. (2019). Going deeper in spiking neural networks: VGG and residual architectures. *Frontiers in Neuroscience*, *13*, 95.

Shahraray, B., & Brown, M. K. (1988, January). Robust depth estimation from optical flow. In *1988 Second International Conference on Computer Vision* (pp. 641-642). IEEE Computer Society.

Shon, D., Im, K., Park, J. H., Lim, D. S., Jang, B., & Kim, J. M. (2018). Emotional stress state detection using genetic algorithm-based feature selection on EEG signals. *International Journal of Environmental Research and Public Health*, 15(11), 2461.

Tan, A. H., Carpenter, G. A., & Grossberg, S. (2007, June). Intelligence through interaction: Towards a unified theory for learning. In *International Symposium on Neural Networks* (pp. 1094-1103). Springer.

Tresp, V., Esteban, C., Yang, Y., Baier, S., & Krompaß, D. (2015). *Learning with memory embeddings.* arXiv preprint arXiv:1511.07972.

Wang, P., Kong, R., Kong, X., Liégeois, R., Orban, C., Deco, G., ... Thomas Yeo, B. T. (2019). Inversion of a large-scale circuit model reveals a cortical hierarchy in the dynamic resting human brain. *Science Advances, 5*(1), eaat7854.

Wang, W., Pedretti, G., Milo, V., Carboni, R., Calderoni, A., Ramaswamy, N., ... Ielmini, D. (2018). Learning of spatiotemporal patterns in a spiking neural network with resistive switching synapses. *Science Advances, 4*(9), eaat4752.

Wang, W., Subagdja, B., Tan, A. H., & Starzyk, J. A. (2010, July). A self-organizing approach to episodic memory modeling. In *The 2010 International Joint Conference on Neural Networks (IJCNN)* (pp. 1-8). IEEE.

Wang, Z., Wu, H., Burr, G. W., Hwang, C. S., Wang, K. L., Xia, Q., & Yang, J. J. (2020). Resistive switching materials for information processing. *Nature Reviews. Materials, 5*(3), 173–195.

Wieser, I., Toprak, S., Grenzing, A., Hinz, T., Auddy, S., Karaoğuz, E. C., ... Wermter, S. (2016, September). A robotic home assistant with memory aid functionality. In *Joint German/Austrian Conference on Artificial Intelligence (Künstliche Intelligenz)* (pp. 102-115). Springer.

Wu, C., Zhang, J., Selman, B., Savarese, S., & Saxena, A. (2016, May). Watch-bot: Unsupervised learning for reminding humans of forgotten actions. In *2016 IEEE International Conference on Robotics and Automation (ICRA)* (pp. 2479-2486). IEEE.

Xia, Q., & Yang, J. J. (2019). Memristive crossbar arrays for brain-inspired computing. *Nature Materials, 18*(4), 309–323.

Zhang, X., Zhuo, Y., Luo, Q., Wu, Z., Midya, R., Wang, Z., ... Yang, J. J. (2020). An artificial spiking afferent nerve based on Mott memristors for neurorobotics. *Nature Communications, 11*(1), 1–9.

Zhang, X. Y., Zhang, X. Z., Lu, F. Y., Zhang, Q., Chen, W., Ma, T., ... Liang, T. B. (2020). Factors associated with failure of enhanced recovery after surgery program in patients undergoing pancreaticoduodenectomy. *Hepatobiliary & Pancreatic Diseases International, 19*(1), 51–57.

Zhou, B., Wu, K., Lv, P., Wang, J., Chen, G., Ji, B., & Liu, S. (2018). A new remote health-care system based on moving robot intended for the elderly at home. *Journal of Healthcare Engineering*, ●●●, 2018.

Chapter 2
Visualizing Neuroscience Through AI:
A Systematic Review

Roohi Sille

https://orcid.org/0000-0003-3031-7693

University of Petroleum and Energy Studies, India

Akshita Kapoor

University of Petroleum and Energy Studies, India

Tanupriya Choudhury

University of Petroleum and Energy Studies, India

Hussain Falih Mahdi

University of Diyala, Iraq

Madhu Khurana

University of Gloucestershire, UK

ABSTRACT

The field of neuroscience explains how the neural networks in the brain work together to perform a variety of tasks, including pattern recognition, relative memory, object recognition, and more. The mental activity that makes different jobs possible is difficult to understand. Understanding the various patterns present in natural neural networks requires a combination of artificial intelligence and neuroscience, which requires less computation. As a result, it is possible to understand a large number of brain reactions in relation to the activity that each person is engaged in. Human brain neurons need to be trained by experience in order to perform activities like moving the hands, arms, and legs while also considering how to respond to each activity. In the past 10 years, artificial intelligence (AI), with its potential to uncover patterns in vast, complex data sets, has made amazing strides, in part by emulating how the brain does particular computations. This chapter reviews the replication of neuroscience via AI in a real-time scenario.

DOI: 10.4018/978-1-6684-6980-4.ch002

INTRODUCTION

Intelligence is described in terms of how an object responds to a circumstance or action. Human intelligence is characterized by abilities in data manipulation and accurate pattern identification. Humans can learn to match patterns by retraining their neural networks in the brain. We call this human intellect. The human brain is made up of one million neurons connected in various ways. Since trained neurons are required for learning, seeing, and analyzing, these skills make up intelligence. In order to infuse systems with human intelligence and teach them to observe, learn from, and respond in accordance with that intelligence, artificial intelligence (AI) tries to imbue them with human cognition. For scientists, mathematicians, and researchers working on AI, the mechanical, anatomical, and functional properties of the brain have served as an inspiration. AI has shown promise in the field of neurology. Artificial intelligence (AI) has led to unexpected learning and perception outcomes when it comes to the data carried by brain neurons due to how challenging it is to comprehend brain neurons. Using this information, abilities like pattern matching, inference, object detection, etc. are developed. Artificially intelligent systems (AIS) would be able to reason, learn on its own, reason, and match patterns, and other cognitive functions if neuroscientists succeed in replicating the human brain in AIS. Pandarinath collaborated with David Sussillo, a computational neuroscientist at the Google Brain Team in San Francisco, California, on his study on latent variables. Sussillo asserts that an artificial neural network is merely a crude analogy of how the brain works. For example, it represents synapses as numbers in a matrix while, in reality, they are intricate bits of biological machinery that interact with their neighbors in dynamic ways and use both chemical and electrical activity to send or terminate impulses. Sussillo claims that "a single integer in a matrix is as far from the truth of what a synapse actually is as you could possibly get" (Quan, 2022).

The artificial intelligence system has developed to the point where it can mimic human thought processes and display what those people are thinking. As a result, AIS are utilized not only in the fields of marketing and data analysis but also in the diagnosis and detection of medical conditions. As a result of these devices' accuracy, operating rooms now use them. A large number of robots are educated to do various surgical procedures. These systems have been trained for great levels of precision, making this conceivable. Artificial intelligence, artificial neural networks, machine learning, and deep learning are just a few of the technologies that the writers focus on in this chapter that have their roots in neuroscience. Understanding the development of these methods, which draw inspiration from the human brain, as well as the various fields in which they are used and have achieved state-of-the-art status, is the main goal.

This chapter focusses on the relationships between neuroscience and AI. It also discusses the AI systems that have been developed to achieve various goals such as visualizing objects, pattern matching, mimicking human knowledge and prediction capabilities. It also analyses the various AI systems to understand the parameters linked to the human brain and the activities performed by them.

The chapter is organized as follows: section (ii) discuss about the background of AI and neuroscience (iii) discusses about the literature survey (iv) discuss about the future scope and conclusion.

Background

The relationship between AI and neuroscience goes both ways, and when it comes to interdependence, AI and neuroscience are dependent on one another in a way that both contribute to a deeper knowledge of the human brain and improve the accuracy of AI systems. The tasks associated with neuroscience include pattern matching, learning, and thinking formation, as well as tasks related to visualization and analysis. AI helps in understanding the human brain with respect to the parameters through which human brain has the capability to perform multiple operations. The fields of neuroscience and artificial intelligence have made remarkable advancements in recent years (AI). AI can be developed in two ways with the support of intensive biological intelligence research. First off, neuroscience can supplement the traditional mathematical and logical methodologies that have mostly dominated Artificial Intelligence, in addition to generating inspiration for new kinds of algorithms and structures. The second benefit of neuroscience is that it can verify current AI methods. It is clear from this that the presence of a recognized algorithm in the brain indicates that it is most likely a crucial component of general intelligence.

LITERATURE REVIEW

As a field of technical psychology and computational neuroscience, there is a distinction between theory-based models (e.g., reinforcement learning, etc.) versus techniques that are data-driven (e.g., deep learning). It should be noted that while the former model contains a great deal of information about biological mechanisms, the probability of success is higher for the latter. Methods with high performance are typically the least explicable, and methods that are easily explained are generally not the most accurate. This area is currently the focus of several efforts: (i) Evaluate the application of neurostimulation-relevant explainable learning solutions to neuroscience and neuropsychiatry datasets, (ii) encourage the formation of an explainable learning community among scholars, and (iii) encourage researchers to share data and theories freely (Jean-Marc et al., 2019).

This essay provides a concise overview of the various applications of artificial intelligence and neuroscience in our daily lives, including managing data and visualizing objects—tasks connected to brain functions—as well as matching patterns, learning from experience, and learning based on experience. Deep examination of neuroscience with regard to learning, visualizing, analysing, and predicting led to the development of the AI approach. Systems with embedded AI function in every way like humans do.

Figure 1. Breakdown of how neuroscience can be visualized through AI in different life scenarios

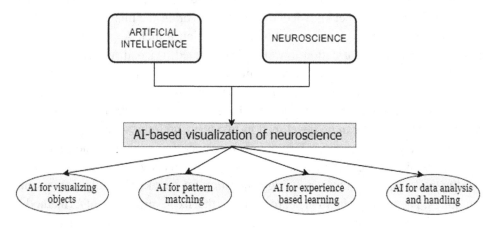

AI for Visualizing Objects

Artificial intelligence also makes use of deep neural networks to decode human thought. With the use of this device, they want to scan deep into the brain to decode and reconstruct images. In order to scan the brain's interior instead of only the surface, scientists develop fMRI (Functional MRI), which is different from regular MRI and exclusively tracks brain activity. Tracking brainwaves and blood flow to the brain is one of fMRI's peculiar behaviours.

The technology decodes the scan's data to determine the subject's state of mind at the time of the scan. Using a sophisticated neural network, data is transformed into picture format. Humans are required to turn on the system in order for it to function. When the machine is trained on how the brain functions, it learns how the human brain thinks and develops a solution. It gathers information from blood flow by monitoring the path, velocity, and direction of the blood toward the brain.

The device generates visuals by monitoring blood flow and using the data it gathers. This approach requires the use of multilayer deep neural networks. DNN includes elements of image processing. The data is then sent to Deep Generator Network (DGN) Algorithm, which uses it to build the image with a high degree of precision and accuracy. Obtaining clean or high-resolution photos is not possible without DGN. DGN can capture faces, eyes, and textual patterns, resulting in the production of high-quality visual cues. Highly similar decoded images are produced by a DGN algorithm when its efficiency is greater than 99% (M UMER Mirza, 2020).

Scientists from Stanford and UCLA have created a computer system that recognises and learns about items in the real world using the same visual learning strategy that people do.

With the aid of this "computer vision" technology, a computer can interpret and recognise visual images. The development of general artificial intelligence systems—computers that can think, learn on their own, and behave more like people—begins with the help of this technology. Although contemporary AI computer vision systems are becoming more powerful and capable, their capacity to recognise what they see is constrained by the amount of training and programming they have received. The method is broken down into three main steps. It starts by dividing each image into discrete units known as "viewlets." The machine then learns how to match each viewlet together after that. Last but not least, the system looks at neighbouring items to see whether they may be used to describe and identify the principal object.

In order to assist the new system "learn" like humans, researchers created a framework based on findings from cognitive psychology and neuroscience. About 9,000 photos, each depicting people and things, were used by the researchers during their testing. The software was able to create a thorough model of the human anatomy without assistance or labelling from other sources. Automobiles, motorbikes, and planes were used for engineering testing. Their system consistently outperformed conventionally taught computer vision systems, or at least came close to it (New AI system mimics how humans visualize and identify objects, 2018).

According to researchers at MIT's Computer Science and Artificial Intelligence Laboratory, robots can also learn to see by touch. Based solely on tactile information, an AI model predicts how the environment will interact based on the movement of the hand. The integration of senses could make the robot more powerful and reduce the amount of data needed to conduct tasks like manipulating things and grasping them. Using Generative adversarial networks (GANs), the team pieced together visual images based on tactile data. There are two parts to GANs: generators that produce samples and discriminators that try to distinguish them from actual data (Wiggers, 2019).

AI for Pattern Matching

The relationship between brain functions and cognitive function is a topic of interest for scientists (such as perception, memory, intelligence, reasoning, and consciousness.) (Kaku 2014)(Kaku, 2014). The neocortex in particular, in the brain, is continually attempting to comprehend the data. If it can't fully comprehend a pattern, the neocortex descends to a lower level. Patterns that are unfamiliar to all levels are referred to as novel patterns.

There are numerous studies being done on the human neocortex. While HBP (Markram, 2012)(Markram, 2012) intends to model the human brain, BRAIN (National Institutes of Health 2016) seeks to create a comprehensive picture of brain activity. In "On Intelligence" (Hawkins and Blakeslee 2007), (Hawkins & Blakeslee, 2004)one of the complementary theories regarding brain functioning, systematic descriptions of the neocortex's role in pattern matching are given. The neocortex is responsible for high level cognitive functions. These ideas suggest that in order to match patterns, the neocortex functions through modules of pattern matching.

The pattern matching problem has been discussed from a variety of angles in the literature. Another strategy comparable to ours is wavelet theory, which employs a series of filters to extract characteristics from an original image at particular spatial frequencies and sizes (Taubman and Marcellin, 2012)(Taubman & Marcellin, 2012). Our model analyses more generic features that are broken down recursively rather than the extraction of intrinsic features in a pattern, in contrast to the wavelet theory, which is used to apply recognition (edges recognition, texture classification, etc.).

Today's machine learning research is seeing the emergence of the field of deep learning. Through deep learning, computers are able to create complex notions from simpler ones. Convolutional neural networks (CNNs) are among the Deep Learning pattern matching methods that have been developed in recent years (LeCun, Bengio, and Hinton 2015)(LeCun et al., 2015), recursive patterns matching model, where the recursive solutions provide a succinct, understandable, and elegant solution (recursivity), but they call for enormous trees, where it is feasible to accelerate execution time through parallelism (Puerto et al., 2018).

First, researchers ask healthy volunteers to spend 20 minutes watching a 10-second YouTube video as part of their investigation. The five video categories—waterfalls, people, faces, forms, moving objects, and motorsports—were chosen at random from a larger pool of movies. The final round of videos includes motorcycle, vehicle racing, water scooter, and snowmobile videos. By examining and comparing the brain waves each movie produced, the researchers were able to use EEG to pinpoint unique brain reactions to different video categories.

They chose three at random from the five categories mentioned above. Recently, neurobiologists created two artificial neural networks.

The first phase is the creation of specific images from noise, and the second is the creation of noise identical to that produced by the EEG. Both systems interacted to produce an actual image. The experiment was then performed for unused videos belonging to the same categories. In this technique, it was possible to generate identical images with an estimated 90% accuracy (M UMER Mirza, 2020).

AI for Experience-Based Learning

A framework for artificial intelligence is being created that will instruct computers how to learn from experience, much like people do. Children, for example, start off by learning to identify things like faces and toys before moving on to learning about communication. They can develop their thinking in this way as they get older. They want AI bots to be able to recognize hazards on their own. As a result, the AI agent may dynamically learn about typical behavior and network traffic patterns, enabling it to recognize and stop assaults before they cause serious harm. Which approach is ideal in this situation? Possibly by learning?

Utilizing a reinforcement learning method, machines examine their surroundings and pick up new information through positive and negative reinforcement. They are able to accomplish a goal by keeping an eye on the future. The use of this kind of algorithm necessitates voluminous and reliable historical data that precisely captures all conceivable configurations and traits for every particular scenario.

There are actions the agent takes, rewards or punishments it receives, and a certain state it is in [St] while it strives to accomplish its goal. The agent chooses an action [At] at this stage of the process based on his observations of the surroundings and his desire to advance to the next state. The agent is first unsure of what the subsequent state will be like. If you advance to the next state, neither you nor your activities can tell you whether the benefits will be greater or worse. Only the current state of their current state and their potential actions depending on the current state are taken into consideration by agents at each phase. In this way, with repeated execution, the agent will learn how the value of his actions changes over time and which ones will yield the largest rewards. As a result, instead of learning how to maximize the goal itself, the agent learns how to come up with the best plan of action to accomplish it.

Exploitation and exploration are crucial components of reinforced learning. Exploration involves choosing random acts. However, employing exploitative methods relies on figuring out whether a particular action is worthwhile at the time in question. Depending on how we want to learn and grow, there will be a range of levels of exploration and exploitation. Every action has a null value in the initial state. It is impossible to forecast the general environment in advance because to the possibility that a state's share availability may differ from state to state. Stocks only increase in value over time. Therefore, investigation is crucial (Online, 2022).

In industry reinforcement, a range of jobs are performed by robots with learning capabilities. These machines are not only safer than people for the duties they carry out, but they are also more productive.

In order to keep Google Data Centers cool, for instance, Deepmind employs AI agents. A 40% decrease in energy use was the effect of this. Without human input, artificial intelligence manages the centers. Experts are still watching over the data center. It operates as follows:

- Deep neural networks are fed data snapshots from data centers every five minutes.
- Then, depending on various combinations, an estimate of future energy use is made.
- A set level of safety must be maintained while identifying the operations that will use the least amount of power possible, and then implementing those actions in the data center (Mwiti, 2022).

AI for Enormous Data Handling and Analysis

Software that is powered by data automatically analyses data from any source and offers insightful information. Data from client interactions can be instructive, influencing product development, enhancing team effectiveness, and identifying what functions well and poorly. Your data analysis can be automatically cleansed, processed, explained, and in the end visualized with artificial intelligence-guided systems.

Asymmetries in data management are the outcome of two things: I public information patterns that some negotiation parties fail to observe, and (ii) difficult to understand acts by an economic actor. The system learns by computations that are automatically improved. These three components—the data to be processed, the connectivity with the cloud and BD, and the computation models—are essential to the machine learning process. These three objectives must all be accomplished using ML, AI, and data science (Serey et al., 2021).

Artificial intelligence-powered data processing systems are distinct from those that use conventional techniques. Artificial intelligence software only initially needs human input; it does not require it continuously. We are working with training data in this situation. AI may analyze data in a variety of ways, such as:

- A bot can produce speedy responses for data analysis using Natural Language Processing (NLP). AI bots are recognized to outperform humans because they work with accumulated stored data, which enables them to respond with pertinent information more quickly.

- Text analysis, a branch of AI/ML, allows machines to comprehend human language and communication. Natural language processing (NLP) is used in text analysis to examine texts and extract information from the data they contain.
- Businesses can diagnose, prescribe, and predict by utilizing AI to analyze qualitative data. Businesses can forecast outcomes by employing numerous strategies at once with the use of machine learning (ML) (Ramakrishnan, 2021).

Another team's research on "Neural Encoding and Decoding with Deep Learning for Dynamic Natural Vision" was published in the journal Cerebral Cortex. Deep learning algorithms were created in order to decode the data stored in the brain.

Over the course of many hours, the researchers observed three women while they watched a range of video clips and recorded their brain activity. Videos regarding avian life, aircraft, and other relevant topics were screened. They received the photos from the cerebral cortex researchers' published studies. Using a functional MRI equipment, researchers monitored signals associated with visual brain activity. Deep learning algorithms predicted brain activity after seeing numerous clips, and it was remarkably comparable to what the women actually performed with their brains. Artificial systems imitate the workings of the brain and, by reacting to particular thoughts, provide tangible outcomes.

Researchers were able to identify the cortical region that governs thought processing thanks to their work. The acquired images were then processed and visually represented using a neural network that had been trained to do so. After the test, the network decoded the brainwaves and provided data with an accuracy rate of more than 50%. In addition, even without scanning a person's brainwaves, the network can create a visual depiction of their thoughts. The experiment's accuracy rate is 25% (M UMER Mirza, 2020).

Based on our research on different life scenarios, three quite used models or algorithm, with their advantage and the year of their introduction are mentioned below.

FUTURE SCOPE IN ARTIFICIAL INTELLIGENCE

Recent AI research has advanced at a remarkable rate. In difficult object identification tests, it has been demonstrated that artificial systems are capable of matching human performance. AI can translate between languages (Wu et al., 2016)(Wu et al., 2016), replicate human speech and, in some cases, natural visuals (Lake et al., 2015)(Lake et al., 2015), and produce neural artwork (Gatys et al., 2015) (Gatys et al., 2015) that is nearly identical to that produced by their human counterparts. AI may also

Table 1. Summary of literature survey

Model/Algorithm/Method	Advantage	Year Introduced
Convolutional neural networks (CNNs)	The fundamental benefit of CNN over its forerunners is that it uses the unique characteristics for every category on its own during pattern matching and automatically determines the significant aspects without human supervision.	1990s
Generative adversarial networks (GANs)	Generative models, which use an unsupervised learning approach, produce data that resembles real data.	June 2014
Deep generator network (DGN) Algorithm	DGNs are able to generate a wide variety of distinctive samples that are fairly convincing, and which helps in better visualization and enlargement of datasets.	2016

be used to learn from the past and forecast the future, which will assist AI systems improve the calibre of their output as they develop.

There is still a lot of work to be done before artificial intelligence reaches human levels, though. The use of neuroscience concepts will be crucial as we seek to close this gap. As a result of their ability to characterise neural circuit computations in great detail, a new generation of techniques for brain imaging and genetic bioengineering are altering our understanding of how mammalian brains work (Deisseroth and Schnitzer, 2013)(Deisseroth & Schnitzer, 2013). With continued research, it is feasible to learn more about the deep-seated brain neurons that react to sensory visions.

CONCLUSION

Brain research has been a major source of inspiration for artificial intelligence research since the turn of the 20th century. Artificial intelligence may be viewed in this sense as an enticing design template given that the brain is capable of sensing, planning, and decision-making. High-dimensional deep neural networks, which can combine memory and visual object identification tasks, frequently include hierarchical brain-inspired architecture. Neuroscience has benefited from the advancement of AI as well (Macpherson et al., 2021).

The importance of the field has been highlighted by our examination of the different ways that neuroscience has assisted AI development. It is vital to remember that when we prepare for future cooperation between the two disciplines, neuroscience's contributions to artificial intelligence have rarely resulted in comprehensive solutions that could be instantaneously put into machines. Instead, by offering insights into the learning and thought processes of animals, neuroscience has traditionally offered a more subtle benefit to researchers researching artificial intelligence. Insights from neuroscience will, in our opinion, help AI research move more swiftly. The most effective method to accomplish this is for AI researchers to actively collaborate with neuroscientists to determine the most crucial challenges that require experimental investigation.

Researchers in these two fields need to work closely together in order to successfully apply the learnings from neuroscience to the development of artificial intelligence algorithms. The researchers in these two domains regularly exchange ideas, which is where these breakthroughs frequently originate. If we can better comprehend the mind by boiling down intelligence to an algorithmic design and contrasting it with the human brain, we may be able to decipher the meaning of creativity, dreams, and even consciousness (Hassabis et al., 2017).

REFERENCES

Deisseroth, K., & Schnitzer, M. J. (2013). Engineering approaches to illuminating brain structure and dynamics. *Neuron*, *80*(3), 568–577. doi:10.1016/j.neuron.2013.10.032 PMID:24183010

Gatys, L. A., Ecker, A. S., & Bethge, M. (2015). *A neural algorithm of artistic style.* arXiv preprint arXiv:1508.06576.

Hassabis, D., Kumaran, D., Summerfield, C., & Botvinick, M. (2017). Neuroscience-inspired artificial intelligence. *Neuron*, *95*(2), 245–258. doi:10.1016/j. neuron.2017.06.011 PMID:28728020

Hawkins, J., & Blakeslee, S. (2004). *On intelligence.* Macmillan.

Jean-Marc, F., Guillermo, S., Andrew, R., Helen, M., & Michele, F. (2019). Explainable Artificial Intelligence for Neuroscience: Behavioral Neurostimulation. *Frontiers in Neuroscience*, *13*, 1346. doi:10.3389/fnins.2019.01346 PMID:31920509

Kaku, M. (2014). *El futuro de nuestra mente: El reto científico para entender, mejorar, y fortalecer nuestra mente.* Debate.

Lake, B. M., Salakhutdinov, R., & Tenenbaum, J. B. (2015). Human-level concept learning through probabilistic program induction. *Science*, *350*(6266), 1332–1338. doi:10.1126cience.aab3050 PMID:26659050

LeCun, Y., Bengio, Y., & Hinton, G. (2015). Deep learning. *Nature*, *521*(7553), 436-444.

Macpherson, T., Churchland, A., Sejnowski, T., DiCarlo, J., Kamitani, Y., Takahashi, H., & Hikida, T. (2021). Natural and Artificial Intelligence: A brief introduction to the interplay between AI and neuroscience research. *Neural Networks*, *144*, 603–613. doi:10.1016/j.neunet.2021.09.018 PMID:34649035

Markram, H. (2012). The human brain project. *Scientific American*, *306*(6), 50–55. doi:10.1038cientificamerican0612-50 PMID:22649994

Mirza. (2020). *AI can Read and Visualize our thoughts*. Retrieved August 17, 2022, from https://thinkml.ai/ai-can-read-and-visualize-our-thoughts/

Mwiti, D. (2022, July 21). *10 Real-Life Applications of Reinforcement Learning*. Retrieved August 22, 2022, from https://neptune.ai/blog/reinforcement-learning-applications/

New AI system mimics how humans visualize and identify objects. (2018). Retrieved August 18, 2022, from https://samueli.ucla.edu/new-ai-system-mimics-how-humans-visualize-and-identify-objects/

Online, D. (2022, May 24). *How can Artificial Intelligence learn from Experience?* Retrieved August 20, 2022, from https://www.dqindia.com/can-artificial-intelligence-learn-experience/

Puerto, E., Aguilar, J., & Chávez, D. (2018). A recursive patterns matching model for the dynamic pattern recognition problem. *Applied Artificial Intelligence*, *32*(4), 419–432. doi:10.1080/08839514.2018.1481593

Quan, J. (2022). Visualization and Analysis Model of Industrial Economy Status and Development Based on Knowledge Graph and Deep Neural Network. *Computational Intelligence and Neuroscience*, *2022*, 2022. doi:10.1155/2022/7008093 PMID:35528336

Ramakrishnan, V. (2021, July 20). *Data Analysis Made Simple through Artificial Intelligence - Aspire Systems*. Retrieved from https://blog.aspiresys.com/digital/big-data-analytics/data-analysis-made-simple-through-artificial-intelligence/

Serey, J., Quezada, L., Alfaro, M., Fuertes, G., Vargas, M., Ternero, R., Sabattin, J., Duran, C., & Gutierrez, S. (2021). Artificial intelligence methodologies for data management. *Symmetry*, *13*(11), 2040. doi:10.3390ym13112040

Taubman, D., & Marcellin, M. (2012). JPEG2000 image compression fundamentals, standards and practice. Academic Press.

Wiggers, K. (2019). *MIT CSAIL's AI can visualize objects using touch.* Retrieved January 10, 2023, from https://venturebeat.com/ai/mit-csails-ai-can-visualize-objects-using-touch/

Wu, Y., Schuster, M., Chen, Z., Le, Q. V., Norouzi, M., Macherey, W., . . . Dean, J. (2016). *Google's neural machine translation system: Bridging the gap between human and machine translation.* arXiv preprint arXiv:1609.08144.

KEY TERMS AND DEFINITIONS

Convolutional Neural Networks (CNNs): It is a Deep Learning algorithm that is capable of receiving image input, weighing the components and elements of the image, and determining which is significant among them.

Electroencephalography (EEG): A device that captures and measures the electrical activity in the brain.

Functional MRI: A functionality of using magnetic resonance imaging for estimating and mapping brain activity based on the measures of circulation and oxygenation.

Natural Language Processing: It is a subfield of computer science (in particular, artificial intelligence) that enables computers to interpret verbal and written information much like humans.

Neocortex: A significant portion of the higher brain functions are concentrated in the layered, complex tissue that comprises the cerebral cortex.

Neural Network: They are a component of deep learning algorithms modeled after brain activity, emulating how neurons communicate with one another.

UCLA: It stands for University of California, Los Angeles.

Chapter 3
Study and Innovative Approach of Deep Learning Algorithms and Architecture

Omprakash Dewangan
Kalinga University, India

ABSTRACT

Deep learning is becoming increasingly important in our everyday lives. It has already made a big difference in industries like cancer diagnosis, precision medicine, self-driving cars, predictive forecasting, and speech recognition, to name a few. Traditional learning, classification, and pattern recognition methods necessitate feature extractors that aren't scalable for large datasets. Depending on the issue complexity, deep learning can often overcome the limitations of past shallow networks that hampered fast training and abstractions of hierarchical representations of multi-dimensional training data. Deep learning techniques have been applied successfully to vegetable infection by plant disease, demonstrating their suitability for the agriculture sector. The chapter looks at a few optimization approaches for increasing training accuracy and decreasing training time. The authors delve into the mathematics that underpin recent deep network training methods. Current faults, improvements, and implementations are discussed. The authors explore various popular deep learning architecture and their real-world uses in this chapter. Deep learning algorithms are increasingly being used in place of traditional techniques in many machine vision applications. Benefits include avoiding the requirement for specific handcrafted feature extractors and maintaining the integrity of the output. Additionally, they frequently grow better. The review discusses deep convolutional networks, deep residual networks, recurrent neural networks, reinforcement learning, variational autoencoders, and other deep architectures.

DOI: 10.4018/978-1-6684-6980-4.ch003

INTRODUCTION

In the field of deep learning, artificial neural networks (ANNs), which are powerful algorithms modeled after human brains, learn from enormous quantities of data. Simply explained, deep learning is the process of teaching computers to learn new knowledge in a manner similar to how people do. Humans perceive information from images, text, and speech using a network of neurons in their brains in addition to their sense organs (eyes, ears, etc.). This process of information exchange between many millions of neurons via electrical and chemical signals (Rosenblatt, 1958). Artificial neural networks convey information utilizing multiple interconnected layers of neurons, similar to how natural neural networks operate (nodes). Neural nets with more than three layers are typically referred to as having "depth" in deep learning (they can have more than 100 layers, just so you know). Despite the fact that the three technologies are interconnected, the terms cannot be interchanged. It is critical to understand how deep learning differs from machine learning and artificial intelligence. Regarding relationships, deep learning is a branch of machine learning, which is a subset of artificial intelligence, which acts as a catch-all term for all smart technologies (Werbos, 1975).

DEEP LEARNING ALGORITHM

Deep learning is a machine learning and artificial intelligence technique designed to scare people and influence their behavior based on specific human brain functions and efficient choices. It is a crucial component of data science that directs it's modeling-based on data-driven methods under statistical and predictive modeling driving such a human-like vehicle In order to work appropriately, there must be some powerful forces that have the We referred to them as algorithms (LeCun et al., 2015).

Deep learning algorithms are dynamically created to run through multiple layers of neural networks, which are nothing more than a collection of decision-making networks that have been trained to fulfill a specific task. Later, each of these is put through straightforward layered representations before moving on to the second layer. However, the majority of machine learning is taught to perform admirably on datasets that must deal with a large number of features or columns. Whether a data set is structured or not depends on (Ng, 2019). The main reason why machine learning frequently fails is that it cannot identify a straightforward image with 800 by 1000 pixels in RGB. It becomes quite difficult for a standard machine learning method to handle an algorithm to deal with these depths (Metz, 2019).

DEEP LEARNING'S IMPORTANCE

Deep learning algorithms are essential for identifying the features and are capable of handling enormous datasets. Numerous procedures for processing data, whether it is structured or not. However, some jobs that may include complicated difficulties can be overkill for deep learning algorithms since they require access to enormous volumes of data in order to operate efficiently. For instance, there is an image net, a well-known picture recognition program with access to 14 billion photos million photographs in its algorithms that are data-driven (Shrestha and Mahmood, 2019). It is an extremely thorough tool that has defined a benchmark for advanced deep learning methods using photos as its target dataset.

Deep learning algorithms are extremely advanced algorithms that discover information about the image that we previously talked about by putting it through each layer of the neural network. The layers are really thick and sensitive to find the image's low-level details, such as pixels and borders, and therefore the Combination layers use this data to create comprehensive representations by comparing it to earlier data (Silver et al., 2015). For instance, the middle layer could be configured to recognize certain unique components of the photograph's subject that other deeply educated layers are set up to recognize specifically dogs, trees, cutlery, and other things (Kingma and M. Welling, 2013).

DEEP LEARNING ARCHITECTURE AND ALGORITHMS

Neural Networks with Convolutions (CNNs)

ConvNets, also known as CNNs, are primarily made up of numerous layers and are utilized in for the processing of images and object detection. Yann LeCun created it in 1998, along with initially known as LeNet. It was created back then to detect numerals and zip code characters. CNNs are frequently used in satellite image identification, medical image processing, anomaly detection and series forecasting (Nevo, 2019).

The data is processed by CNNs by going through several layers and extracting features to display. Convolutional processes Rectified Linear Units (ReLUs), which are part of the convolutional layer, are used to correct the feature map. These feature maps are corrected for the following feed using the pooling layer. Pooling is often a down-sampled sampling procedure that minimizes the feature map's dimensions. Later, the outcome produced comprises 2-D arrays made up of flattened in the map of a single, long, continuous, and linear vector. The subsequent layer, that is, the flattened matrix or 2-D array retrieved from the fully connected layer, which Pooling Layer takes the image as input and classifies it to identify it (Esteva et al., 2017).

Figure 1. Neural networks with convolutions (CNNs)

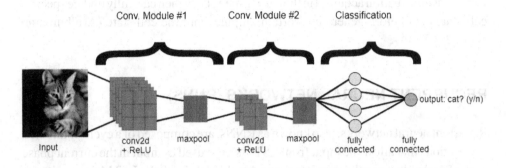

NETWORKS WITH LONG-SHORT TERM MEMORY (LSTMS)

Recurrent Neural Networks (RNN) that are programmed to learn and remember are known as LSTMs. For the long term, adjust for dependencies. It has a stronger ability to memorize and recall previous data. It is its only behavior, period, and is what it does by default. LSTMs are created to hold up over time and they are therefore mostly utilized in time series forecasts as a result of their ability to limit memory or antecedent inputs (LeCun et al., 1998).

Figure 2. Networks with Long-Short Term Memory (LSTMs)

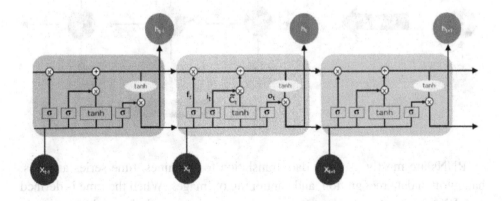

This comparison is made due to their chain-like structure, which consists of four interconnected layers that communicate with one another in various ways. There are further uses for They can be used to create voice recognizers, advance medicinal research, and even create musical loops time series prediction (Taylor et al., 2010).

The LSTM operates on a series of events. First, they have a tendency to forget irrelevant information acquired in the earlier state. They then carefully update specific cell-state data before generating certain outputs from the cell state (Arulkumaran et al., 2017).

RECURRENT NEURAL NETWORKS (RNNS)

Recurrent neural networks, also known as RNNs, are composed of a cycle of directed connections that allow the input from LSTMs to be used as input in the current phase of the RNNs. Because these inputs are so deeply ingrained, the LSTMs' capacity for memorization allows them to be temporarily stored in the internal memory. RNNs consequently rely on the inputs that LSTMs preserve and operate in accordance with the synchronization phenomenon of LSTMs (Gheisari et al., 2017).

Figure 3. Recurrent Neural Networks (RNNs)

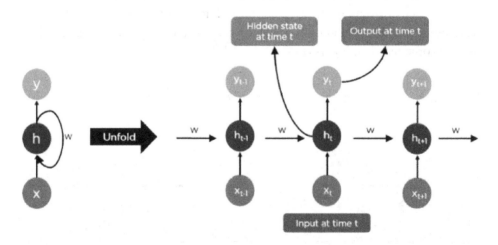

RNNs are mostly used for data translation to machines, time series analysis, handwritten data recognition, and captioning of images. When the time is defined as t, RNNs put output feeds at (t-1) time in accordance with the work strategy. At input time t+1, the output determined by t is then fed. Similar operations are carried out for all inputs, regardless of input length. RNNs have the additional property of storing historical data; hence, even if the model size is expanded, the input size remains constant. RNNs resemble this when they are fully unfolded (Pouyanfar, 2018).

GANS (GENERATIVE ADVERSARIAL NETWORKS)

GANs are deep learning algorithms that are used to create new instances of data that closely resemble the training data. A GAN typically has two parts: a generator that learns to produce fake data and a discriminator that evolves by taking lessons from this false data. Since they are widely employed to sharpen astronomical images and simulate lensing the gravitational dark matter, GANs have grown significantly in popularity over time. Additionally, it is used in video games to boost the visual appeal of 2D textures by producing new versions of them in higher resolutions, such as 4K. They are also employed in the production of lifelike cartoon characters, as well as the representation of human faces and 3D objects (Vargas et al., 2017).

Figure 4. GANs (Generative Adversarial Networks)

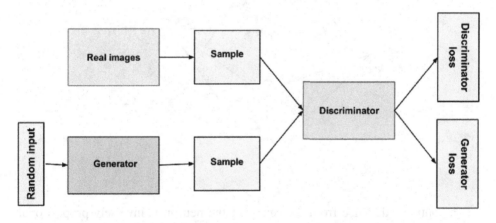

By creating and comprehending both fake and real data, GANs function in simulation. The discriminator quickly learns to adapt and recognize it as false data throughout the training to grasp this data, while the generator produces various types of phony data. These identified results are then transmitted to GANs for updating (Buhmann, 2003), (Akinduko et al., 2016).

RADIAL BASIS FUNCTION NETWORKS (RBFNS)

Radial Basis Function Networks are a particular class of neural networks that employ radial functions as activation functions and adhere to a feed-forward methodology. They are typically used for time-series prediction, regression testing, and classification and have three layers: the input layer, hidden layer, and output layer (Chen, 2015). By analyzing the similarities found in the training data set, RBFNs do these tasks. In most cases, they have an input vector that feeds these data into the input layer, validating the identification and disseminating results by comparing prior data sets. In fact, the input layer's neurons are sensitive to this data, and the layer's nodes are effective at categorizing the data class. Although they act in tight integration with the input layer, neurons are initially present in the hidden layer (Ng and Jordan, 2001).

Figure 5. Radial Basis Function Networks (RBFNs)

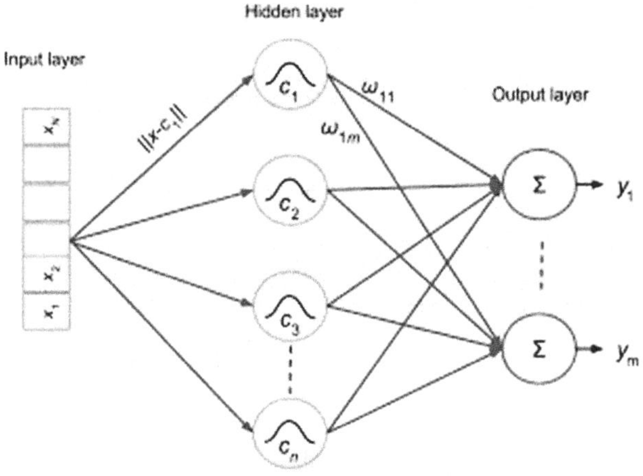

The output's distance from the center of the neuron is inversely proportional to the Gaussian transfer functions in the hidden layer. The output layer consists of linear combinations of radial-based data, where output is produced using Gaussian functions that are supplied as parameters to the neuron. Consider the illustration provided below to fully comprehend the procedure (LeCun et al., 1998).

Figure 6. Multilayer Perceptrons

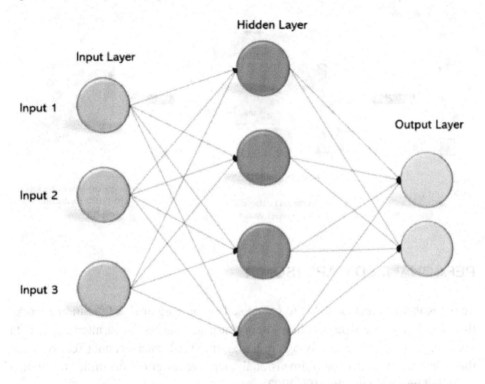

MULTILAYER PERCEPTRONS

MLPs, or multilayer perceptrons, are the cornerstone of deep learning technology. It belongs to a group of feed-forward neural networks with a number of perceptron-filled layers. These perceptrons each have a different activation function. Input and output layers in MLPs are also connected and have the same number of layers. Between these two strata, there is another layer that is still undiscovered. MLPs are primarily used to create voice and picture recognition software, as well as various kinds of translation software (Schuler et al., 2013).

The data is fed into the input layer to begin the operation of MLPs. The layer's neurons come together to create a graph that creates a link that only goes in one direction. It is discovered that there is weight for this input data between the hidden layer and the input layer. Activation functions are used by MLPs to identify the nodes that are prepared to fire. The tanh function, the sigmoid, and the ReLUs are some of these activation mechanisms. In order to produce the required output from the given input set, MLPs are mostly utilized to train the models and determine what kind of correlation the layers are serving (Radford et al., 2015).

Figure 7. Personalized Maps (SOMs)

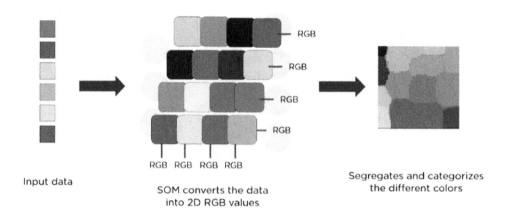

PERSONALIZED MAPS (SOMS)

Teuvo Kohenen created SOMs to create self-organizing artificial neural networks that could visualize data and help users grasp its aspects. Most attempts at data visualization for problem-solving are based on what humans cannot see. Because these data are typically multidimensional, there are fewer opportunities for human error and involvement (Jolliffe, 2002).

SOMs aid in data visualization by choosing random vectors from the provided training data after initializing the weights of various nodes. So that dependencies may be understood, they look at each node to determine the respective weights. The best matching unit is used to choose the winning node (BMU) (Noda, 2013). These winning nodes are later found by SOMs, but they gradually disappear from the sample vector. Therefore, there is a greater likelihood that the node will detect the weight and perform additional tasks the closer it is to the BMU. To make sure that no node that is closer to BMU is overlooked, numerous iterations are also performed. The RGB color is one such illustration mixtures that we employ in our regular work. Think about the illustration below to comprehend how they function (Hinton and Salakhutdinov, 2006).

Networks of Deep Belief (DBNs)

DBNs are referred to as generative models because they contain a variety of latent as well as stochastic elements. Because the latent variable has binary values, it is referred to as a hidden unit. Due to the fact that the RGM layers are piled on top of one another, DBNs are also known as Boltzmann Machines and others to create communication with lower levels and those above it. DBNs are utilized in applications for capturing moving objects as well as video and picture recognition (Wang et al., 2016).

Figure 8. Networks of Deep Belief (DBNs)

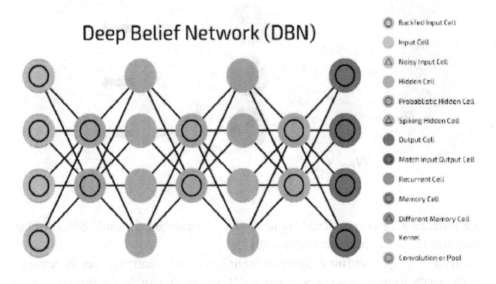

Algorithms that are Greedy power DBNs. The layer-by-layer method involves learning through The most typical operation of DBNs is a top-down method to weight generation. DBNs employ Gibbs sampling is applied step-by-step to the top buried two-layer. The following steps An ancestor sampling model is used to select a sample from the observable units. DBNs gain knowledge from the values that are present in the latent value from each layer after the bottom-up pass method (Teh and Hinton, 2001).

RESTRICTED BOLTZMANN MACHINES (RBMS)

Geoffrey Hinton created RBMs, which mimic stochastic neural networks and learn from the input set's probability distribution. In the field, this algorithm is primarily employed topic modeling, classification, regression, and dimension reduction are thought to be the components that make up DBNs. The visible layer and the concealed layer are both present in RBIs layer. Bias units attached to both of these layers' hidden units provide a connection between them. nodes that are responsible

Figure 9. Restricted Boltzmann Machines (RBMs)

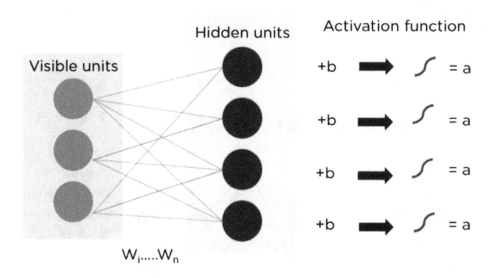

for producing the output. RBMs typically have two stages, forward and backward, backward pass and pass (Naul et al., 2018).

By taking inputs and turning them into numbers, RBMs carry out their operations, such that the forward pass encrypts inputs. RBMs account for the importance of each input, and the backward pass further transforms these input weights into reconstructed weights inputs. Both of these translated inputs are afterwards mixed with their respective weights. These after that, inputs are directed toward the visible layer, where activation occurs, and output is that is easily reconstruct able is generated. Consider the graphic below to get a better idea of this procedure (Najafabadi et al., 2015).

AUTOENCODERS

Inputs and outputs are typically found in particular types of neural networks called autoencoders identical. It was created in order to primarily address issues with unsupervised learning. Highly trained neural networks called autoencoders reproduce the data. Because of this, In general, input and output are equivalent. They help with tasks like pharmaceutical discovery, population forecasting and image processing (Goodfellow et al., 2016).

The encoder, the code, and the decoder are the three parts that make up an autoencoder the decryptor. Autoencoders are designed with a structure that allows them to accept inputs and change them into different representations (Gavin, 2016).

Figure 10. Autoencoders

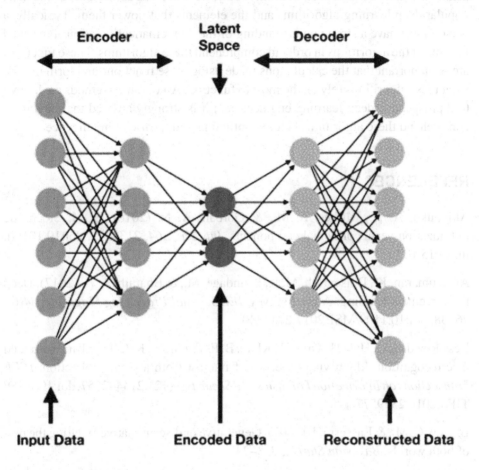

The endeavors to duplicate the original contribution made by reconstructing them yields more precise results. They accomplish this by encrypting the input or image, lowering the size. If the image is not clearly visible, it is sent to the neural network for explanation. The image is then referred to as being "reconstructed" and is as exact as possible. See the illustration provided below to comprehend this intricate process (Glorot and Bengio, 2010).

CONCLUSION

In this chapter, deep learning and the algorithms that support it are the key topics. In the beginning, we discovered how deep learning transforms the job at a dynamic speed with vision to produce intelligent software that can replicate it and work like a human brain. In a later section of this essay, we will learn about some of the most popular deep learning algorithms and the elements that power them. Typically, a person must have a strong understanding of the mathematical functions presented in some of the algorithms in order to comprehend these algorithms. These functions are so important that the calculations made using these functions and formulas are what these algorithms rely on the most to function. All of these methods are known to a prospective deep learning engineer, and it is strongly advised that beginners comprehend these algorithms before continuing with artificial intelligence.

REFERENCES

Akinduko, A. A., Mirkes, E. M., & Gorban, A. N. (2016). SOM: Stochastic initialization versus principal components. *Inf. Sci.*, *364*, 213–221. doi:10.1016/j. ins.2015.10.013

Arulkumaran, K., Deisenroth, M. P., Brundage, M., & Bharath, A. A. (2017). Deep reinforcement learning: A brief survey. *IEEE Signal Processing Magazine*, *34*(6), 26–38. doi:10.1109/MSP.2017.2743240

Best-Rowden, L., Han, H., Otto, C., Klare, B. F., & Jain, A. K. (2014). Unconstrained face recognition: Identifying a person of interest from a media collection. *IEEE Transactions on Information Forensics and Security*, *9*(12), 2144–2157. doi:10.1109/TIFS.2014.2359577

Bishop, C. M., & Lasserre, J. (2007). Generative or discriminative? Getting the best of both worlds. *Bayesian Statist.*, *8*, 3–24.

Buhmann, M. D. (2003). *Radial Basis Functions*. Cambridge Univ. Press. doi:10.1017/CBO9780511543241

Chen, K. (2015). *Deep and modular neural networks" in Springer Handbook of Computational Intelligence*. Springer.

Cybenko, G. (1989). Approximation by super positions of a sigmoidal function. *Mathematics of Control, Signals, and Systems*, *2*(4), 303–314. doi:10.1007/BF02551274

Duchi, J., Hazan, E., & Singer, Y. (2011). Adaptive subgradient methods for online learning and stochastic optimization. *Journal of Machine Learning Research*, *12*, 2121–2159.

Escalante, H. J., Montes, M., & Sucar, L. E. (2009). Particle swarm model selection. *Journal of Machine Learning Research*, *10*, 405–440.

Esteva. (2017). *Dermatologist-level classification of skin cancer with deep neural networks*. Academic Press.

Gavin. (2016). *The Levenberg-Marquardt method for nonlinear least squares curve-fitting problems*. Academic Press.

Gheisari, M., Wang, G., & Bhuiyan, M. Z. A. (2017). A survey on deep learning in big data. *Proc. IEEE Int. Conf. Computing. Sci. Eng. (CSE),* 173-180. 10.1109/CSE-EUC.2017.215

Glorot, X., & Bengio, Y. (2010). Understanding the difficulty of training deep feed forward neural networks. *Proc. 13th Int. Conf. Artif. Intell. Statist.,* 249-256.

Goldberg, D. E. (2013). *The Design of Innovation: Lessons from and for Competent Genetic Algorithms*. Springer.

Goodfellow, I., Bengio, Y., & Courville, A. (2016). *Deep learning. In Adaptive Computation And Machine Learning*. MIT Press.

Guo, Y., Cai, Q., Samuels, D. C., Ye, F., Long, J., Li, C.-I., Winther, J. F., Tawn, E. J., Stovall, M., Lähteenmäki, P., Malila, N., Levy, S., Shaffer, C., Shyr, Y., Shu, X., & Boice, J. D. Jr. (2012). The use of next generation sequencing technology to study the effect of radiation therapy on mitochondrial DNA mutation. *Mutation Research/Genetic Toxicology and Environmental Mutagenesis, 744*(2), 154–160. doi:10.1016/j.mrgentox.2012.02.006 PMID:22387842

Hadsell, R., Chopra, S., & LeCun, Y. (2006). Dimensionality reduction by learning an invariant mapping. *Proc. IEEE Comput. Soc. Conf. Computing Vis. Pattern Recognition (CVPR),* 1735-1742. 10.1109/CVPR.2006.100

He, K., Zhang, X., Ren, S., & Sun, J. (2016). Deep residual learning for image recognition. *Proc. IEEE Conf. Comput. Vis. Pattern Recognit. (CVPR),* 770-778. 10.1109/CVPR.2016.90

Hinton, G. E. (2007). Learning multiple layers of representation. *Trends in Cognitive Sciences, 11*(10), 428–434. doi:10.1016/j.tics.2007.09.004 PMID:17921042

Hinton, G. E., & Salakhutdinov, R. R. (2006). Reducing the dimensionality of data with neural networks. *Science, 313*(5786), 504–507. doi:10.1126cience.1127647 PMID:16873662

Hornik, K. (1991). Approximation capabilities of multilayer feed forward networks. *Neural Networks, 4*(2), 251–257. doi:10.1016/0893-6080(91)90009-T

Huang, G.-B., Zhu, Q.-Y., & Siew, C.-K. (2006). Extreme learning machine: Theory and applications. *Neurocomputing, 70*(1-3), 489–501. doi:10.1016/j.neucom.2005.12.126

Huang, L., Joseph, A. D., Nelson, B., Rubinstein, B. I. P., & Tygar, J. D. (2011). Adversarial machine learning. *4th ACM Workshop Secur. Artif. Intell.*, 43-58.

Ioffe & Szegedy. (2015). *Batch normalization: Accelerating deep network training by reducing internal covariate shift.* Academic Press.

Jolliffe, I. T. (2022). *Principal component analysis in Mathematics and Statistics.* Springer.

Jordan, M. I., & Mitchell, T. M. (2015). Machine learning: Trends perspectives and prospects. *Science, 349*(6245), 255–260. doi:10.1126cience.aaa8415 PMID:26185243

Kingma & Ba. (2014). *Adam: A method for stochastic optimization.* Academic Press.

Kingma, D. P., & Welling, M. (2013). *Auto-encoding variational Bayes.* https://arxiv.org/abs/1312.6114

Kuo, Hariharan, & Malik. (2015). *Deep Box: Learning object ness with convolutional networks.* Academic Press.

Larrañaga, P., Kuijpers, C. M. H., Murga, R. H., Inza, I., & Dizdarevic, S. (1999). Genetic algorithms for the travelling salesman problem: A review of representations and operators. *Artificial Intelligence Review, 13*(2), 129–170. doi:10.1023/A:1006529012972

LeCun, Y., & Bengio, Y. (1998). *Convolutional networks for images speech and time series. In The Handbook of Brain Theory and Neural Networks.* MIT Press.

LeCun, Y., Bengio, Y., & Hinton, G. (2015). Deep learning. *Nature, 521*(7553), 436–444. doi:10.1038/nature14539 PMID:26017442

LeCun, Y., Bottou, L., Bengio, Y., & Haffner, P. (1998). Gradient-based learning applied to document recognition. *Proceedings of the IEEE, 86*(11), 2278–2324. doi:10.1109/5.726791

Letsche, T. A., & Berry, M. W. (1997). Large-scale information retrieval with latent semantic indexing. *Inf. Sci., 100*(1-4), 105–137. doi:10.1016/S0020-0255(97)00044-3

Lin, C.-T., Prasad, M., & Saxena, A. (2015). An improved polynomial neural network classifier using real-coded genetic algorithm. *IEEE Transactions on Systems, Man, and Cybernetics. Systems, 45*(11), 1389–1401. doi:10.1109/TSMC.2015.2406855

Martens, J. (2010). Deep learning via Hessian-free optimization. *Proc. 27th Int. Conf. Int. Conf. Mach. Learn.*, 735-742.

Metz, C. (2019). Turing Award Won by 3 Pioneers in Artificial Intelligence. *New York Times*, p. B3.

Miikkulainen. (2017). *Evolving deep neural networks*. Academic Press.

Nagpal. (2018). *Development and validation of a deep learning algorithm for improving Gleason scoring of prostate cancer*. Academic Press.

Najafabadi, M. M., Villanustre, F., Khoshgoftaar, T. M., Seliya, N., Wald, R., & Muharemagic, E. (2015). Deep learning applications and challenges in big data analytics. *Journal of Big Data*, 2(1), 1. doi:10.118640537-014-0007-7

Naul, B., Bloom, J. S., Pérez, F., & van der Walt, S. (2018). A recurrent neural network for classification of unevenly sampled variable stars. *Nature Astron.*, 2(2), 151–155. doi:10.103841550-017-0321-z

Nevo. (2019). *ML for flood forecasting at scale*. Academic Press.

Ng. (2019). *Machine learning yearning: Technical strategy for ai engineers in the era of deep learning*. Academic Press.

Ng, A. Y., & Jordan, M. I. (2001). On discriminative vs. generative classifiers: A comparison of logistic regression and naive Bayes. *Proc. 14th Int. Conf. Neural Inf. Process. Syst.*, 841-848.

Noda, K. (2013). Multimodal integration learning of object manipulation behaviors using deep neural networks. *Proc. IEEE/RSJ Int. Conf. Intell. Robots Syst.*, 1728-1733. 10.1109/IROS.2013.6696582

Pouyanfar. (2018). A survey on deep learning: Algorithms techniques and applications. *ACM Comput. Survey, 51*(5), 92.

Radford, Metz, & Chintala. (2015). *Unsupervised representation learning with deep convolutional generative adversarial networks*. Academic Press.

Razali, N. M., & Geraghty, J. (2010). Genetic algorithm performance with different selection strategies in solving TSP. *Proc. world Congr. Eng.*, 1-6.

Rosenblatt, F. (1958). The perceptron: A probabilistic model for information storage and organization in the brain. *Psychological Review*, 65(6), 386–408. doi:10.1037/h0042519 PMID:13602029

Salakhutdinov, R., & Hinton, G. (2009). Deep Boltzmann machines. *Proc. 12th Int. Conf. Artif. Intell. Statist.*, 448-455.

Sampson, J. R. (1976). Adaptation in Natural and Artificial Systems. SIAM, 18, 529-530.

Sastry, Goldberg, & Kendall. (2005). *Genetic Algorithms.* Academic Press.

Schuler, C. J., Burger, H. C., Harmeling, S., & Scholkopf, B. (2013). A machine learning approach for non-blind image deconvolution. *Proc. IEEE Conf. Comput. Vis. Pattern Recognit.*, 1067-1074. 10.1109/CVPR.2013.142

Shrestha & Mahmood. (2016). Improving genetic algorithm with fine-tuned crossover and scaled architecture. *J. Math., 10.*

Shrestha, A., & Mahmood, A. (2019). Enhancing siamese networks training with importance sampling. *Proc. 11th Int. Conf. Agents Artif. Intell.*, 610-615. 10.5220/0007371706100615

Silver. (2016). Mastering the game of go with deep neural networks and tree search. *Nature, 529*(7587), 484.

Simpson, (2015). *Uniform learning in a deep neural network via 'oddball' stochastic gradient descent.* Academic Press.

Srivastava, N., Hinton, G., Krizhevsky, A., Sutskever, I., & Salakhutdinov, R. (2014). Dropout: A simple way to prevent neural networks from overfitting. *Journal of Machine Learning Research, 15,* 1929–1958.

Tang, J., Deng, C., & Huang, G.-B. (2015). Extreme learning machine for multilayer perceptron. *IEEE Transactions on Neural Networks and Learning Systems, 27*(4), 809–821. doi:10.1109/TNNLS.2015.2424995 PMID:25966483

Taylor, G. W., Fergus, R., LeCun, Y., & Bregler, C. (2010). *Convolutional learning of spatio-temporal features in Computer Vision.* Springer.

Teh, Y. W., & Hinton, G. E. (2001). Adv. Neural Inf. Process. Syst.: Vol. 908-914. Rate-coded restricted Boltzmann machines for face recognition. Academic Press.

Vargas, Mosavi, & Ruiz. (2017). Deep learning: A review. *Proc. Adv. Intell. Syst. Comput.*, 1-11.

Wang, M., Li, H.-X., Chen, X., & Chen, Y. (2016). Deep learning-based model reduction for distributed parameter systems. *IEEE Transactions on Systems, Man, and Cybernetics. Systems, 46*(12), 1664–1674. doi:10.1109/TSMC.2016.2605159

Werbos. (1975). *Beyond Regression: New tools for prediction and analysis in the behavioral sciences*. Academic Press.

Whitley, D. (1994). A genetic algorithm tutorial. *Statistics and Computing, 4*(2), 65–85. doi:10.1007/BF00175354

Yu, D., & Deng, L. (2015). *Automatic Speech Recognition: A Deep Learning Approach*. Springer. doi:10.1007/978-1-4471-5779-3

Chapter 4
Enhancing Brain Imaging Using Super Resolution:
Challenges and Benefits

Madhulika Bhadauria
iD https://orcid.org/0000-0001-6833-5657
Amity University, India

Rishita Khurana
Amity University, India

Supavadee Aramvith
Chulalongkorn University, Thailand

ABSTRACT

Super-resolution reconstruction creates one or more high-resolution images from a collection of low-resolution frames. This chapter examines a number of super-resolution methods proposed over the last two decades and provides an overview of the contributions made recently to the broad super-resolution problem. During the procedure, a thorough examination of numerous crucial elements of super-resolution is presented, which are frequently overlooked in the literature. The authors have also outlined various advancements and studies that have been done in the particular domain. The prime focus of this chapter is to highlight the importance and application of super resolution in brain MRI and explore all the work that has been done in the field so far. The experiments on simulated and actual data are used to support novel strategies for tackling the difficulties faced while implementing the technique. Finally, several prospective super-resolution difficulties are identified, and methodologies are presented.

DOI: 10.4018/978-1-6684-6980-4.ch004

INTRODUCTION

The ability of a sensor to notice or measure the smallest or littlest item by relying on the pixel size is referred to as resolution of an image. Higher-resolution digital images are continuously appealing in a variety of applications. The imaging methods have quickly evolved somewhat recently; also, the resolution has arrived at another level. The critical question is whether or not the techniques for increasing an image's resolution are necessary. Although the top-quality showcases as of late have arrived at another level, the need for resolution improvement can't be disregarded in numerous applications; medical imaging being one of them. Medical imaging, sometimes referred to as radiography, is a field of medicine where clinical staff takes pictures of various body parts for therapeutic or diagnostic purposes. Concerning this, inside each imaging methodology, explicit actual laws are in charge, characterizing the significance of commotion and the affectability of the imaging process. It is still not possible to generate 3D models of the human structure from high-resolution photographs without increasing radiation exposure. Considering these realities, the current methods can't yet fulfill the requests. Super resolution is subsequently still vital.

Super resolution may have various implications relying upon the application space or perspective. For example, every one of the calculations managing super resolution depends on the requirements that a super resolution picture ought to produce low resolution input pictures when suitably distorted and down-tested to demonstrate the picture development process. As a result, it is the method used the most frequently to frame a higher-resolution image by combining several low-resolution images. This examination is less substantial in terms of medical imaging. Medical images are always the consequence of correlations between a tissue and a physical abnormality, such as a wave or an ionizing molecule. Because of high indicative capacity and natural models, imaging organic miniature designs of sub-micron size has been a significant objective lately for some imaging modalities. There are primarily two limits intrinsic and extrinsic from which the low resolution in medical images originates. Intrinsic resolution limitation starts from an actual connection between the tissue and the actual peculiarity (wave or rudimentary molecule). It is restricted both by the attributes of this communication, like lessening, dissipating, and so forth, and by the qualities of the sensors like frequency, its temperament and course of action (spatial distance between identifiers). The annoyance of the picture accounts causes extrinsic resolution limitation. It is limited by non-constrained and unconstrained tissue or patient rhythms such as developments, heart rate, and breathing rate.

The super-resolution provides a number of advantages but also some drawbacks that are typically looked at in medical imaging. Due to constraints, medical images' spatial resolution is insufficient. To resolve the issues, diverse techniques of super-resolution have been proposed, for example, advancement or learning-based methodologies.

As of late, different techniques have turned into flourishing innovations and are emerging remarkably. Different deep learning methods and strategies are discussed briefly in this chapter which solves super-resolution problems. The applications of super-resolution are also discussed.

LITERATURE REVIEW

The main purpose of super-resolution imaging is to reconstruct a high-resolution image based on a series of images acquired from the same scene (referred to as 'low-resolution' images) to avoid image limitations and/or posed to overcome the conditions. An image captures process to facilitate better content visualization and scene recognition. This section provides a comprehensive overview of SR imaging and video reconstruction methods developed in the literature and highlights future research challenges. The SR image approach reconstructs a single high-resolution image from a given set of low-resolution images, while the SR video approach reconstructs a high-resolution image sequence from a group of adjacent low-resolution frames. Additionally, several applications of SR are discussed to provide insightful comments on future SR research directions. A comparison of the prior SR methods used in various studies is provided in Table 1.

Background

The development of the charge-coupled gadget created another period of imaging where optical pictures could be effectively caught by various strong state indicators and stored as computerized data. The size and number of these indications determined the resolution of the captured image. Most imaging applications relied upon high-resolution symbolism. It was not considered a feasible methodology to increase the resolution by improving detector array resolution. While advancements in semiconductor fabrication resulted in higher-resolution picture sensors, shrinking pixel sizes reduced signal-to-noise ratios and light responsiveness. Besides, commonsense expense and actual limits limited the capacity to change identifiers for most inheritance imaging frameworks. The community of image processors created a set of methods known as super-resolution to overcome the difficulties and produce high-resolution symbolism from frameworks with lower-resolution imaging finders. These calculations joined an assortment of low-resolution pictures containing associating curios and re-established high-resolution pictures.

Table 1. Literature review

Author	Year	A	B	C	D	E	F	Application	Key Finding
El-Khamy et al. (El-Khamy, 2005)	2005	✓	✓	✗	✗	✗	✗	A wavelet domain-based SR method that enrols data first then merges wavelet coefficients of low resolution to produce a lone picture.	To recreate an HR photo of size 256256, three pictures of size 128128 and low-resolution are utilized. The PSNR obtained is 32.2dB.
D. Zhang and Xiaolin Wu. (Zhang & Wu, 2006)	2006	✗	✗	✓	✗	✗	✗	An edge-directed non-linear interpolation method which is based on a combination of data and directional channel to save sharpness of edge and decrease ringing antiquities.	The proposed technique is applied to Lena, Butterfly, Pepper, Hole and Cloth images. These images have PSNRs of 29.28, 29.28, 28.11, 29.30, and 25.18, respectively, which is more than 2dB when using standard approaches.
Li, Min, and Truong Q. Nguyen. (Li & Nguyen, 2008)	2008	✗	✗	✓	✗	✗	✗	An edge-coordinated interpolation approach is proposed in light of MRF model, which delivers perfect sharpness across edges.	PSNR value obtained for 3×3 is 34.03, 5×5 is 34.25, 7×7 is 34.37 and 9×9 is 34.28.
Demirel et al. (Demirel & Anbarjafari, 2010)	2010	✓	✓	✗	✗	✗	✗	Low-resolution images are enhanced using SWD.	The accomplished PSNR for Lena is 34.82, Pepper is 33.06 and Baboon is 23.87.
Xu, Hongteng et al. (Xu et al., 2013)	2013	✗	✗	✓	✗	✗	✗	The proposed methodology, neighbourhood fractal investigation is based on super-resolution computation for a single image. The image is sharpened in accordance with how the image gradient is exhibited as a gauge of a collection of fractals.	The approach was tested on photos of a child, a koala, and a Kodak, with RMSEs of 22.14, 12.94, and 17.38, respectively.
Kumar, Neeraj, and Amit Sethi. (Kumar & Sethi, 2016)	2016	✗	✗	✗	✗	✓	✓	A single high-resolution (HR) image is produced from a single low-resolution (LR) image by means of a learning based SISR technique.	HR reconstruction with little information and result fix sizes not just makes learning more proficient; it likewise demonstrates that SISR is a profoundly nearby issue.
Sun, Na et al. (Sun & Li, 2019)	2019	✗	✗	✓	✓	✗	✓	A new algorithm, a mixture of traditional and deep learning-based algorithms, is proficient in obtaining super-resolution reconstruction of images.	The outcomes show that the calculation significantly affects the MSE and PSNR. The proposed method has better execution than the customary interpolation method and single profound learning method.
Zhang, Jing, et al. (Zhang et al., 2020)	2020	✗	✗	✗	✓	✗	✓	A multi-residual network and multi-feature SCSR (MRMFSCSR) is paired with a proposed picture super-resolution reconstruction calculation to improve image resolution and be used in image processing.	According to the findings, the MRMFSCSR algorithm outperforms the VDSR approach at picture reconstruction.
Fukami, Kai et al. (Fukami et al., 2021)	2021	✗	✗	✓	✓	✗	✓	The current model recreates high-settled violent streams from extremely coarse information in space, and repeats the worldly advancement for a suitably-picked period.	These key outcomes recommend that the current technique can play out a scope of stream recreations on the side of computational and exploratory endeavors.
Fang, Linjing, et al. (Fang et al., 2021)	2021	✗	✗	✗	✗	✗	✓	Model predictions are improved with the PSSR approach in which information is used in adjacent frames.	Point-scanning image acquisition is facilitated by the PSSR approach with an unobtainable resolution, speed, and sensitivity.

Abbreviation/Explanations
A/ Wavelet domain-based
B/ Frequency domain-based
C/ Spatial domain-based
D/ Reconstruction-based
E/ Example-based
F/ Learning-based

49

The capacity to rise above the principal resolution cut-off points of sensors utilizing super-goal calculations has also shown tremendous progress and demonstrated competence in the space of visual imaging. By a long shot, most of uses utilizing super-resolution innovation have been in the space of visual symbolism for one or the other customer or guard-type applications.

Researchers are now working on techniques to use the super-resolution system in various clinical imaging applications. In a few fundamental ways, clinical imaging applications differ from visual imaging. To begin with, unlike ocular imaging, clinical imaging frequently employs extremely controlled brightness of the human body during image acquisition. SNR increases with more grounded enlightenment energy, as with any imaging framework. However, because of the need to avoid tissue damage in clinical imaging, illumination radiation is limited, lowering the SNR well below that of visual imaging. Second, as opposed to visual applications, clinical imaging applications place a greater emphasis on imaging speed. Third, rather than providing externally appealing symbols, therapeutic imaging aims to collaborate with the discovery or discovery of illness.

OVERVIEW, TECHNIQUES, APPLICATIONS

Overview

The idea behind super-resolution is that by stitching together a number of low-resolution images of a scene, a high-resolution image or series can be created.

As a result, it makes an effort to transform a set of low-resolution photos into a high-resolution image that mimics the scene of the original photograph. The formula for comparing high resolution and poor resolution is as follows:

Low resolution = degradation (high-resolution)

Therefore, the overall methodology is to consider the resulting low-resolution pictures from resampling a high-resolution picture. When the picture of high resolution is resampled depending upon the input pictures and the imaging model, the objective is to recuperate it as it will produce observed low-resolution pictures. As a result, the accuracy of an imaging model is critical for super-resolution. Furthermore, erroneous showing, or movement, can further degrade the image. The images seen could be from a single or multiple cameras, or frames from a video sequence. These images should follow a standard reference outline. Registration is the term for this procedure. The super-resolution approach can be applied to a region of interest in the altered composite picture. The path to successful super-resolution entails careful

Figure 1. Stages in a super-resolution model

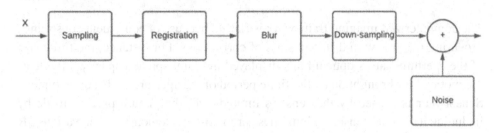

planning and alignment, such as registration and detailing a suitable forward picture model. The stages of the super-resolution process are depicted in Figure 1.

A super-resolution has various applications in diverse fields; it is famously utilized in the accompanying applications:

- Observation/Surveillance: to recognize, distinguish, and perform facial acknowledgment on low-resolution pictures obtained from surveillance cameras.
- Clinical: catching high-resolution MRI pictures can be precarious checking the time, spatial inclusion, and signal-to-noise ratio (SNR).
- Media: As media can be delivered at a lesser resolution and up scaled, it can be used to save server costs.

Techniques

Image enhancement utilizing super-resolution techniques has been a hot research topic for a long time. The necessity for image resolution augmentation has prompted a lot of research, and different solutions have been developed over the previous three decades. The techniques cover a wide range of topics, from signal processing to machine learning, from frequency to spatial domain. Early super-resolution research focused on the shift and associating features of the Fourier transform, which was based on the idea of (Tsai, 1989). However, the picture perception or image observation model with which these frequency domain suggestions can deal is quite limited, and true concerns are significantly more complex. Specialists nowadays generally address the issue in the spatial space for its adaptability to demonstrate a wide range of picture debasements. The picture observation model serves as the starting point for our discussion of various techniques.

Image Observation Model

The computerized imaging framework is flawed because of equipment constraints, procuring pictures with different sorts of corruptions. For instance, the finite size of the aperture causes optical blue, displayed by Point spread capacity. In videos, the motion blur brought on by the finite period of the aperture is also quite typical. Sensor blur is caused by the sensor's limited size; the picture pixel is made by including it over the sensor region. These problems are demonstrated in various SR methods. Figure 2 shows the model relating the HR picture with LR video outlines. The contribution of the imaging framework is constant normal scenes, very much approximated as band-restricted signals.

Figure 2. Image observation model

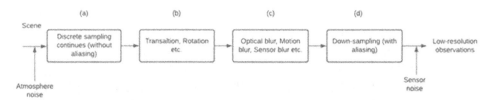

Before arriving at the imaging framework, these signals might be polluted by barometrical disturbance. Examining the proceeds with signal past the Nyquist rate produces a high-resolution advanced picture. In our SR setting, there typically exists movement between the camera and scene of some sort to catch. The contributions to the camera are different casings of the scene, associated by conceivably neighborhood or worldwide movements. Going through the camera, these movements related to high-resolution casings will cause various obscuring impacts, such as optical haze and movement obscure. These obscured pictures are then down sampled at the picture sensors into pixels. These down sampled pictures are additionally impacted by the sensor commotion furthermore shading sifting commotion. The frames finally caught by the low-resolution imaging frameworks are obscured, destroyed, and noisy adaptations of the hidden genuine scene. If X signifies the HR picture, and Y is the k-th observation of LR, then X and Y are addressed in lexicographical order. Eq. (1) shows the relationship of LR observations with HR.

$$Y \text{ (kth observation)} = \{D_k H_k F_k X + V_k\};$$

X represents the scene, F_k signifies the information of motion, H_k signifies the blurs, D_k signifies the operator for down sampling and V_k signifies the noise.

In simple terms, it can be concluded as:

$$Y = MX + V$$

Frequency Domain-Based

The frequency domain-based SR methods use the following methodology: The LR picture(s) are translated to the frequency domain before the HR image is measured in that domain. The reconstructed HR image is then transferred back to the spatial domain. Based on the method used to translate the pictures into the frequency domain, these computations are split into two categories: methods based on the Fourier transform and methods based on the Wavelet transform, which are discussed in greater detail in the subsections that follow.

Tsai and Huang's (Tsai, 1989) initial frequency domain-based technique transforms low-resolution satellite pictures into discrete Fourier change (DFT) space. The relationship between the pertinent DFT coefficients of the high-resolution image of the undiscovered planet and those of the low-resolution image is used to combine these images. To obtain high-resolution images, the reverse DFT (IDFT) is applied to the images to convert them back to spatial space. A quick super-resolution remake based on a frequency domain registration and non-uniform interpolation was suggested by Vandewalle et al. (Vandewalle et al., 2004).

The frequency domain-based technique has several advantages, some of which are given below.

- Low computational complexity.
- Extrapolation of the high-frequency information found in low-resolution photographs to improve the high-frequency information in the images.

The disadvantage of this SR method is that it cannot deal with modern applications, which during the image collecting procedure merely call for a global relocation between the scene images and the linear space-invariant blur. Another issue is that sharing previous information used to resolve the SR issue is difficult. Because the SR issue is poorly described, it is critical to join previous data to improve outcomes.

Spatial Domain-Based

Three categories can be found in the spatial area-based methodologies:

- Interpolation-based methodology

- Reconstruction-based methodology
- Learning-based methodology

Interpolation-Based

The image interpolation process is the most important activity in image processing when using an interpolation-based methodology. The function values are resolved in the interpolation step by fitting the function in discrete samples. A smooth kernel function is used to interpolate the HR image from the LR in an interpolation-based approach. Interpolation-based SR approaches use parametric or nonparametric techniques to enhance the size of LR. This group of methods evaluates the pixels in the HR lattices to produce a better resolution image using a base work or an interpolation bit. This procedure contains both non-adaptive and adaptive procedures.

Non-adaptive Interpolation: In this method, pixels are straightforwardly controlled as considering the picture substance of highlights. Some examples of this method are: Nearest neighbor, Bilinear and Bicubic.

The interpretation of realized pixel esteems included in the nearest neighbor. When the image has high-resolution pixels, it produces excellent results. Some data is lost at the edges as a result of this. The average value of the closest pixels on either side is used in the bilinear approach. It's an easy procedure to follow. This method outperforms the closest neighbor method and takes less time to calculate than the bicubic interpolation method. The interpretation of a weighted normal of the closest pixels is included in bicubic interpolation. This technique produces better results, but it takes longer to compute. A unique class of piecewise polynomial is used in spline interpolation as the interpolant.

Unfortunately, these techniques suffer from inadequate protection of spatial features in the image, resulting in lower picture quality, despite their low computational complexity. On the other hand, interpolation-based SR approaches, work well in low-frequency regions but ineffectively in high-frequency regions due to their proclivity for concealing and jaggy curios along edges. As a result, interpolation-based SR approaches' SR capacity is limited.

Reconstruction-Based

In reconstruction-based methodology, earlier information on progressive LR picture frames of a similar scene is used and tackles an inverse problem that is not presented well. This methodology can be characterized into two classes: deterministic methodology and stochastic methodology.

The deterministic methodology uses constrained least squares to regularize the arrangement while encoding information displaying the appearance of high-resolution images. The standard method is to use regularization on top of a least-squares augmentation after forcing smoothness. Regularization ensures an arched and differentiable improvement function. Along with this, an optimal solution can be calculated utilizing various standard techniques like gradient descent. The output is an improvement over the low-resolution image, but retaining smoothness isn't always the best choice, especially if different priors can be built that better safeguard high-frequency features (Deshpande & Patavardhan, 2019).

The stochastic techniques that treat SR reconstruction as a factual assessment issue have quickly acquired noticeable quality because they give a strong hypothetical system for incorporating a-priori constraints fundamental for agreeable arrangement of the SR inverse problem which is not presented well.

The factual procedures expressly handle earlier data and commotion. The incorporation of earlier information is generally more regular utilizing a stochastic methodology.

An adaptable and advantageous approach to model prior information about the final arrangement can be achieved using Bayesian methodology with the stochastic reconstruction method. This technique can be applied when the posterior likelihood density function of the first picture can be assessed. The gauge for which the posterior likelihood is the greatest is what the maximum a posteriori (MAP) method looks for when evaluating the super-resolution. It is common practice to use Markov random field (MRF) picture models as the prior term.

The advantage of this method is that it integrates well with other well-liked image processing jobs including de-noising, augmentation, and de-convolution. The high-resolution image is repeatedly generated utilizing the difference between the observed low-resolution picture and the simulated low-resolution picture according to Irani and Peleg's iterative back-projection approach (Irani & Peleg, 1991). Due to how badly the SR problem has been explained, it seems unlikely that this technique will result in a novel solution.

Learning-Based

Since the minute details of real-world pictures are hard to catch systematically, analysts are investigating a learning-based approach for super-resolving pictures. This strategy comprises two stages:

- Training
- Super-resolution

A glossary of picture patches is created in the training step, and the other step includes sampling utilizing the dictionary as input for image patching. There are two types of dictionaries: external and internal. The external dictionary can be created by combining several external training images, whereas the internal dictionary can be created without additional images.

The learning-based SR technique assembles the previously undiscovered high-resolution picture using functions subordinate priors. There are two categories of the low-resolution input image: overlapping and non-overlapping. The best match is then chosen from the training dataset. Using appropriate HR patches, the resulting HR image is recreated. (Genitha & Vani, 2010) introduces a learning-based picture super-resolution technique.

APPLICATIONS

Satellite Image Processing

It is often wanted to have pictures of high resolution in satellite imaging. Super-resolution plays a vital role in executing this task. Information extraction, image rectification, restorations and enhancement constitute satellite image processing. This multitude of regions commonly needs the procedures of super-resolution. The number of pixels is increased in super-resolved images, improving the digital pictures presentation i.e., visual understanding increments. Additionally, it could help in the expulsion of bends and topographical data can be additionally upgraded. In further handling, SR can likewise be joined in additional order of regions or topographical areas. It could likewise incorporate learning-based methods which are valuable.

The mapping of satellite pictures with super-resolution utilizing Hopfield neural networks has been proposed. (Zhang et al., 2014) have utilized neural-based techniques for the grouping of spatial fields. It gives exact and powerful technique for identifying objective fields utilizing remote detecting symbolism. It is one of the use cases of SR in mapping by utilizing satellite imaging.

Multipoint remote sensing imaging is one of the other applications of SR. Multipoint data of the region may have comparable data yet not precisely the same. It may be utilized for getting additional data from pictures by utilizing SR. The adaptive-based strategies have been proposed to join the multipoint data (Zhang et al., 2014). A versatile weighted super-resolution remaking procedure has been utilized to diminish the limitations of the various resolutions. Another area of satellite picture incorporates the characterization of various regions which could likewise be upgraded with SR.

Medical Image Processing

A super-resolution has gained a lot of importance in the field of the medical industry. Several great works have been done to enhance the quality of medical pictures. SR strategies are highly required in various medical tests including CT scans, MRI etc. (Robinson, 2017). These tests require high resolution and a great upgrade of a picture which SR techniques can only provide (Robinson, 2017).

Many of the medical field's pictures are of low resolutions, low contrast, and geometric deformation. For example, X-ray has lower contrast and ultrasound has boisterous pictures. Therefore, super-resolution pictures can be involved to eliminate all the issues faced (Sable & Gaikwad, 2012). At present, a significant number of clinical imaging applications are quick and exact with the contribution of SR. It is dependably attractive to identify the illness at the beginning phase. However, at that early time imaging of the matter is as a rule with lower contrast. It has been made conceivable to have higher resolution and early perception of conclusion for clinical and clinical scientists with the appearance of novel imaging techniques.

Some applications of SR in the medical field include Functional MRI, positron emission tomography imaging system, Optical Coherence Tomography and X-ray digital mammography (Kennedy et al., 2007; Kennedy et al., 2006; Peeters et al., 2004).

Medical imaging is significant for diagnosis. In, this manner, having a higher resolution essentially works on restorative treatment. In addition, a higher resolution may considerably work on programmed identification and image segmentation (Greenspan, 2009). In medical imaging, various algorithms are used for diagnosis, which is also based on the SR technique. This chapter explores a major application of Super Resolution in brain MRI and all the medical modalities and SR techniques in detail.

Super Resolution in Brain MRI

Because low-field MRI scanners are significantly more affordable than high-field MRI scanners, anyone in the globe can use MRI technology. Low-field MRI scanners have lower signal-to-noise ratios; hence images acquired with them have an inferior resolution. This project's purpose is to boost image resolution. To achieve this goal, the authors have described a deep learning-based strategy for transforming low-resolution low-field MR data into high-resolution MR images. In order to do single picture super-resolution reconstruction, pairings of noisy low-resolution images and their noise-free high-resolution counterparts from the publicly accessible NYU fastMRI library were used to train CNN. The network was then applied to noisy MRI pictures acquired with a low-field scanner after that. Tesla-range fields are typically used in clinical settings by high-field MRI scanners. The high price, large size, and infrastructure requirements of high-field MRI scanners can be attributed to the need for superconducting magnets to produce extremely strong and uniform fields. Clear, ultra-high-resolution images with the majority of the high-frequency components recovered were obtained by the trained Convolutional network. Finally, the authors have shown that a deep learning-based approach holds great promise for enhancing low-field MR image resolution (Zeng et al., 2018).

Developing low-field MRI scanners is critical for increasing the accessibility of MRI scanners. Low-field scanners are far less expensive and do not rely on superconducting magnets. Furthermore, because they have fewer infrastructure requirements, they can be made portable, allowing them to be transported to people living in rural areas in low- and middle-income nations. The low-field scanner was created as part of a larger attempt to build a platform for pediatric imaging hydrocephalus in impoverished countries. As a result, the scanner was made to fit the heads infants' heads. MRI scan times are generally long, and much of today's MRI research is focused on speeding up the acquisition process. Infants have a harder time remaining still for long periods of time than adults do. As a result, every attempt should be taken to complete the scan quickly while maintaining acceptable quality of an image. When assuming that the spatial frequency domain, or k-space, has been completely swept, a shorter scan length correlates to a lower resolution image. The goal of super-resolution image reconstruction techniques is to take one or more low-resolution (LR) images and turn them into a high-resolution (HR) image. Since the attention will be on single image super-resolution (SISR), only one LR image will be used. Since one LR image may correlate to several separate HR photographs, SISR is an ill-posed problem for which there is no one solution (Yang et al., 2014).

Assuming that the image is sparse in some transform domain and sampling only a portion of k-space, compressed sensing (CS) methodologies could be utilized to reduce scan time while still reconstructing a high-quality image, according to the research performed by the authors. Instead, the authors will focus on picture reconstruction with super-resolution (SR). This choice was made because the SR problem was easier to solve than the CS problem: low-resolution photos can be used in SR, whereas in CS, k-space data must be used. In addition, in CS, the k-space sampling pattern must be considered. After being trained on LR-HR image pairs, the neural network should be able to increase image quality as intended by the authors. Interpolation can be used in a variety of methods for SISR, including bicubic interpolation, Lanczos interpolation, and zero-padding the k-space data, which is prevalent in MRI scans (Yang et al., 2014). Although these methods are quick and simple to apply, their results can be erroneous when recovering high-frequency components. The problem is commonly treated as a minimization problem in reconstruction-based SR techniques, with historical knowledge of the solution, including restricting the solution space. Reconstruction-based approaches have the drawbacks of being computationally expensive and requiring the adjustment of hyper parameters.

The third strategy for addressing the SISR problem is learning-based (or example-based) solutions. Machine learning is used in these techniques to extract correlations between LR and HR images. They are quick and usually perform well in terms of calculations. Some examples of these methods include MRF, neighbor embeddings and sparse representations. Deep learning (DL) techniques perform better than any other learning- and reconstruction-based techniques. Convolutional neural networks such as SRCNN, SRDenseNet, and SRGAN are only a few of the neural networks that have been used in SISR. In this study, the authors performed SISR on MR brain images using a Convolutional neural network from the SRDenseNet architecture.

The work's main contribution and innovation is its application: the authors focus on low-field MR brain images. Low-field MRI is a young discipline that has a lot of potential, but it also faces some difficulties. This study demonstrates how deep learning-based algorithms can overcome low-field MR imaging difficulties. Because of its non-invasive imaging and potent properties, magnetic resonance imaging (MRI) is one of the greatest procedures for providing exact clinical results and obsessive investigation. It is utilized to display anatomical information about the body's tissues, tumors, muscles, brain, and heart. In neurological and brain research, MRI is quite useful. However, low spatial and resolution resolutions are recurring issues with MRI that impair the diagnosis and post-processing processes. In medical imaging, there are numerous issues to contend with. High-quality MRI images are generally accompanied by a long sampling time, patient discomfort, a larger magnetic field, and higher costs. Clinically, such things are difficult to do and infrequent.

In the field of computer vision, SR techniques have become increasingly prevalent in the recent decades. Many works of literature have recently been offered to improve image quality. Single image super-resolution (SISR) and multiple image super-resolution (MISR) are examples of SR techniques (MISR). A single LR photo is used to create the SR image with SISR. By merging the accuracy of several LR photos, the SR image is rebuilt in MISR. The main drawback of the MISR approach is the difficulty of collecting many photos of the same object, making it therapeutically impracticable due to patient comfort. SISR techniques include model-based SR, reconstruction-based SR, and learning-based SR.

Model-based SR methods use interpolation algorithms like the closest neighbor, bicubic, and bilinear to estimate the pixel values in the HR grids and reconstruct the HR features from the LR images. It creates fuzzy edges, irritating artifacts, and incredibly smooth reconstructed images with missing minute details, even though it provides HR images with excellent computing efficiency. Reconstruction-based

SR addresses the problem of blurred edges by using exact prior HR information. Prior knowledge such as edge, gradient, and global means is used to rebuild HR pictures. However, at high magnification, the reconstructed images lack fine features. Learning-based SR employs a variety of machine learning approaches to learn the SR-to-LR mapping. It has also been found that before proceeding to apply SR, it is very important to correct the distortions of an image because images of three-dimensional objects are frequently distorted - an image of a three-dimensional object will be squashed or pulled in ways that do not reflect the object's true appearance - but when the image is of a brain and its purpose is to understand disease or disorder, this is especially important to correct. Some distorted and undistorted images are shown in Table 2.

Due to the quick development of machine learning, deep learning models have proven to be successful in image classification and are becoming more and more effective at bringing out the concealed features of a picture.

Many different types of literature on SR studies have been proposed due to deep learning's potential. Deep learning models like CNN, RNN, and GANs are included in the present literature. Super-resolution CNN, fast super-resolution CNN, deep recursive CNN, very deep CNN, and super-resolution GANs are some of the deep learning models that are available in the literature right now. These methods might work well for recreating HR natural photos but are inappropriate for MRI images. The state-of-the-art study also includes SR techniques for MRI picture improvements. They do, however, cause inconsequential artifacts and distortions. For MRI pictures, SR techniques should give relevant artifacts and therapeutically important features. As a result, the challenges of creating an SR method for MRI images are clear because current methods fall short of all necessary criteria, making the creation of a new SR method necessary.

A deep learning model called Auto-Encoder is able to represent images on its own. The Auto-Encoder-based SR models produce good outcomes with little computational effort. The phrase "auto encoder" refers to a device that performs both encoder and decoder operations. After learning the input images, the encoder converts them into a latent space representation. The image is solely reconstructed by the decoder using the latent space representation. The SR model suggested by Dong et al. is based on sparse coding. Sparse coding assumes that the HR image's sparse representation from the HR dictionary is equivalent to the LR image patch's sparse representation from the LR dictionary. Using nonlocal means to estimate HR representations from LR representations is proposed as a way to overcome this assumption using sparse representation noise. However, they generally use the dictionary training approach, in which the LR image patch can be directly or indirectly considered as HR image patches. Another key disadvantage of the current study is that simple linear mapping is difficult to describe complicated interactions.

Table 2. Distorted and undistorted images

Deep Learning-Based SR Techniques

The success of SR methods in NIP has led to the development of deep learning-based SR techniques for MR imaging domains. In MRI SR, GAN-based and CNN-based SR techniques have been frequently deployed. Du, Jinglong, et al. (Du et al., 2020) offers a CNN-based SR technique for brain MRI. Enhanced Deep Residual Network is proposed by WANG, Xiang-hai et al. (Wang, 2022) to improve ResNet-based synthetic multi-orientation of brain MRI images. In order to reconstitute the HR characteristics of brain MRI using neural network design, Chen et al. (Chen, 2018) suggested utilizing a 3D densely connected super-resolution network. An FSRCNN-based 3D CNN was presented by Mane et al. (Mane et al., 2020) to reconstruct the image. The complexity of the network grows as it grows deeper. Özyurt et al. (Özyurt et al., 2020) suggested a fuzzy C means SR CNN approach for segmenting high-quality brain MRI images. This method made use of the squeezeNet network, which had been pre-trained. Song et al. (Song et al., 2022) present a GAN-based SR technique, in which MRI pictures are enlarged using frequently used SR algorithms, and GAN is trained to generate SR MRI images. The SR images are then finalized using the ensemble learning process.

Microscopy Image Processing

SR is likewise assuming a significant part in microscopic image processing. A lot of progress has been made in this domain according to the literature. Biological structures such as cells and tissue can be visualized in an efficient manner using this technique. One of the extremely critical fields in microscopy imaging is SR fluorescence microscopy. Fluorescence magnifying lens is one of the fundamental instruments for assessing the pathways, organic atoms, living cells, tissues, and surprisingly entire subjects in of the past time (Huang et al., 2009). It is more helpful when contrasted with electron microscopy. Other procedures like MRI or OCT can give resolutions in 10s of centimeters and micrometers.

SR-based procedures may likewise give the data up to a nanometer scale. It incorporates a few strategies like switchable fluorophores and strong restriction calculations. Here, different pictures taken in exchanging mode can be joined to give higher resolution. Therefore, SR is being proved as very helpful in microscopic image processing.

Multimedia Industry and Video Enhancement

In the present time, media-based applications are expanding every day. Super-resolution is additionally being included in the interactive media industry (Malczewski

& Stasiński, 2009). In the present time films, activities, and visual impacts all need HD information. So, SR can likewise be demonstrated as a helpful procedure in video upgrades. Numerous strategies utilized in interactive media-based applications involve the SR technique for upgrading pictures and recordings. Wireless-based applications like pictures or recordings likewise include SR-based strategies to upgrade their quality.

Astrological Studies

Super-resolution is moreover involved as the critical procedure in astrological studies. High resolution

Galactic pictures are beneficial all the time for better calculation. Many obscured and boisterous pictures can be consolidated to improve the view. (Payne et al., 2003) has involved the SR for improvement of nature of visionary pictures. Some firmly gathered stars and distant articles can be envisioned in a better way using SR. In this space, commonly numerous unidentified items could likewise be envisioned better.

Other Application Areas

According to the study, it has been found that SR has numerous applications practically in each space of advanced picture handling. A lot of research has now been associated with this region. SR is likewise playing a huge job in the modern applications. Additionally, with association of programming-based methods, no equipment adjustment is required, so it is conceivable to redesign the past frameworks. It very well may be anticipated that in future there would be considerably more extent of super resolution methods in overhauling of computerized picture handling.

CONCLUSION

According to the research, it may be inferred that SR has numerous practical applications in each space of advanced image processing. Great exploration has proactively been engaged in this area. In late present-day applications SR is additionally assuming a huge part. In addition, with the inclusion of programming-based procedures no equipment adjustment is required, so redesigning the past systems is conceivable. It very well may be anticipated that in the future, there will be significantly more extent of super-resolution strategies in redesigning advanced image processing.

REFERENCES

Chen, Y. (2018). Brain MRI super resolution using 3D deep densely connected neural networks. In *2018 IEEE 15th International Symposium on Biomedical Imaging (ISBI 2018)*. IEEE. 10.1109/ISBI.2018.8363679

Demirel, H., & Anbarjafari, G. (2010). Image resolution enhancement by using discrete and stationary wavelet decomposition. *IEEE Transactions on Image Processing, 20*(5), 1458–1460. doi:10.1109/TIP.2010.2087767 PMID:20959267

Deshpande, A., & Patavardhan, P. P. (2019). Survey of super resolution techniques. *ICTACT Journal on Image & Video Processing, 9*(3).

Du, J., Wang, L., Liu, Y., Zhou, Z., He, Z., & Jia, Y. (2020). Brain MRI super-resolution using 3D dilated Convolutional encoder–decoder network. *IEEE Access: Practical Innovations, Open Solutions, 8*, 18938–18950. doi:10.1109/ACCESS.2020.2968395

El-Khamy, S. E. (2005). Regularized super-resolution reconstruction of images using wavelet fusion. *Optical Engineering, 44*(9).

Fang, L., Monroe, F., Novak, S. W., Kirk, L., Schiavon, C. R., Yu, S. B., Zhang, T., Wu, M., Kastner, K., Latif, A. A., Lin, Z., Shaw, A., Kubota, Y., Mendenhall, J., Zhang, Z., Pekkurnaz, G., Harris, K., Howard, J., & Manor, U. (2021). Deep learning-based point-scanning super-resolution imaging. *Nature Methods, 18*(4), 406–416. doi:10.103841592-021-01080-z PMID:33686300

Fukami, K., Fukagata, K., & Taira, K. (2021). Machine-learning-based spatial-temporal super resolution reconstruction of turbulent flows. *Journal of Fluid Mechanics*, 909.

Genitha, C. H., & Vani, K. (2010). *Super resolution mapping of satellite images using hopfield neural networks. In Recent Advances in Space Technology Services and Climate Change 2010 (RSTS & CC-2010)*. IEEE.

Greenspan, H. (2009). Super-resolution in medical imaging. *The Computer Journal, 52*(1), 43–63. doi:10.1093/comjnl/bxm075

Huang, B., Bates, M., & Zhuang, X. (2009). Super-resolution fluorescence microscopy. *Annual Review of Biochemistry, 78*(1), 993–1016. doi:10.1146/annurev.biochem.77.061906.092014 PMID:19489737

Irani, M., & Peleg, S. (1991). Improving resolution by image registration. *CVGIP. Graphical Models and Image Processing, 53*(3), 231–239. doi:10.1016/1049-9652(91)90045-L

Kennedy, J. A., Israel, O., Frenkel, A., Bar-Shalom, R., & Azhari, H. (2007). Improved image fusion in PET/CT using hybrid image reconstruction and super-resolution. *International Journal of Biomedical Imaging, 2007*, 2007. doi:10.1155/2007/46846 PMID:18521180

Kennedy, J. A., Israel, O., Frenkel, A., Bar-Shalom, R., & Haim Azhari. (2006). Super-resolution in PET imaging. *IEEE Transactions on Medical Imaging, 25*(2), 137–147. doi:10.1109/TMI.2005.861705 PMID:16468448

Kumar, N., & Sethi, A. (2016). Fast learning-based single image super-resolution. *IEEE Transactions on Multimedia, 18*(8), 1504–1515. doi:10.1109/TMM.2016.2571625

Li, M., & Nguyen, T. Q. (2008). Markov random field model-based edge-directed image interpolation. *IEEE Transactions on Image Processing, 17*(7), 1121–1128. doi:10.1109/TIP.2008.924289 PMID:18586620

Malczewski, K., & Stasiński, R. (2009). Super resolution for multimedia, image, and video processing applications. In *Recent Advances in Multimedia Signal Processing and Communications* (pp. 171–208). Springer. doi:10.1007/978-3-642-02900-4_8

Mane, V., Jadhav, S., & Lal, P. (2020). Image super-resolution for MRI Images using 3D faster super-resolution convolutional neural network architecture. *ITM Web of Conferences, 32*. 10.1051/itmconf/20203203044

Özyurt, F., Sert, E., & Avcı, D. (2020). An expert system for brain tumor detection: Fuzzy C-means with super resolution and convolutional neural network with extreme learning machine. *Medical Hypotheses, 134*, 109433. doi:10.1016/j.mehy.2019.109433 PMID:31634769

Payne, H. E., Jedrzejewski, R. I., & Hook, R. N. (2003). Astronomical Data Analysis Software and Systems XII. *Astronomical Data Analysis Software and Systems, 12*, 295.

Peeters, R. R., Kornprobst, P., Nikolova, M., Sunaert, S., Vieville, T., Malandain, G., Deriche, R., Faugeras, O., Ng, M., & Van Hecke, P. (2004). The use of super-resolution techniques to reduce slice thickness in functional MRI. *International Journal of Imaging Systems and Technology, 14*(3), 131–138. doi:10.1002/ima.20016

Robinson, M. D. (2017). *New applications of super-resolution in medical imaging. In Super-resolution imaging.* CRC Press.

Sable & Gaikwad. (2012). A Novel Approach for Super Resolution in Medical Imaging. *International Journal of Emerging Technology and Advanced Engineering, 2*(11).

Song, L., Li, Y., & Lu, N. (2022). ProfileSR-GAN: A GAN based Super-Resolution Method for Generating High-Resolution Load Profiles. *IEEE Transactions on Smart Grid, 13*(4), 3278–3289. doi:10.1109/TSG.2022.3158235

Sun, N., & Li, H. (2019). Super resolution reconstruction of images based on interpolation and full convolutional neural network and application in medical fields. *IEEE Access: Practical Innovations, Open Solutions, 7*, 186470–186479. doi:10.1109/ACCESS.2019.2960828

Tsai, R. Y. (1989). Multiple frame image restoration and registration. *Advances in Computer Vision and Image Processing, 1*, 1715–1989.

Vandewalle, P., Süsstrunk, S., & Vetterli, M. (2004). *A frequency domain approach to super-resolution imaging from aliased low-resolution images.* Technical Journal.

Wang. (2022). *Single Image Super-Resolution Reconstruction Using Deep Residual Networks with Non-decimated Wavelet Edge Learning.* ACTA ELECTONICA SINICA.

Xu, H., Zhai, G., & Yang, X. (2013). Single image super-resolution with detail enhancement based on local fractal analysis of gradient. *IEEE Transactions on Circuits and Systems for Video Technology, 23*(10), 1740–1754. doi:10.1109/TCSVT.2013.2248305

Yang, C.-Y., Ma, C., & Yang, M.-H. (2014). Single-image super-resolution: A benchmark. In *European conference on computer vision.* Springer.

Zeng, K., Zheng, H., Cai, C., Yang, Y., Zhang, K., & Chen, Z. (2018). Simultaneous single-and multi-contrast super-resolution for brain MRI images based on a convolutional neural network. *Computers in Biology and Medicine, 99*, 133–141. doi:10.1016/j.compbiomed.2018.06.010 PMID:29929052

Zhang, H., Yang, Z., Zhang, L., & Shen, H. (2014). Super-resolution reconstruction for multi-angle remote sensing images considering resolution differences. *Remote Sensing, 6*(1), 637–657. doi:10.3390/rs6010637

Zhang, J., Shao, M., Yu, L., & Li, Y. (2020). Image super-resolution reconstruction based on sparse representation and deep learning. *Signal Processing Image Communication, 87*, 115925. doi:10.1016/j.image.2020.115925

Zhang, L., & Wu, X. (2006). An edge-guided image interpolation algorithm via directional filtering and data fusion. *IEEE Transactions on Image Processing, 15*(8), 2226–2238. doi:10.1109/TIP.2006.877407 PMID:16900678

Chapter 5
Overview on Incorporating Computer–Aided Diagnosis Systems for Dementia:
Early Detection of Alzheimer's Disease

Vania Karami
https://orcid.org/0000-0003-2492-6185
University of Camerino, Italy

Giulio Nittari
University of Camerino, Italy

Sara Karami
New York Institute of Technology, Canada

Seyed Massood Nabavi
Royan Institute, Iran

ABSTRACT

Dementia is one of the major issues in public health all over the world. Alzheimer's disease (AD) is its most common and famous form. Late detection of AD has irreparable effects for the people suffering from it. Cognitive assessment tests are the conventional approach to detect AD. They are quick to do, and not costly. However, they have low predictive values. Therefore, other ways such as magnetic resonance imaging (MRI) are used. Recently, advances in computer-aided diagnosis system (CADS) using MRI have provided useful information in the quantitative evaluation of AD at an early stage. Although it cannot be substituted with the doctors, but it helps. Many algorithms for CADS were presented, which means CADS is one of the growing techniques in this field. Because there is no standardized approach to determine the best one, it is essential to be familiar with general approaches to design a CADS. This chapter deals with a general approach for design and develop a reliable CADS using biomarkers extracted from MRI. The advancement of using CAS and MRI for AD are discussed.

DOI: 10.4018/978-1-6684-6980-4.ch005

INTRODUCTION

Alzheimer's Disease (AD) and Its Diagnostic Approaches

One of the greatest challenges that neuropsychologists have encountered in the last 50 years has been determining the cognitive and behavioral aspects of dementia and their relationship to underlying brain dysfunction (Bondi et al., 2017). With the ageing of the population and the age-related nature of many dementias and neurodegenerative disorders, this problem has become increasingly difficult.

Even though the concept of dementia has existed for many years, the main important clinical syndromes and related changes were first discovered not long ago (Mahandra, 1984).

Dementia is related to more than 70 diverse causes of brain dysfunction, but Alzheimer's disease (AD) is the most common cause for half of all cases (Cumming & Benson, 1992). AD is the foremost common shape of dementia, caused by build-up of beta amyloid plaques within the brain (Alzheimer's Disease Facts and Figures, 2010).

AD is regularly confused with normal aging and dementia. Serious memory loss, characteristic of AD, is not an indication of typical aging (Toepper, 2017). Healthy aging may include the gradual hair loss, weight, height, and muscle mass. It is common to have a slight decrease in memory, such as slower review of information, but cognitive decline that affects standard of daily living is not an ordinary portion of the aging process; it is characterized as the noteworthy loss of cognitive abilities efficiently serious to interfere with social functioning (Pini et al., 2016).

Because AD advances slowly, there are three main stages of the disease, each with its own set of problems and symptoms. Identification of these stages in a patient can help for a better decision; Early-stage AD: this stage lasts 2 to 4 years, it is often when the disease is first diagnosed. In this step, family and friends may start to understand the patient's cognitive ability decline (Choo et al., 2019).

Moderate AD: this is the longest stage and usually lasts 2 to 10 years. Patients often faced difficult problems regarding memory and daily living activities (Deardorff, Grossberg, 2019).

Severe AD: in this final level, decrement of cognitive capacity continues, and physical ability is severely affected. This stage can last 1 or 3 years and due to the difficulty for families to care for the patient, this step results in nursing home or long-term care in other related places (Block et al., 2016).

LITERATURE REVIEW

There is no standardized approach to determine the best computer-aided diagnosis system (CADS), therefore, it is essential to be familiar with general approaches to design a CADS. Study of different methods for specific application can help to design and develop in an appropriate way. Lately, deep learning techniques for segmenting the structure of the brain and categorizing AD have drawn attention. As a result, deep techniques are now favored over cutting-edge deep learning techniques because they can produce useful results over a vast quantity of data (Khojaste-Sarakhsi et al., 2022). The retrieved features from MRI had a big effect on how well-known earlier methods were (A° et al., 2022). A recent related survey provided the current state of using classification methods on MRI for early detection of AD (Fathi et al., 2022). The review of deep models, modalities, feature extraction strategies showed that most studies have reported the normal control and AD classification with desirable results (Fathi et al., 2022).

There are other group of CADS that have ability to offer an AD conversion diagnosis in longitudinally monitored cohorts of mild cognitive impairment (MCI) patients. This is significant because primary care doctors might employ CADS to monitor MCI patients. In these investigations, a pipeline for pre-processing and prediction that is computationally effective is created to identify patterns related to AD conversion. A recent study to identify the AD conversion point in MCI subjects using CADS in MRI data achieved area under curve (AUC)=84.7 while cognitive tests and demographics alone achieved AUC=80.6, a significant difference (n=669, $p < 0.05$) (Pena et al., 2022).

Computer-Aided Diagnosis System (CADS) in Early Detection of AD Using MRI

In the medical field, computer-aided diagnosis system (CADS) helps clinicians make better decisions (Chang et al., 2021). Recently, in order to improve the quantitative evaluation of the disease and decrease the reporting time, different CADS have been designed to provide a hand for physicians (Fei, 2017). Though CADS cannot be substituted with the doctors but absolutely it is helpful for them to decide better and to play a supporting role in clinical detection (Karami et al., 2019).

Each CADS has several main parts that needed to be designed accurately because the output of each part is the input for another part and can affect its accuracy and finally affects the total function of the system (Figure 1). The overall framework of CADS includes:

MRI as Input

First part of each CADS is preparation of input data. One of the promising areas for detection of AD is Neuroimaging (Ten Kate et al., 2018), (Zeng et al., 2021). In this chapter, we will discuss the use of magnetic resonance imaging (MRI) of the human brain as input dataset. Brain scans such as MRI, can give useful information about the brain's condition (Pini et al., 2016). Even before clinical symptoms appear, hippocampus shrinkage is a common cause of AD (Emilien et al., 2004). Gosche and colleagues (2002), as one of the first studies, used postmortem MRI scans of participants with different types of cognitive impairment in order to reveal hippocampal volume's effect on AD neuropathology (Gosche et al., 2002). Their results showed that the scans could be used to identify non-demented elderly with AD dementia which have not yet presented with memory impairment (Gosche et al., 2002). This AD risk identification before the appearance of symptoms helps physicians to administer treatment to slow down the disease progression.

MRI Biomarkers for AD

Recently, the term biomarker definition has broadened to include biological characteristics that can be measured objectively and assessed as an indicator of normal biological processes, pathogenic processes or pharmacological responses to therapeutic intervention (Naylor, 2003). In practical terms, biomarkers are tools that help to understand the prediction, cause, detect, progression, regression, or outcome of the disease treatment. In the AD, an efficient ideal biomarker should have the detection ability of AD neuropathology feature, be sensitive and specific to diagnostic, confirmed by neuropathological validation, and be precise with good reproducibility for follow-up after treatment (Kantarci & Jack, 2004). Recent studies have shown the ability to extract features of MRI in AD (Zeng et al., 2021).

Image Processing

In the medical field, image processing is a crucial step since images are acquired in the basic modality to not harm the human body (Karami et al., 2019).

Feature Extraction

An initial set of raw data will be the result of processing step. Feature extraction is a process of dimensionality reduction of this raw data set to a reduced manageable group of features while it still accurately and completely explains the original dataset (Karami et al., 2019). One of the main benefits of this step is reducing and facilitating the processing time without losing important information and machine's efforts for learning and generalization of the classification step (Figure 2)

Feature Selection

Feature selection is done to filter irrelevant or redundant variables (Adutwum & Harynuk, 2014). It is usually used after feature extraction and the difference is that feature selection keeps a subset of the original features while in feature extraction, it creates new and smaller ones (Karami et al., 2019).

Classification

The last part which leads to results denoted as classification that assigns a class to the selected features (El Houby, 2018). Classification needs an algorithm known as classifier. The classifier uses a training data to identify appropriately the class of the unknown data. Figure 1 shows the overall framework of CADS.

This chapter deals with a general approach for design and develop a reliable CADS using biomarkers extracted from MRI. In the next section, some of the general approaches for design and develop a reliable CADS using biomarkers extracted from MRI are presented. As results, the advancement of using CADS and MRI for AD are presented. Then, the results of the CADS for early detection of AD are discussed.

METHODS

In the previous part of this chapter, we introduced CADS and its principle for early detection of AD using MRI. In this section, we will explain how CADS can be used in prediction modeling of AD.

CADS for Early Detection of AD Using MRI

As you read in the previous sections, the first step is data preparation to provide an appropriate dataset. As shown in Figure 2, data preparation has several steps that each step is as input for the next step.

Different datasets with different types of images and clinical information can be chosen based on the goal of the study. Raw MRI images need to be preprocessed. Image preprocessing includes different steps. Based on the type of data and the aim of the studies, every study uses different methods. During data preparation, volume segmentation is also used whenever it is needed to differentiate tissue to white matter (WM), gray matter (GM), and cerebrospinal fluid (CSF).

Figure 1. General framework of CADS. This overall framework of CADS shows the interrelation between each part. CADS has different steps that the output of each step is used as the input of next part

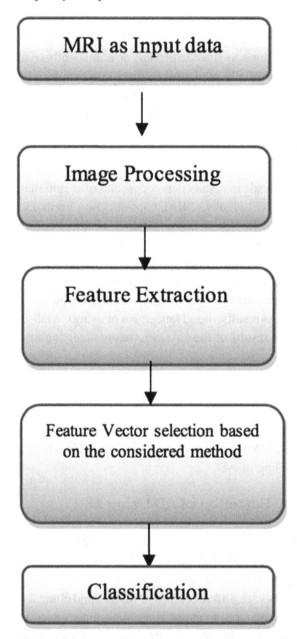

Figure 2. Diagram of data preparation. The results of this step are the inputs of the CAS

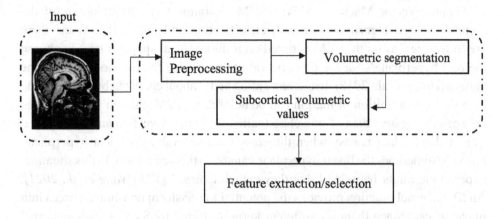

MRI measurements have been used as a method to extract biomarkers based on the changes of volume in the clinical detection of AD (Pini et al., 2016). Morphometric MRI have investigated the brain volume abnormalities that are associated with AD using voxel-based morphometry (VBM). The results of VBM can be used as volume evaluation beside other useful markers in CADS (Juottonen et al., 1998). These morphological changes in the brain can be measured using manual, semi-automated, and automated volumetric techniques to study the brain and then can be considered as biomarkers for the extent of neurodegeneration. Volumetric MRI studies have shown the volume decrement in AD compared to controls (Bobinski et al., 1999) and the volume has been approved as a good discriminator among controls and AD. In addition, hippocampal atrophy and its rate have consistently been shown to increase in AD (Killiany et al., 2002).

The results of the subcortical volumetric values can be the quantified volume for different parts of the brain as the region of interest. The results of previous studies showed Total Intracranial Volume (TIV; cm3), GM (cm3), WM (cm3), CSF (cm3), left hippocampus (L-Hippocampus; cm3), right hippocampus (R-Hippocampus; cm3), total hippocampus (T-Hippocampus; cm3), cortical GM (Cortex; cm3) are the variables that can differentiate the AD groups with healthy (Karami et al., 2021), (Pini et al., 2016). The differences were checked using statistical analysis. The results of the statistical investigation to extract appropriate feature approved that AD and control groups could be distinguished by these variables and therefore, they can be used as input for the classification. These values as AD biomarkers are the selected features for training and testing for classification. Therefore, it is time to develop a prediction model for classification. An algorithm is used to learn these features that were most representative. There are different machine learning - and deep learning-based algorithms. This chapter provides an overview of some of the main algorithms that showed better results for classification of MRI features in our investigations.

Support Vector Machine (SVM): SVM (Karami et al., 2019) is one of the commonly used algorithms for both classification and regression. When there are 'n features' as input, SVM is based on n-dimensional space; It tries to choose the best hyperplane/s for the classification to maximize the division between the classes (Huang et al., 2018). In understanding better about choosing best hyperplane by SVM, the definition of margin can be helpful. In SVM, margin is the distance between the nearest data of one class (called the support vector) and hyperplane. This understanding is easy when the classes are separable by linear hyperplane; however sometimes the linear hyperplane cannot do this separation. In this situation, hyper-circle might be helpful that they called it *kernel SVM (Wang et al., 2021).* An SVM kernel function provides the potential to transform non-linear spaces into linear spaces. Since there are different kernels offered by SVM, choosing kernel is one of the important steps in classification using SVM. In order to choose the right kernel, it is suggested to start with a quadratic polynomial and then increase using more complex one. If you start to use the most complicated kernel from the beginning, it can increase computational time in addition to the high probability of overfitting. Kernel is one of the advantages of the SVM to provide the possibility for classification in the condition that the data have an unknown or non-regular distribution *(Wang et al., 2021).*

Gradient Boosted Trees: Gradient boosted trees (Zhang & Jung, 2021) are a group of algorithms that combine several Decision Trees (DTs) to create a strong classifier. These models are effective at classification of complex datasets, and this is one of the reasons to becoming popular. Boosting empowered the accuracy of the performance but it has negative effect on the interpretability.

Random Forests (RF): RF (Sipper & Moore, 2021) is part of the DT algorithms. DT is a type of machine learning method that breaks up a complex decision into a union tree structure of simple binary decisions. Each node represents one input variable. The tree's branching continues until leaves determine the final label. A DT can be compared to a tree with a root (top node) that branches into possible outcomes; The internal nodes (non-leaf nodes) are the outcomes of the branches, and each node is a feature, and each branch is made using the comparison between testing value and a threshold value of the node (Karami et al., 2021). The term random corresponds to the using different subsets of the training data in the training step. In addition, each node in the decision tree is split by random selected variables of the data. As an advantage of DT, using different decision trees in training decreases the probability of overfitting, but RF usually does not work well with smaller training datasets (Liu et al., 2020).

Generalized Linear Model (GLM): GLM (Abramovich & Grinshtein, 2016) is an extension of ordinary linear regression. GLM allows for a variety of distributions while linear model follows a conditionally normal distribution. This is because of the potential of GLM to incorporate a multitude of effects, its flexibility to manage categorical and continues variables (Pernet, 2018). In GLM, the dependent variables can be defined as a linear combination of independent variables. Therefore, due to the linearity, the relation between variables can be shown by a line in 2D, a plan in 3D, and a hyperplane in 4D, and above. GLM is important in health science studies due to its ability to model binary outcomes or count data, however, it needs to be checked for overfitting and noise (Pernet, 2018).

Naive Bayes: In predictive modeling, Naive Bayes (Zhang, 2016) is a simple, fast, and surprisingly powerful algorithm for both two and multi-class classification. The term 'Naive Bayes' refers to simple tractable calculation of the probabilities for each hypothesis. It is known that learning Naive Bayes model from training data is fast because the probability of each class and the probability of each class given different input values need to be calculated while no coefficients need to be fitted by optimization procedures. Naive Bayes is appropriate for classification of multiclass groups.

Performance Assessment of Different classification Approaches for Early Detection of AD

The classification performance is evaluated in the test set using different metrics including accuracy, sensitivity, and specificity. To compute these metrics, it is better to create a table as a confusion matrix (Figure 3) for visualizing a classification model's performance (Zhang, 2016).

True Positive (TP): Observation is positive, and the prediction is also positive. False Negative (FN): Observation is positive but is predicted negative. True Negative (TN): Observation is negative and is predicted negative. False positive (FP): Observation is negative but is predicted positive.

Another statistic for evaluating classification success is the area under the receiver operating characteristic (ROC) curve (AUC); On a ROC curve, sensitivity and false positive rate are depicted, and AUC is derived from ROC to show the real positive rate against the false positive rate (Karami et al., 2019).

One of our recent studies examined the efficacy of several machine learning algorithms using volumetric characteristics collected from an MRI dataset of AD and healthy people (Karami et al., 2021). Table 1 depicts the outcomes for the performances of the above-mentioned algorithms in the same MRI dataset.

In this part, we presented the characteristics of the listed algorithms. As shown in Figure 3, the final outputs of the classifiers are presented as accuracy, specificity,

Figure 3. Confusion matrix for a classification model's performance

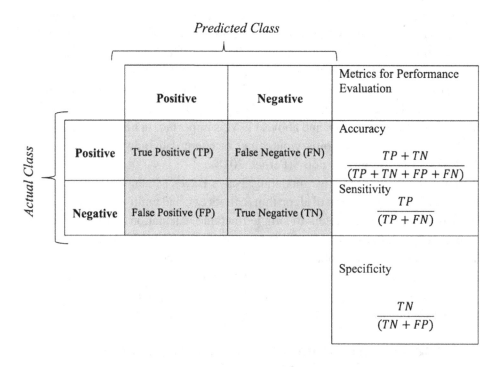

sensitivity, and AUC. It should be mentioned that according to the results of Figure 3, each algorithm has a different performance in the same dataset, and it is better to find the one which optimizes the outcomes. There is no perfect algorithm or an exact rule for choosing a specific algorithm. In the next part of this chapter, the

Table 1. Machine learning methods are used to evaluate the classification of MRI data: Generalized Linear Model (GLM), Naive Bayes, Random Forest, Gradient Boosted Tress, Support Vector Machine (SVM)

Method	Accuracy (%)	Sensitivity (%)	Specificity (%)	AUC (%)
GLM (Generalized Linear Model)	65.3±3	73.3±18.1	60±25.3	74.73±7.6
Random Forest	83.3±0	83.3±15.6	83.323.6	85.8±12
Naive Bayes	72±10.7	71.7±18.3	70±18.3	73.3±16.8
Gradient Boosted Tress	60±9.1	26.7±25.3	100±0	96.7±7.5
SVM (Support Vector Machine)	62.7±12.8	26.7±0	100±0	85.8±9.1

advancement and improvement of the detect of AD using CADS and MRI will be discussed.

RESULTS

In order to detect early symptoms of AD in MCI participants, researchers have been examining biomarkers based on neuroimaging in conjunction with computational methods for years. Computer-based techniques such as CADS are more suitable for detection of abnormalities, feature extraction, and classification. This is significant because primary care doctors might employ CAD systems to monitor AD patients. The method outlined in this paper addresses this gap and presents a computationally efficient pre-processing and prediction pipeline, and is designed for recognizing patterns associated with AD conversion.

Current research's focuses were the design and development of a system that uses medical imaging. To design this system, we needed: 1) digital image, 2) image processing tools, 3) techniques of classification. All these can detect the abnormality of features, classify them, and provide visual proof to the radiologists.

One of the crucial applications of CADS is finding abnormalities automatically in the human body. In this chapter explain a CADS that uses MRI data and VBM analysis to predict the conversion to AD years before clinical diagnosis. Among all these, detection of AD from healthy patients has been important due to the significant effect of detect of AD at early stage. A clinical treatment plan for a subject or the evaluation of a clinical trial for first-line medications to treat AD can both benefit from this prediction. The early detection can help to have better quality of life with higher peace both for patient and family, and economical treatment.

Using a variety of techniques, including morphometry, many researchers have employed MRI feature extraction for AD classification or the prediction of MCI-to-AD conversion. VBM analysis is a popular method for this purpose, and it has been used extensively to predict early conversion to AD using data from brain MRI. To this aim, using the suggested feature-selection procedure, the extracted raw-feature vectors are subsequently converted to lower-dimensional feature vectors for classification. The performance evaluation of a CADS is a continuous process by which data are assessed and analyzed to demonstrate the scientific validity, and analytical and clinical performance of the device for its intended purpose as stated by the designer. Later levels of evaluation focus on the diagnostic accuracy of a test in a relevant dataset.

FUTURE DIRECTION

CADS to Improve Early Detection Of AD

The fact that CADS incorporates factors frequently utilized in clinical settings and has a quick picture processing and prediction pipeline makes it easily adaptable to the healthcare sector. For patients who are at a high risk of developing AD conversion, this device may be employed as an effective tool. However, CADS could be translated into the healthcare setting as an objective AD diagnostic tool for patients but it cannot substitute the doctor. It surely leads to making a better decision in health care environment. It plays a supporting and interpretative role in detection using clinical data.

In this chapter, the effectiveness of CADS is discussed in terms of evaluation criteria. The results showed that CADS is more capable of distinguishing between AD and healthy with excellent classification accuracy when it uses MRI. This approved its efficiency as a second opinion besides the neurologist.

Although machine learning methods for brain MRI analysis have a lot of potential, they nevertheless have certain drawbacks. On comparatively small datasets, it doesn't show competitive outcomes. Numerous researches have demonstrated that when the size of the training datasets is increased, the majority of approaches consistently produce improved results (Cho et al., 2015). Due to legal and privacy concerns, gathering a significant amount of brain MRI data is difficult. Consequently, it is essential to create a deep learning approach using a variety of datasets. Adding more data to the existing dataset is one approach. In order to achieve this, deep learning techniques use data augmentation, which enlarges the dataset by applying random alterations to the original data, including translation, flipping, deformation, and rotation. Data augmentation benefits include introducing random variations to the original data and reducing overfitting, as demonstrated by numerous studies (Salvatore et al., 2015).

Regarding the efficiency of the MRI, it has both advantages and disadvantages. It is non-invasive, painless, and can detect abnormality without X-ray radiation. Although, some patients have problems with the small space inside the machine. In some cases which have metallic objects inside their body, they cannot use the MRI system with its strong magnetic field. In addition, it is a very expensive process that may not be supported by insurance. This leads to longtime intervals between tests. The lack of short time between tests may miss early detection of AD because they require comparison of serial results. Longtime intervals between tests permit symptom presentation to vary or even disappear. To solve this problem, behavioral data such as speech recognitions in verbal interactions/dialogues, eye movements associated with AD besides MRI might provide the possibility to check a complete set of different cognitive aspects. This can extend the predictive variables (e.g., based on biomarkers, social interactions, and mood disturbances). Different input features derived from MRI, communication, or both could be considered and the importance of each class of features can be evaluated. This makes CADS for AD more important in clinical practice soon. Depending on the available type of features, it might be possible to improve the classification accuracy.

CONCLUSION

In the first section of this chapter, the review of more diverse and latest articles providing the implementation details of deep learning in various applications like feature extraction, object detection and classification, and tracking is done. This provided the principal knowledge about complete overview of CADS. In addition, identification of brain's changes using quantitative and volumetric MRI measurements is reviewed. The microstructural damages of WM, GM, and CSF might be a useful tool to monitor AD progression.

The results of these studies have shown different biomarkers as appropriate raw features. These features will be used as the input of CADS. The core results of this chapter confirmed the working hypothesis that CADS using MRI has the potential to be used for the identification of regional atrophy pattern in AD.

REFERENCES

Abramovich, F., & Grinshtein, V. (2016). Model Selection and Minimax Estimation in Generalized Linear Models. *IEEE Transactions on Information Theory*, *62*(6), 3721–3730. doi:10.1109/TIT.2016.2555812

Adutwum, L. A., & Harynuk, J. J. (2014). Unique ion filter: A data reduction tool for GC/MS data preprocessing prior to chemometric analysis. *Analytical Chemistry*, *86*(15), 7726–7733. doi:10.1021/ac501660a PMID:25002039

Alzheimer's Disease Facts and Figures. (2010). *Rep* (Vol. 6). Alzheimer's Association.

Block, V. A., Pitsch, E., Tahir, P., Cree, B. A., Allen, D. D., & Gelfand, J. M. (2016). Remote Physical Activity Monitoring in Neurological Disease: A Systematic Review. *PLoS One*, *11*(4), e0154335. doi:10.1371/journal.pone.0154335 PMID:27124611

Bobinski, M., de Leon, M. J., Convit, A., De Santi, S., Wegiel, J., Tarshish, C. Y., Saint Louis, L. A., & Wisniewski, H. M. (1999). MRI of entorhinal cortex in mild Alzheimer's disease. *Lancet, 353*(9146), 38–40. doi:10.1016/S0140-6736(05)74869-8 PMID:10023955

Chang, C. H., Lin, C. H., & Lane, H. Y. (2021). Machine Learning and Novel Biomarkers for the Diagnosis of Alzheimer's Disease. *Int J Mol Sci., 22*(5), 2761. doi:10.3390/ijms22052761 PMID:33803217

Cho, J., Lee, K., Shin, E., Choy, G., & Do, S. (2015). *How much data is needed to train a medical image deep learning system to achieve necessary high accuracy.* arXiv. 20151511.06348

Choo, I. H., Chong, A., Chung, J. Y., & Kim, H. (2019). Association of Subjective Memory Complaints with the Left Parahippocampal Amyloid Burden in Mild Cognitive Impairment. *Journal of Alzheimer's Disease, 7*(Nov), 1261–1268. doi:10.3233/JAD-190816 PMID:31707367

Cummings, J. L., & Benson, D. F. (1992). *Dementia: A clinical approach.* Butterworth-Heinemann.

Deardorff & Grossberg. (2019). A fixed-dose combination of memantine extended-release and donepezil in the treatment of moderate-to-severe Alzheimer's disease. *Drug Des Devel Ther., 10*, 3267-3279.

El Houby, E. M. F. (2018). Framework of Computer Aided Diagnosis Systems for Cancer Classification Based on Medical Images. *Journal of Medical Systems, 42*(8), 157. doi:10.100710916-018-1010-x PMID:29995204

Emilien, G. R. (2004). *Alzheimer Disease: Neuropsychology and Pharmacology.* Birkhauser. doi:10.1007/978-3-0348-7842-5

Hamdi, Bourouis, Rastislav, & Mohmed. (2022, February 7). Evaluation of Neuro Images for the Diagnosis of Alzheimer's Disease Using Deep Learning Neural Network. *Frontiers in Public Health, 10*, 834032. doi:10.3389/fpubh.2022.834032 PMID:35198526

Fathi, S., Ahmadi, M., & Dehnad, A. (2022, July). Early diagnosis of Alzheimer's disease based on deep learning: A systematic review. *Computers in Biology and Medicine, 146*, 105634. doi:10.1016/j.compbiomed.2022.105634 PMID:35605488

Fei, B. (2017). Computer-aided diagnosis of prostate cancer with MRI. *Curr Opin Biomed Eng., 3*, 20–27. doi:10.1016/j.cobme.2017.09.009 PMID:29732440

Gosche, K. M., Mortimer, J. A., Smith, C. D., Markesbery, W. R., & Snowdon, A. D. (2002). Hippocampal Volume as an Index of Alzheimer Neuropathology: Findings from the Nun Study. *Neurology*, *58*(10), 1476–1482. doi:10.1212/WNL.58.10.1476 PMID:12034782

Huang, S., Cai, N., Pacheco, P. P., Narrandes, S., Wang, Y., & Xu, W. (2018). Applications of Support Vector Machine (SVM) Learning in Cancer Genomics. *Cancer Genomics & Proteomics*, *15*(1), 41–51. doi:10.21873/cgp.20063 PMID:29275361

Juottonen, K., Laakso, M. P., Insausti, R., Lehtovirta, M., Pitkanen, A., Partanen, K., & Soininen, H. (1998). Volumes of the entorhinal and perirhinal cortices in Alzheimer's disease. *Neurobiology of Aging*, *19*(1), 15–22. doi:10.1016/S0197-4580(98)00007-4 PMID:9562498

Kantarci, K., & Jack, C. R. (2004). Quantitative magnetic resonance techniques as surrogate markers of Alzheimer's disease. *NeuroRx*, *1*(2), 196–205. doi:10.1602/neurorx.1.2.196 PMID:15717020

Karami, V., Nittari, G., & Amenta, F. (2019). Neuroimaging Computer-Aided Diagnosis Systems for Alzheimer's Disease. *International Journal of Imaging Systems and Technology*, *29*(1), 83–94. doi:10.1002/ima.22300

Karami, V., Nittari, G., Traini, E., & Amenta, F. (2021). An Optimized Decision Tree with Genetic Algorithm Rule-Based Approach to Reveal the Brain's Changes During Alzheimer's Disease Dementia. *Journal of Alzheimer's Disease*, *84*(4), 1–8. doi:10.3233/JAD-210626 PMID:34719494

Khojaste-Sarakhsi, M., Haghighi, S. S., Ghomi, S. M. T. F., & Marchiori, E. (2022, August). Deep learning for Alzheimer's disease diagnosis: A survey. *Artificial Intelligence in Medicine*, *130*, 102332. doi:10.1016/j.artmed.2022.102332 PMID:35809971

Killiany, R. J., Hyman, B. T., Gomez-Isla, T., Moss, M. B., Kikinis, R., Jolesz, F., Tanzi, R., Jones, K., & Albert, M. S. (2002). MRI measures of entorhinal cortex vs hippocampus in preclinical AD. *Neurology*, *58*(8), 1188–1196. doi:10.1212/WNL.58.8.1188 PMID:11971085

Lerch, J. P., Pruessner, J. C., Zijdenbos, A., Hampel, H., Teipel, S. J., & Evans, A. C. (2005). Focal decline of cortical thickness in Alzheimer's disease identified by computational neuroanatomy. *Cerebral Cortex (New York, N.Y.)*, *15*(7), 995–1001. doi:10.1093/cercor/bhh200 PMID:15537673

Li, L., Lee, C. C., Zhou, F. L., Molony, C., Doder, Z., Zalmover, E., Sharma, K., Juhaeri, J., & Wu, C. (2021). Performance assessment of different machine learning approaches in predicting diabetic ketoacidosis in adults with type 1 diabetes using electronic health records data. *Pharmacoepidemiology and Drug Safety*, *30*(5), 610–618. doi:10.1002/pds.5199 PMID:33480091

Liu, B., Guo, W., & Xin, C. (2020). Morphological Attribute Profile Cube and Deep Random Forest for Small Sample Classification of Hyperspectral Image. *IEEE Access: Practical Innovations, Open Solutions*, *8*, 117096–117108. doi:10.1109/ACCESS.2020.3004968

Mahandra, B. (1984). *Dementia: A survey of the syndrome of dementia*. MTP.

Mathis, Wang, Holt, Huang, Debnath, & Klunk. (2003). Synthesis and evaluation of 11C-labeled 6-substituted 2-arylbenzothiazoles as amyloid imaging agents. *Journal of Medicinal Chemistry*, (46), 2740–2754.

Naylor, S. (2003). Biomarkers: Current perspectives and future prospects. *Expert Review of Molecular Diagnostics*, *3*(5), 525–529. doi:10.1586/14737159.3.5.525 PMID:14510173

Pena, D., Suescun, J., Schiess, M., Ellmore, T. M., & Giancardo, L. Alzheimer's Disease Neuroimaging Initiative. (2022, January 3). Toward a Multimodal Computer-Aided Diagnostic Tool for Alzheimer's Disease Conversion. *Frontiers in Neuroscience*, *15*, 744190. doi:10.3389/fnins.2021.744190 PMID:35046766

Pernet C, (2018). Brain Morphometry: Methods and Clinical Applications. *The General Linear Model: Theory and Practicalities*.

Pini, L., Pievani, M., Bocchetta, M., Altomare, D., Bosco, P., Cavedo, E., Galluzzi, S., Marizzoni, M., & Frisoni, G. B. (2016). Brain atrophy in Alzheimer's Disease and aging. *Ageing Research Reviews*, *30*, 25–48. doi:10.1016/j.arr.2016.01.002 PMID:26827786

Salvatore, C., Cerasa, A., Battista, P., Gilardi, M. C., Quattrone, A., & Castiglioni, I. (2015). Magnetic resonance imaging biomarkers for the early diagnosis of Alzheimer's disease: A machine learning approach. *Frontiers in Molecular Neuroscience*, *9*, 270. doi:10.3389/fnins.2015.00307 PMID:26388719

Sipper, M., & Moore, J. H. (2021). Conservation machine learning: a case study of random forests. *Sci Rep.*, *11*(1), 3629. doi:10.103841598-021-83247-4 PMID:33574563

Ten Kate, M., Ingala, S., Schwarz, A. J., Fox, N. C., Chételat, G., van Berckel, B. N. M., Ewers, M., Foley, C., Gispert, J. D., Hill, D., Irizarry, M. C., Lammertsma, A. A., Molinuevo, J. L., Ritchie, C., Scheltens, P., Schmidt, M. E., Visser, P. J., Waldman, A., Wardlaw, J., ... Barkhof, F. (2018). Secondary prevention of Alzheimer's dementia: Neuroimaging contributions. *Alzheimer's Research & Therapy*, *10*(1), 112. doi:10.118613195-018-0438-z PMID:30376881

Toepper, M. (2017). Dissociating Normal Aging from Alzheimer's Disease: A View from Cognitive Neuroscience. *Journal of Alzheimer's Disease*, *57*(2), 331–352. doi:10.3233/JAD-161099 PMID:28269778

Wang, B., Zhang, X., Xing, S., Sun, C., & Chen, X. (2021). Sparse representation theory for support vector machine kernel function selection and its application in high-speed bearing fault diagnosis. *ISA Transactions*, *118*, 207–218. doi:10.1016/j.isatra.2021.01.060 PMID:33583570

Zeng, H. M., Han, H. B., Zhang, Q. F., & Bai, H. (2021). Application of modern neuroimaging technology in the diagnosis and study of Alzheimer's disease. *Neural Regeneration Research*, *16*(1), 73–79. doi:10.4103/1673-5374.286957 PMID:32788450

Zhang, Z. (2016). Naïve Bayes Classification in R. *Annals of Translational Medicine*, *4*(12), 241. doi:10.21037/atm.2016.03.38 PMID:27429967

Zhang, Z., & Jung, C. (2021). GBDT-MO: Gradient-Boosted Decision Trees for Multiple Outputs. *IEEE Transactions on Neural Networks and Learning Systems*, *32*(7), 3156–3167. doi:10.1109/TNNLS.2020.3009776 PMID:32749969

Chapter 6
Ambient Assisted Living (AAL) Systems to Help Older People

Rita Komalasari

(iD) https://orcid.org/0000-0001-9963-2363

Yarsi University, Indonesia

ABSTRACT

There is significant interest in the development and implementation of smart and intelligent ambient assisted living (AAL) systems that can give daily support to help older people live independently in their homes. Additionally, such systems will lower the expense of healthcare that governments must bear in order to provide support for this group of residents. It also relieves families of the burden of constant and often tedious round-the-clock surveillance of these individuals, allowing them to focus on their own lives and commitments. As a result, recognition, classification, and decision-making for such people's daily activities are critical for the development of appropriate and successful intelligent support systems capable of providing the essential assistance in the correct manner and at the right time.

INTRODUCTION

This chapter contains reviews based on the concept of the book. Both academics and the general public will benefit greatly from this chapter. For example, a health professional dealing with older people. To aid the elderly, this chapter explores ambient assisted living (AAL) technologies. The structure of the chapter is as follows: First, a literature-based method was briefly explained. Second, the author presents the literature review results in the results section. Third, an evidence-fusion theory-based technique is provided in the discussion section—this evidence includes the

DOI: 10.4018/978-1-6684-6980-4.ch006

usefulness of AAL systems to help older people. Finally, a conclusion and future research recommendations are presented in the conclusion section.

AAL technologies are being developed to assist the elderly in prolonging their time spent in their current residences. In addition, the cost of health care for this population will be reduced if governments implement such systems. It also relieves families of the burden of constant and often tedious round-the-clock surveillance of these individuals, allowing them to focus on their own lives and commitments. Because of this, it's important to recognize, categorize, and decide about these people's daily activities to make intelligent support systems that can help them in the right way and at the right time.

METHODOLOGY

In terms of the method, the review presents a meta-ethnographic synthesis of studies on ambient assisted living (AAL) technologies. Qualitative research reporting on the experiences of using AAL systems to aid the elderly was the focus of the present review. The author paid particular attention to professional understandings of AAL, whether they influence practice and the hurdles and facilitators that older people face when seeking help for AAL. By combining the perspectives of experts with different roles and responsibilities, we may better understand the situation in which older people seek AAL's aid. The goal is that this information will shed light on effective strategies used by experts and show where more AAL help needs to be given.

The following were the criteria for inclusion and exclusion:

The researcher carefully read each piece. Using our proforma review approach, it was decided if they were pertinent enough to the study to merit further investigation. Use this tool to gather data on the arguments made in each item, their conclusions, and an assessment of their attributes. As a result, the assessment procedure carefully assessed the overall calibre of the research (Komalasari et al., 2022). The following figure 1 illustrates the specific method.

RESULT

According to a literature study, this section summarizes the results. Automated home systems use a distributed sensory system to collect information about human environments, then decide and activate actuators based on that data to control specific home gadgets, perform specific activities, or share data with other systems outside the house. There is a strong connection between the AAL home name and this central concept. A smart space, a warehouse, or an AAL home that uses collaborative

Figure 1. the specific method

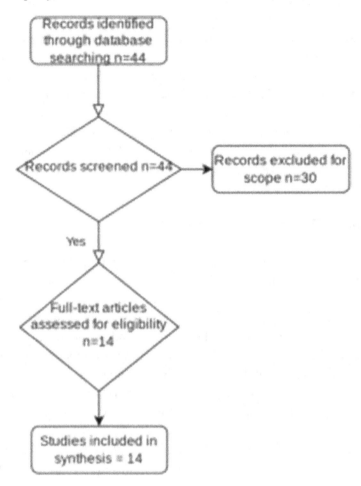

ambient intelligence are all terms that may describe an AAL home. Elderly people may get a variety of home support, controlled medicine, fall prevention, and security measures from AAL houses with these characteristics. These solutions help elderly individuals feel safe and comfortable in their own homes. With AAL, family members may keep tabs on their elderly loved ones from anywhere they have Internet access (Scataglini & Imbesi 2021).

Across the globe, there are a variety of laboratory studies, initiatives, and industrial demonstrations using AAL houses that have many of the same characteristics. Looking at the goals these initiatives strive for, there are many technologies, information sources, methods of validating results, and results they use.

TECHNOLOGY'S ADVANCEMENT

Three Types of AAL Home Technology

Systems of Social Connectivity

The most important people were those whose goal was to encourage social interaction, networking, and the discovery of social efficiencies. Enhancement of Security in AAL Homes Those focusing on emergency and drug management systems for the individual. They aim AAL Health Monitoring Residences at addressing long-term issues. The package also includes Continual Health Records and active telehealth engagement with patients. Many projects are going on worldwide, and I will briefly describe some of them in the following paragraph.

The University of Virginia developed AlarmNet, a wireless sensor based AAL system, to monitor one's health while living alone (Stucki et al., 2014). It includes wearable sensors, wireless sensors, user interfaces, decision-making algorithms, and a database. Portable and stationary devices are both used for communicating and alerting. They may collect data from an accelerometer and other sensors using a wearable sensor. Anonymized and aggregated personal data are collected from all residents and used following their needs. If a patient's medical circumstances change, the system may be changed to notify certain people or the patient themselves. To gather information like temperature, dust content, light intensity, and a resident's precise location through embedded sensors, devices are dispersed throughout the surroundings. For example, pressure sensors on the ground may monitor a person's footfall to identify an increased danger of falling, even if a set of bed sensors can keep tabs on their resting breathing, heart rate, and movement. AlarmNet's adaptability makes it possible to expand the system if additional sensors are installed, or new situations emerge that need monitoring (Padikkapparambil et al., 2020). AlarmNet's system design needs to be improved despite its novel approach to activity analysis. Because AlarmNet has a closed architecture, it cannot use third-party sensors or software.

The University of Washington launched the Assisted Cognition Environment (ACE) project (Al-Shaqi et al., 2016) to understand better how artificial intelligence might improve and assist the everyday lives of older people with cognitive problems. They may provide patient support by using the established system to detect their immediate surroundings, locate them, analyse their behaviour patterns, and provide them with both verbal and physical help. The system can also let caretakers know about certain conditions if it needs to.

There are two primary components to the system. That it can construct an activity supervision model that aids patients in lessening the suffering from spatial disorientation in and out of their home environment is a major benefit of the system. Structured prompter: This second feature helps individuals with daily multi-step chores (Al-Shaqi et al., 2016). At the United States Georgia Institute of Technology, a project called AWARE Home is underway to understand the aging population's unique needs better. By introducing ubiquitous computing, they may provide their family members worried about their well-being while living alone with critical information. By using so-called "smart floor" technology, which captures footstep patterns, the study aimed to differentiate one specific person from others and pinpoint their exact position. The "ground reaction forces (GFR)" profiles derived from the data collected from the tiles serve as the foundation for reconstructing each person's footprints. For each person, they compare the GFR model against fresh GFR data. A basic feature-vector average method and a hidden Markov model (HMM) are used in the analysis. Another aim of this research was to use radio-frequency tags to track down "often misplaced commodities like keys and eyeglasses throughout the home. Scientists placed floor vibration sensors to keep tabs on the flow of people and commodities in the lab. They also used smart floor measurements and the GFR method to determine how people lose their things in space (Al-Shaqi et al., 2016).

The University of Florida researchers created CareWatch, a program that monitors the health and well-being of the elderly. The system monitored cognitively impaired people's sleeping habits, triggering several alert systems for caregivers. One of the most common signs of cognitive decline and dementia is a shift in a person's sleep patterns, which impacts their mental and physiological well-being and places additional demands on their caregivers (İnçki & Ari, 2018).

CareWatch is a program that educates caregivers on how to best care for elderly adults with dementia. As of this writing, all of them are still living at home. CareWatch is a preventative initiative. unauthorized house escapes, particularly at night, and eases some of the stress on caregivers. Informal caregivers, such as family members, may use CareWatch, a new technology to assist in the care of the elderly. To date, it is flexible and versatile. Patients and caregivers alike will benefit from the system's night-time features, which will help them sleep better and feel more rested throughout the day.

Independent Living Technology started the University College Dublin, Ireland, Research Group (Bal et al. 2011). Open-source software and hardware make up the bulk of the project. That may be used for biomedical research in a short period. Software developed by Genoa University researchers for gesture recognition, movement analysis, and multimodal interfaces is available under the GNU Public License (GPL). This provides the foundation for the BioMOBIUS research project. They monitor physiological parameters via the BioMOBIUS platform, which includes a sensor structure. They transformed measures into clinically useful and expressive data using a multi-method data processing framework and a smart agent. Monitors are used to keep tabs on things like heart rate variability, blood pressure, gait stability, and attentiveness to danger. The system's broad use of an interface that uses both wired and wireless connection mechanisms makes it adaptable to many devices.

The goal of the Casas study was to use machine learning methods to recognize and analyse the specific behaviours of older adults with dementia (Ahamed et al., 2020). In a test environment, a person's emotions and other sensors are recorded to define "cognitive health" and "dementia" behaviour in older adults who are in good cognitive health and those who have been diagnosed with dementia. The results show that the learning algorithm can pick up on changes in how different tasks are done, but it can't tell the difference between confusion caused by dementia and a mistake made by accident.

The method Lotfi and co-workers used to detect anomalous behaviour in dementia patients was to use a new form of monitoring. Observed signals from many places were used to characterize the flow of inhabitant activities in residence and their time length. Clustering techniques are used to examine daily activity patterns based on collected data. Compared to Ahamed et al. (2020), their approach shows a clearer separation between abilities. An ICT technology transfer laboratory in Bologna performed the Casattenta project to research whether residents' daily activities may be monitored via AIT, sensor systems fusion, as well as wireless communication networks (WANs). An array of fixed sensors, a collection of wearable sensors, and a platform for communication make up their system. The system's primary goal was to keep an eye on the health and daily routines of its people, those who are elderly and live alone (Farella et al., 2010). All the system's parts were assembled using a wireless method called ZigBee data transmission. This made it possible for the system to monitor and pick up on critical situations for the elderly, like the risk of falling and being unable to move.

A wide range of healthcare applications may benefit from wireless sensor networks, including stroke rehabilitation and disaster response, according to a study by academics at Harvard University (Rawat et al., 2014). Battery-powered sensors were improved with sufficient processing and communication modules for usage in the project's wireless sensor network (WSN). By using the WSN, it was possible to automate the real-time censoring. Vital signs are collected, processed, and integrated into a patient's medical record system. This project used TinyOS, a commercially available operating system, to incorporate medical sensors, including gyroscopes and EMG sensors, pulse oximeters, and EKG sensors (Soh et al., 2015). Secure software architecture allows patients to share information with wireless medical equipment securely.

Georgia Tech's aware house research program started A smart home initiative called Georgia-. Innovative designs enhanced relationships between senior citizens, their families, and the wider community in the Georgia-Tech smart home. Basic

RFID sensors and vision systems were used to enable indoor positioning tracking. As part of the Georgia-Tech initiative, a group of researchers developed an activity recognition system that focuses on everyday activities like watching TV, reading a book, or putting together a meal.

Centre Scientific and Technical Bâtiment (CSTB) led the GERHOME gerontological smart house initiative (CSTB), a French research organization (CSTB, 2011).

The entire system helped those who lost their ability to make decisions. Real-time video surveillance and sensor data were used to automate the identification of human actions using GERHOME's software. An intelligent agent architecture was used to establish a communication infrastructure for the project. This infrastructure makes integrating many existing systems with several sorts of sensors easy. To better comprehend the daily patterns of the elderly, they equip GERHOME with the installation of sensors, both wired and wireless, into household furnishings and appliances.

A thorough examination of the data gathered identifies any anomalies or shifting patterns in behaviour. For elderly people, delaying their admission to nursing homes was an important goal of the GERHOME project. Three steps have to be examined to achieve this aim. The 3D geometric information of the observed subject is used to construct a knowledge library of reference behaviours, subsequently used to evaluate the frailty of the aged. It is also important that the system can identify potentially dangerous scenarios, such as falls. The third stage is to create a human behaviour profile and compare it to the topic reference profile. The principal goal of the system was to find changes in health status early by using computers to interpret sensor data with help from devices like camcorders.

The University of Illinois started an assistive-living initiative called I-LivingTM to build an assistive-living architecture that allows dispersed wireless sensing devices to work together safely. It was developed to offer a wide range of services for older individuals with varying levels of independence and/or assisted living needs to improve their well-being. With RFID, location, and presence identification modules, this project aimed to make an open system architecture.

A project of the University of Texas is called MavHome. at Austin, which aims to automate the house to aid with everyday living tasks by using machine learning to understand the patterns of an individual's actions (VandeWeerd et al. 2020). The project aimed to optimize "Managing an Adaptive Versatile Home" occupant satisfaction at all costs while minimizing hardware and software investment expenses. The system recognizes and expects the everyday behaviours of the occupants to achieve its aim.

MavHome uses various smart activity identification algorithms that use nearby sensors and actuators. An information layer collects and stores sensor data. There is a MITHouse project focusing on smart home design and associated technologies to better serve elderly people in the future at the Institute for Technology at MIT. Construction of an experimental facility outfitted with sensors in various places around MIT began in 2013. Implementing a software platform allowed the creation of new user interfaces. EThere is a need for environmental monitoring and new building solutions to maintaining a healthy weight via regular physical exercise. The sensors used varied, including biometric and infrared transmitters, which were used to gather information about the people who used them and the surroundings in which they lived. Initially, researchers used sensors to keep tabs on lab activity to see how people react to new technology placed in their immediate surroundings. It created user interfaces for various mobile devices and data visualization.

ORCATECH supports the monitoring and help of older people's health and well-being. Ingenious bed sensors included in the gadget detected when an old person was about to get out of bed and immediately turned on the room lights to keep them safe. The device also provides remote control telepresence for elderly people living alone, allowing them to receive health and social support from family members and caregivers far away(Thomas et 2021).

Oregon Health & Science University. The project aimed to create technology for a wide variety of needs in terms of self-sufficient living. It focused on consumer technology to enhance the lives of the elderly. To better serve the aging population's needs, the project team investigated a variety of real-world applications, including locating objects, dispensing medications, monitoring vital signs, detecting patterns, sending alerts, and deploying robots to increase dexterity and teachability. RFID tags, interrogators, smartphones, and WSNs were all used in these investigations.

The author focused on researching and creating interactive medical technologies for use at home by students at the University of Rochester. The project's purpose is to create new technologies that can better identify and expect problems with healthcare outcomes for patients in the future. The system included "Chester the Pill," an interactive medical advice system that includes patients and existing healthcare providers to meet their needs for help in a medically advanced home. Chester the Pill. With a voice recognition and artificial intelligence algorithm, the interactive system uses interactive real-time queries and responses to help residents detect possible illnesses. People and caregivers may better grasp a physician's orders thanks to the system's knowledge of medications, their negative effects, and other health conditions.

SOPRANO is an initiative of the European Union (EU) that aims to create an environment for the elderly called "ambient assisted living" to help them stay independent. An experience-and application-based method has been developed to recognize the difficulties and demands of older people's participation in communal life. They urged older adults to engage in focus groups, one-on-one interviews, and the evaluation process throughout the study process.

At Carleton University, TAFFETA (Third-age-friendly technology) was born. In 2002, they installed a smart home, sensors, and actuators to monitor and control the immediate surroundings. Some of the various sensors used were temperature sensors, motion sensors, microphones, magnetic switches, and RFID tags (Knoefel. 2005).

While in the apartment, TAFFETA sensors tracked movement on the floor, in beds, and on the sofa. They also monitored the respiration rates of the individuals using the bed mats. Based on their medical history, the device also let the passenger know if there was a potential health problem.

Virginia Tech's medical automation research centre began the program. In the WellAware project in 2000 (Bal et al., 2011a). They combined sensory systems and user interfaces in the WellAware project to allow professional carers to monitor the elderly and aid them. Proximity and motion sensors were spread around the smart home and communicated using the ZigBee wireless protocol with the major computer. A system that uses wireless data networking, sensor monitoring, and software to compare senior behaviours to normalcy. These are all major components of the WellAware system. Caretakers may check the health of elderly individuals remotely and decide on the early intervention needed for dangerous medical illnesses using the website access given by the system.

In the TeleCARE project, an architecture for an assisted living environment is presented. Third-party hardware drivers and other peripherals are no longer required because of the project's abstraction. Even though TeleCARE's distributed and environmental fault-tolerant topology allows for reduced overall system power consumption by grouping the sensor nodes, it does not. The framework's hardware requirements remain a mystery. This is a crucial consideration when designing a system to help elderly people and facilitate real-time contact between them and their families.

The primary focus of the CAALYX project is on the system's usability for the elderly population. Measuring its usefulness from the perspective of an elderly user. To accommodate the elderly population's demands, special hardware is used to house the CAALYX project sensors. Because the project relied on mobile phones, a battery issue arose. Older individuals may forget to charge their phones, endangering the system. In contrast, CAALYX delivers a more refined experience. A user-friendly option that can be set upright on the TV.

It is clear from the preceding sections that imaging as part of a system that uses all data and senses to create a fully personalized assistive system for older individuals, particularly those with memory impairments, is non-existent. This chapter discusses how older people, especially those with limited mobility, can benefit from the latest home automation technologies. We need to examine how they can do so.

TECHNOLOGY'S CHALLENGES

For home assistive technology, one important challenge is using wearable sensors for real-time vital signs and health monitoring. Acceptance, durability, usability, communication, and power needs are all issues that must be addressed to make wearable technologies more widely accepted. For example, such devices must, when assessing any patient, deliver vital signs measures and a careful diagnosis of the disease. They must be able to. At the same time, being lightweight, it should have little impact on the wearer's skin and be easy to use in daily routines. The battery life and connectivity capabilities should be long enough to avoid the need for recharging for days or weeks at a time. It should resist impact, heat, cold, and water and be fault-tolerant. When these needs are met in wearable devices, sensor technology developers face a major challenge that might propel new systems of home-assisted technology to new heights of performance.

Standards for identifying aspects of assisted living technology are like a non-entity. As a result, the flexibility of multiple system components, such as there is no standardization in the development of sensors, communication methods, and topic engagement techniques or languages, If there are such standards, it will be easier for system designers and people who make goods to meet the demand to work together. As a general rule, older individuals are more sensitive to their privacy and the potential for intrusion. Consequently, older patients may have difficulty accepting AAL devices since they may see them as intrusive. Overwhelmingly, the reviewed study needs to pay attention to this and assume that end users would accept the system's architecture in its current form, which is different. Because of a dearth of research and surveys on the subject, this assumption is only sometimes held in high regard. The level of social acceptance varies from one civilization to the next, according to the culture. According to Etemad et al. (2019), gender and age affect how people perceive space, which might impact whether or not a system is acceptable when people's behaviour is being watched regularly. Therefore, determining user approval is a significant challenges for system engineers.

SOLUTIONS AND RECOMMENDATIONS

Technology for ambient assisted living (AAL) is highly sought after to help older people's independence and quality of life. AAL can offer various solutions to enhance older people's quality of life, enable them to live healthier, more independent lives, and support older people.

FUTURE RESEARCH DIRECTIONS

This chapter serves as a basis for additional research. The development of an assisted living technology system that employs wearable sensors for the environment and environmental monitoring devices for older people's daily activities should be discussed by caregivers, professionals, individuals, and family members.

CONCLUSION

Ambient Assisted Living (AAL) solutions to aid the elderly are discussed in this chapter. The author has presented a lot of literature research on assisted-living facilities and the influence of modern technology to minimize damage and forecast dangers. This chapter is a starting point for further investigation. Caretakers, professionals, people, and family members should discuss the need for assisted living technology to develop a system that uses wearable sensors for the environment and environmental monitoring devices for the everyday activities of elderly people. Activities to be built during the design stage of the system.

REFERENCES

Ahamed, F., Shahrestani, S., & Cheung, H. (2020). Internet of things and machine learning for healthy ageing: Identifying the early signs of dementia. *Sensors (Basel)*, *20*(21), 6031. doi:10.339020216031 PMID:33114070

Al-Shaqi, R., Mourshed, M., & Rezgui, Y. (2016). Progress in ambient assisted systems for independent living by the elderly. *SpringerPlus*, *5*(1), 1–20. doi:10.118640064-016-2272-8 PMID:27330890

Allen, J., Ferguson, G., Blaylock, N., Byron, D., Chambers, N., Dzikovska, M., Galescu, L., & Swift, M. (2006). Chester: Towards a personal medication advisor. *Journal of Biomedical Informatics*, *39*(5), 500–513. doi:10.1016/j.jbi.2006.02.004 PMID:16545620

Bal, M., Shen, W., Hao, Q., & Xue, H. (2011, June). Collaborative smart home technologies for senior independent living: a review. In *Proceedings of the 2011 15th International Conference on Computer Supported Cooperative Work in Design (CSCWD)* (pp. 481-488). IEEE. 10.1109/CSCWD.2011.5960116

Etemad-Sajadi, R., & Dos Santos, G. G. (2019). Senior citizens' acceptance of connected health technologies in their homes. *International Journal of Health Care Quality Assurance, 32*(8), 1162–1174. Advance online publication. doi:10.1108/ IJHCQA-10-2018-0240 PMID:31566513

İnçki, K., & Ari, I. (2018). Democratization of runtime verification for the internet of things. *Computers & Electrical Engineering, 68*, 570–580. doi:10.1016/j. compeleceng.2018.05.007

Knoefel, F., Emerson, V., & Schulman, B. (2005, March). TAFETA: an inclusive design for tele-health. *Proceedings of the Technology and Persons with Disabilities Conference*.

Padikkapparambil, J., Ncube, C., Singh, K. K., & Singh, A. (2020). Internet of Things technologies for elderly health-care applications. In *Emergence of pharmaceutical industry growth with industrial IoT approach* (pp. 217–243). Academic Press. doi:10.1016/B978-0-12-819593-2.00008-X

Rawat, P., Singh, K. D., Chaouchi, H., & Bonnin, J. M. (2014). Wireless sensor networks: A survey on recent developments and potential synergies. *The Journal of Supercomputing, 68*(1), 1–48. doi:10.100711227-013-1021-9

Scataglini, S., & Imbesi, S. (2021). Human-centered design smart clothing for ambient assisted living of elderly users: considerations in the COVID-19 pandemic perspective. In *IoT in Healthcare and Ambient Assisted Living* (pp. 311–324). Springer. doi:10.1007/978-981-15-9897-5_15

Soh, P. J., Vandenbosch, G. A., Mercuri, M., & Schreurs, D. M. P. (2015). Wearable wireless health monitoring: Current developments, challenges, and future trends. *IEEE Microwave Magazine, 16*(4), 55–70. doi:10.1109/MMM.2015.2394021

Stucki, R. A., Urwyler, P., Rampa, L., Müri, R., Mosimann, U. P., & Nef, T. (2014). A web-based non-intrusive ambient system to measure and classify activities of daily living. *Journal of Medical Internet Research, 16*(7), e3465. doi:10.2196/jmir.3465 PMID:25048461

Thomas, N. W., Beattie, Z., Riley, T., Hofer, S., & Kaye, J. (2021). Home-based assessment of cognition and health measures: The collaborative aging research using technology (CART) initiative and international collaborations. *IEEE Instrumentation & Measurement Magazine, 24*(6), 68–78. doi:10.1109/MIM.2021.9513638

VandeWeerd, C., Yalcin, A., Aden-Buie, G., Wang, Y., Roberts, M., Mahser, N., Fnu, C., & Fabiano, D. (2020). HomeSense: Design of an ambient home health and wellness monitoring platform for older adults. *Health and Technology*, *10*(5), 1291–1309. doi:10.100712553-019-00404-6

ADDITIONAL READING

Komalasari, R. (2022). A Social Ecological Model (SEM) to Manage Methadone Programmes in Prisons. In Handbook of Research on Mathematical Modeling for Smart Healthcare Systems (pp. 374-382). IGI Global. doi:10.4018/978-1-6684-4580-8.ch020

Komalasari, R. (2022). Pemanfaatan Kecerdasan Buatan (Ai) Dalam Telemedicine: Dari Perspektif Profesional Kesehatan. *Jurnal Kedokteran Mulawarman*, *9*(2), 72–81.

Komalasari, R. (2023). Telemedicine in Pandemic Times in Indonesia: Healthcare Professional's Perspective. In N. Vajjhala & P. Eappen (Eds.), *Health Informatics and Patient Safety in Times of Crisis* (pp. 138–153). IGI Global. doi:10.4018/978-1-6684-5499-2.ch008

Komalasari, R. (2023). Designing Health Systems for Better, Faster, and Less Expensive Treatment. In *Exploring the Convergence of Computer and Medical Science Through Cloud Healthcare*. IGI Global. doi:10.4018/978-1-6684-5260-8.ch001

Komalasari, R. (in press). Digital twin elderly healthcare services. In *Digital Twins and Healthcare: Trends, Techniques, and Challenges*. IGI Global.

Komalasari, R. (in press). History and Legislative Changes Governing Medical Cannabis in Indonesia. In *Medical Cannabis and the Effects of Cannabinoids on Fighting Cancer, Multiple Sclerosis, Epilepsy, Parkinsons and Other Neurodegenerative Diseases*. IGI Global.

Komalasari, R. (in press). The ethical consideration of using Artificial Intelligence (AI) in medicine. In *Advanced Bioinspiration Methods for Healthcare Standards, Policies, and Reform*. IGI Global. doi:10.4018/978-1-6684-5656-9.ch001

Komalasari, R. (in press). Postnatal mental distress, exploring the experiences of mothers navigating the health care system. In *Perspectives and Considerations on Navigating the Mental Healthcare System*. IGI Global.

Komalasari, R. (in press). Treatment of menstrual discomfort in young women and a cognitive behavior therapy (CBT) program. In *Perspectives on Coping Strategies for Menstrual and Premenstrual Distress*. IGI Global.

Komalasari, R. (in press). Literature Review: Health Aspects and Legal Protection for Children in Scotland and Indonesia. *Buana Gender: Jurnal Studi Gender dan Anak*.

Komalasari, R. (in press). Manfaat Positif Allium Sativum L. (Bawang Putih) Dalam Kaitannya Dengan Berbagai Penyakit. *Jurnal Farmasimed*.

Komalasari, R. (in press). Pelatihan Kesehatan dan Pengembangan Profesional Berkelanjutan untuk Pendidik Olah Raga. *Jurnal Ilmiah STOK Bina Guna Medan*.

Komalasari, R. (in press). Persepsi Hakim tentang Rehabilitasi Pengguna Narkoba:Tantangan dan Peluang. *Arena Hukum*.

Komalasari, R., & Mustafa, C. (2021). Meningkatkan Pelayanan Administrasi Publik di Indonesia. *PaKMas: Jurnal Pengabdian Kepada Masyarakat, 1*(1), 20–27. doi:10.54259/pakmas.v1i1.29

Komalasari, R., & Mustafa, C. (2021). Pendidikan Profesi dan Pengabdian Masyarakat di Indonesia. *PaKMas: Jurnal Pengabdian Kepada Masyarakat, 1*(1), 28–36. doi:10.54259/pakmas.v1i1.30

Komalasari, R., & Mustafa, C. (2022). Empowerment of Women with Narcotic Cases. *Buana Gender: Jurnal Studi Gender dan Anak, 7*(1). doi:10.22515/bg.v7i1.5378

Komalasari, R., Nurhayati, N., & Mustafa, C. (2022). Insider/Outsider Issues: Reflections on Qualitative Research. *Qualitative Report, 27*(3), 744–751. doi:10.46743/2160-3715/2022.5259

Komalasari, R., Nurhayati, N., & Mustafa, C. (2022). Enhancing the Online Learning Environment for Medical Education: Lessons From COVID-19. In Policies and procedures for the implementation of safe and healthy educational environments: Post-COVID-19 perspectives (pp. 138-154). IGI Global. doi:10.4018/978-1-7998-9297-7.ch009

Komalasari, R., Nurhayati, N., & Mustafa, C. (2022). Kebijakan Penanganan Penyintas HIV/AIDS Di Lembaga Pemasyarakatan. *Jurnal Kesehatan Kartika, 17*(1), 19–27.

Komalasari, R., Nurhayati, N., & Mustafa, C. (2022). Professional Education and Training in Indonesia. In *Public Affairs Education and Training in the 21st Century* (pp. 125–138). IGI Global. doi:10.4018/978-1-7998-8243-5.ch008

Komalasari, R., Wilson, S., & Haw, S. (2021). A systematic review of qualitative evidence on barriers to and facilitators of the implementation of opioid agonist treatment (OAT) programmes in prisons. *The International Journal on Drug Policy*, *87*, 102978. doi:10.1016/j.drugpo.2020.102978 PMID:33129135

Komalasari, R., Wilson, S., & Haw, S. (2021). A social ecological model (SEM) to exploring barriers of and facilitators to the implementation of opioid agonist treatment (OAT) programmes in prisons. *International Journal of Prisoner Health*, *17*(4), 477–496. Advance online publication. doi:10.1108/IJPH-04-2020-0020

Komalasari, R., Wilson, S., Nasir, S., & Haw, S. (2020). Multiple burdens of stigma for prisoners participating in Opioid Antagonist Treatment (OAT) programmes in Indonesian prisons: A qualitative study. *International Journal of Prisoner Health*. Advance online publication. doi:10.1108/IJPH-03-2020-0018

Mustafa, C. (2021). The Challenges to Improving Public Services and Judicial Operations: A unique balance between pursuing justice and public service in Indonesia. In Handbook of research on global challenges for improving public services and government operations (pp. 117-132). IGI Global. doi:10.4018/978-1-7998-4978-0.ch007

Mustafa, C. (2021). Key finding: result of a qualitative study of judicial perspectives on the sentencing of minor drug offenders in Indonesia: Structural inequality. *Qualitative Report*, *26*(5), 1678–1692. doi:10.46743/2160-3715/2021.4436

Mustafa, C. (2021). The view of judicial activism and public legitimacy. *Crime, Law, and Social Change*, *76*(1), 23–34. doi:10.100710611-021-09955-0

Mustafa, C. (2021). Qualitative method used in researching the judiciary: Quality assurance steps to enhance the validity and reliability of the findings. *Qualitative Report*, *26*(1), 176–186. doi:10.46743/2160-3715/2021.4319

Mustafa, C. (2021). The News Media Representation of Acts of Mass Violence in Indonesia. In *Mitigating Mass Violence and Managing Threats in Contemporary Society* (pp. 127–140). IGI Global. doi:10.4018/978-1-7998-4957-5.ch008

Mustafa, C., Malloch, M., & Hamilton Smith, N. (2020). Judicial perspectives on the sentencing of minor drug offenders in Indonesia: Discretionary practice and compassionate approaches. *Crime, Law, and Social Change*, *74*(3), 297–313. doi:10.100710611-020-09896-0

Suhariyanto, B., Mustafa, C., & Santoso, T. (2021). Liability incorporate between transnational corruption cases Indonesia and the United States of America. *Journal of Legal, Ethical and Regulatory Issues*, *24*(3).

Suhariyanto, B., & Mustafa, C. (2022). Analysis And Evaluation Of Legal Aid In The Indonesian Court. *Jurnal Hukum dan Peradilan, 11*(2), 176-194. doi:10.25216/jhp.11.2.2022.176-194

KEY TERMS AND DEFINITIONS

Ambient Assisted Living (AAL): Is the use of tools and strategies to make sure that elderly residents of the home remain secure and may age in situ. Smart gadgets, wireless networks, software, computers, and medical sensors are all included.

Intelligent Support Systems (ISS): Systems with intelligent support help people make decisions that call for the application of knowledge, instinct, experience, and competence.

Chapter 7

Brain–Inspired AI to a Symbiosis of Human Intelligence and Artificial Intelligence

Omprakash Dewangan
Kalinga University, India

ABSTRACT

Brain-based artificial intelligence has been a popular topic. Applications include military and defense, intelligent manufacturing, business intelligence and management, medical service and healthcare, and others. In order to strengthen their national interests and capacities in the global marketplace, many countries have started national brain-related projects. Numerous difficulties in brain-inspired computing and computation based on spiking-neural-networks, as well as various concepts, principles, and emerging technologies in brain science and brain-inspired artificial intelligence, are discussed in this chapter (SNNs). The advances and trends section covers topics such as brain-inspired computing, neuromorphic computing systems, and multi-scale brain simulation, as well as the brain association graph, brainnetome, connectome, brain imaging, brain-inspired chips and devices, brain-computer interface (BCI) and brain-machine interface (BMI), brain-inspired robotics and applications, quantum robots, and cyborgs (human-machine hybrids).

INTRODUCTION

The goal of neuromorphic engineering is to create a computing architecture that is

DOI: 10.4018/978-1-6684-6980-4.ch007

inspired by the brain as a substitute for the von Neumann processor. For unsupervised learning using flash memory synaptic array and spike-timing-dependent plasticity (STDP) synapse array, a hardware-based SNN architecture has been developed. The statistical theory's probability strategy often matches cognitive computing. It is a technique that understands and analyzes unstructured data by reasoning with goals, learning at scales, interacting naturally with humans (Kang et al., 2019).

A fundamental cognitive process called associative learning connects discrete and frequently different perceptions. Learning paradigms for equivalency that are guided by the auditory and multisensory systems were introduced. Humans can learn through guided associations in three different ways: auditory, visual, and multisensory. The best performance in cognitive learning is elicited by multi-sensory (audiovisual) stimuli. Because multisensory information processing can improve participant performance, the test phase is typically a more challenging cognitive activity than the acquisition phase (Eördegh et al., 2019).

The development of memcomputing and neuromorphic applications can benefit from the usage of phase-change memory devices because of their multi-level storage capability and proven large-scale manufacturing viability. Phase-change materials can reversibly transition from the crystalline to the amorphous phase using electrical pulses. Information is stored using the resistance shift brought on by the structural phase configuration change. Phase-change materials are used in both the writing and retrieval phases of this traditional approach, which is where its primary advantages reside. Although phase-change materials offer excellent phase-transition properties, the method's disadvantage is that their high defect density and extremely disordered nature render them sensitive to highly unfavorable electrical effects (such as noise and drift) (Liu & Zheng, 2017).

A completely new "brain war" combat style can be developed with the aid of military brain science. With the following objectives (Koelmans et al., 2015),

1) It addresses various brain activity patterns and affecting elements. Understanding the brain means being aware of the risk factors for brain damage;
2) Preserving the brain means focusing on preventing brain damage;
3) Monitoring the brain means keeping an eye on how the brain is working using gadgets and technology
4) Brain damage—encouraging the creation of brain-damaging weapons (such as those that explode, emit light, or use magnetic fields);
5) Brain interference—causing brain dysfunction or a loss of control;
6) Brain repair—carrying out the reconstruction of brain functions using cutting-edge technology;
7) Utilizing a variety of techniques (such as magnetism, sound, and electricity) to increase the brain function of individuals engaged in a certain work;

8)   Mimicking the brain through techniques like brain-inspired robot intelligence;

9)   Arming the brain through an emphasis on brain-machine interfaces (BMIs).

This paper's primary goal is to present emerging brain science and brain-inspired artificial intelligence technologies (such as brain-inspired chips, brain-inspired computing, neuromorphic computing systems, BCI and BMI, brain-inspired robotics, quantum robots, and cyborg); their advancements and trends; and some difficulties in brain-inspired computing and SNNs-based computation (Jin et al., 2018).

MULTI-SCALE BRAIN SIMULATION, NEUROMORPHIC COMPUTING SYSTEMS, AND BRAIN-INSPIRED COMPUTING

Computers Inspired by The Brain

The human brain can do complex computational tasks (such as recognition, cognition, and learning) with a very low frequency of neural spiking and a very small amount of power. This

is the outcome of extremely parallel processing and event-driven computation techniques. Only when and where it is necessary for the processing of information is energy utilized. Replicating the time-dependent plasticity of synapses and achieving high connectivity in neuron networks are two major issues in brain simulation. Resistive-switching memory (RRAM) devices can be used in nanodevices that combine high computational power and density scalability (Ielmini, 2018).

A neuromorphic system inspired by the human brain must have electronic synapses that are both long-term and short-term flexible. Short-term plasticity is linked to essential computational processes in biological systems, while long-term plasticity forms the basis of learning and memory responses (Sun et al., 2018).

The electronic synapse, the main component supporting brain-inspired neuromorphic computing, can convincingly mimic long- and short-term plasticity as well as voltage sensitivity in the bio-synapse.

High-dimensional (HD) vector computation, also known as hypervector computation, is a brain-inspired alternative to scalar computation. Well-defined hypervector arithmetic operations, scalability, quick learning, generality, resilience, and widespread parallel operations are some of the key characteristics of HD computing. It was demonstrated how to speed up HD computing with the best operations and memory accesses on a parallel, ultra-low power architecture.

A large associative memory with reliable retrieval and inspiration from the brain has been introduced. Columnar Organized Memory (COM) is made up of spiking winner-take-all (WTA) networks, which are the neocortex's building blocks. Spiking neurons connected by inhibitory synapses make up a spiking WTA. A COM's message storage also contains pattern association and pattern storage. Simulation was used to analyze and assess a COM's capabilities. It was shown that a COM's capacity and a spiking WTA's capacity are linearly connected (Montagna et al., 2018).

For an unmanned autonomous system and an earth observation system, target classification and recognition (TCR) of high resolution remote sensing images is crucial. Deep learning and cognitive computing were used to develop a brain-inspired computing model for TCR. Based on hierarchical latent Dirichlet allocation and deep spiking convolutional neural networks, an ensemble learning algorithm was created.

The Wisdom Web of Things (W2T) offers a social-cyber-physical setting for interactions and activities among people. Big data is produced by W2T during the connectivity of computers, people, and objects. In order to realize a harmonic symbiosis, it mixes big data about human activities and big data about the brain in a social-cyber-physical arena. The main method for carrying out such an endeavor is provided by brain informatics, which offers informatics-enabled brain research and applications in the social-cyber-physical domain, thereby producing a brain big data cycle (Shamsi et al., 2018).

Systems for Neuromorphic Computing

Computers, gadgets, and models inspired by the interconnectedness, energy efficiency, and performance of the brain are referred to as neuromorphic devices or models. The distribution of memories follows a neuromorphic pattern. A brain system's adaptive and learning mechanisms are mediated by many types of "plasticity." Homeostatic plasticity, structural plasticity, long-term potentiation, short-term plasticity mechanism, and long-term depression mechanism are the most prevalent forms.

Memory and learning depend on the activation of synapses between the pre-neuron and post-neuron. In hippocampus neurons, STDP is a crucial learning rule that modifies synaptic weight (or connection strength). A memristor has been a promising contender for artificial synaptic components in neuromorphic computing that is inspired by the brain. Different initial resistance states were used to fulfill various state dependent STDP functions. For brain-inspired computing, a multilayer memristor was created as an artificial synapse component. Devices with different starting resistance states have multiple STDP types and can be used to spike neural networks (Amunts et al., 2016).

A multi-core computer called the SpiNNaker system was created to carry out real-time simulation of the activities of up to a billion neurons. The von Neumann architecture is not used in the IBM "TrueNorth" spiking neural network ASIC. The TrueNorth chip's synapses lack any plasticity mechanisms, making them incapable of implementing online learning or creating memories. Co-localizing computation and memory while reducing the von Neumann bottleneck is only partially successful. In order to replicate large-scale brain models' operations in real time, the NeuroGrid system was created. The physics of field-effect transistors driven in the subthreshold regime is used to directly simulate crucial synaptic and neuronal functions (such as integration, thresholding, exponentiation, and temporal dynamics). The technique used in the BrainScales project is an additional technique for modeling large-scale brain models. A wafer-scale neuronal simulation platform is what BrainScales aims to provide.

Figure 1. The Human Brain Project seeks to understand the brain's multilevel organization

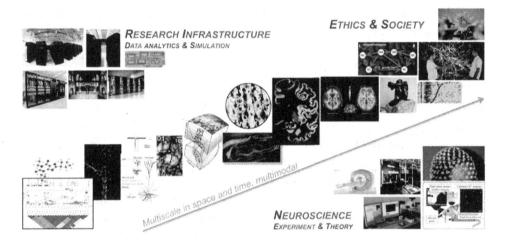

Research and Multi-scale Brain Simulation

The Human Brain Project (HBP), a ten-year European Flagship for reconstructing the multiscale organization of the brain, has been established. The HBP's IT design is centered on cloud-based platforms for collaboration that include workflow management tools, databases, supercomputers, and petabyte storage. The HBP uses a variety of methods, equipment, techniques, etc. to study the brain at multiple spatial dimensions (from molecules to vast networks) and temporal scales (from milliseconds to years) (shown in Figure 1). The HBP initially consists of the platforms listed below, which are coupled via the "Collaboratory" (COLLAB) interface: Medical Informatics, Neuroinformatics, Brain Simulation, Neuromorphic Computing, High-Performance Analytics and Supercomputing, and Neurorobotics (Hasan et al., 2018).

THE BRAINNETOME AND BRAIN ASSOCIATION GRAPH

Brain Association Diagram

The topological properties of complex brain networks have been quantified using theoretical graph approaches. A set of graph metrics can be used to describe hubs that are significant in the brain network (e.g., degree, participation coefficient, and betweenness centrality). Network nodes can be classified as several hub types based on the graph metrics (e.g., connector and provincial hubs). The connectivity of regional hubs in the brain is influenced by stress, however the majority of connections are integrative in character since they traverse different modules. There needs to be agreement on appropriate parcellation techniques that are used to define nodes with biological meanings, thresholding or weighing edges for computing graphs, or the validity of graph metrics before applying graph theory to neuroimaging data. There are still significant research gaps in areas including the comprehensive assessment of the effects of stressor types and timing on teenage brain development, the critical consideration of sex differences, and prospective studies of the effects of stress on children and adolescents. A strategy that allows for comparisons across multimodal data in order to gain new insights has been offered as a valuable measure for understanding how stress affects the brains of adolescents (Indiveri & Liu, 2015).

Brainnetome and the Connectome

An effective paradigm for investigating the functional and structural networks of the brain at various spatiotemporal scales is the brainnetome. The connectome, which is the collection of neuronal connections in the brain, aids in understanding how the brain works normally and how disorders affect it. It also aids in determining a person's intelligence, how effectively their brain recovers from injuries, and how susceptible their brain is to neurodegeneration and severe stress. The connectome is viewed in connectomics as a mathematical graph with nodes that correspond to the gray matter of the brain and linkages that correspond to the white matter tracts. The functional or structural connectedness of the link is represented by its weight. Measures from graph theory can serve as biomarkers for neurological and mental conditions (Lu et al., 2018).

Pathological changes in particular sub-networks or individual connections frequently lead to diseases. Noninvasive measurements of the macroscale functional and structural connectome are possible. Functional brain connection can be expressed as correlation coefficients between electrical activity traces from different parts of the brain. Diffusion tensor imaging can assess structural connectivity (DTI). For a compressive image of the macroscopic connectome, connectivity measures from several modalities must be combined (Amunts et al., 2016).

It has become possible to undertake a graph-theoretic analysis of the human connectome by mapping brain imaging data to networks, where nodes denote anatomical parts of the brain and edges show the existence of fiber tracts between them. The connectome has been shown to have a complex structure and a hyperbolic geometry on the scale between edges and mesoscopic anatomical communities inside cerebral hemispheres. The higher-order connection between distinct brain regions is described by this structure, which contains simplicial complexes of different sizes and cycles (Yin et al., 2019).

The brain's neural wiring patterns are the subject of the connectome. In systems neuroscience, the impact of its components on the dynamics is a key topic. The crucial significance of particular structural connections between neuronal populations for the overall stability of cortex was examined, and the connection between experimentally measured activity and anatomical structure was clarified. A paradigm was put forth to analyze the rapidly expanding corpus of connection data based on fundamental restrictions on brain activity and combine physiological and anatomical information to produce a coherent representation of cortical networks (Ho et al., 2018).

BRAIN IMAGING

After comparing the individual's data with a population dataset made up of individuals ranging in age, brain imaging and pertinent information from other sources can be helpful in determining "brain age," or an individual's apparent age. It is possible to determine whether a brain has aged by calculating the difference between the brain age and the actual age (the "delta").

Although imaging techniques like electroencephalography (EEG) and X-ray computed tomography have been used to investigate neurological systems and clinical services, their spatial resolution is constrained and has little bearing on the cellular activity of the neuron network. Microelectrode arrays can be implanted into the deep brain or utilized on the cortex surface to monitor neuronal activity by recording intracellular and extracellular signals. To investigate the optical performance of an implantable thin-film image sensor for analyzing deep brain neuronal fluorescence activity, a mathematical model was developed. The accuracy of this condensed model, which is based on the photon transport theory, is comparable to that of the traditional Monte Carlo ray tracing technique. Functional neuroimaging enables the measurement of the brain's electrical, hemodynamic, and metabolic activity with regard to the functional networks in the brain. Patients with awareness issues can quantify their compromised brain networks with the aid of these exercises (DOC).

Table 1. A few brain imaging techniques and results in DOC

Methods	Usages	Findings in DOC
Electroencephalography (EEG)	Records electrical activities and explores neural oscillations/interactions or potential fluctuations time.	1. Several indexes of functional brain networks in delta and alpha bands indicate correlations with the consciousness level. 2. Enhanced delta power and reduced theta and alpha power in the DOC. 3. Mismatch negativity, P3, etc. provide the information of the consciousness level.
Positron Emission Tomography (PET)	Detects local metabolic processes or the changes of blood flow in the brain in a task or resting state.	1. Frontoparietal networks and their connections to thalamus nuclei are significant for the occurrence of consciousness. 2. Global brain metabolism cannot be a sensitive marker for tracing the consciousness level.
Functional Magnetic Resonance Imaging (fMRI)	Detects brain activity through measuring blood-oxygen-level-dependent changes and explores functional connections between brain areas.	1. Functional connections in the default mode network (DMN) and between the DMN and executive control network can be the key for the DOC prognosis/diagnosis. 2. A number of resting state networks are disrupted in the DOC.
Diffusion Magnetic Resonance Imaging (dMRI)	Measures the diffusion of water along axon, estimates major fiber tracts between brain areas.	1. Fibers that connect cortical regions within the DMN and between DMN regions and thalamus are correlated to consciousness levels. 2. DOCs with various etiologies reveal different distributions of impaired white matters.
Functional Near-infrared Spectroscopy (fNIRS)	Detects brain activity according to the attenuation changes of near infrared through one's cortex, explores functional connections.	fNIRS has a unique value for quantifying the brain network activity and therapeutic effects in the DOC.

Diffusion MRI is a non-invasive technology that shows the micro-geometry of nervous tissues and explores the connection of white-matter fibers in relation to the anatomical networks in the brain. Some techniques for brain imaging and results in DOC are listed in Table 1.

DEVICES AND CHIPS INSPIRED BY THE BRAIN

Hardware acceleration for brain-inspired computing is referred to as neuromorphic computing. It mimics the neuro-biological architecture of the nervous system using a VLSI (very-large-scale integration) technology and electronic analog circuits. A crucial topic is how to increase the power efficiency and decrease the power consumption of neuromorphic computing systems (NCS). Utilizing hardware designed specifically for neuromorphic computing, such as developing nonvolatile memory and neuromorphic processors, is one method. Additionally, optimizing hardware-aware algorithms reduces energy consumption and enhances the functionality of new gadgets. The future of the NCS architecture is massive parallelism with "spikes," or the brief pulses that transfer information across neurons. Spike-based NCS and digitalized NCS will be developed quickly (Smith et al., 2019).

Nanoscale memristors have been proposed for use as synapses in a computer system that is inspired by the human brain. It has been proposed a synapse structure that can work in both an inhibitory and an excitatory manner. This structure exhibits learning behavior that is exponential-like. By discretizing the neuron spike in time, users may regulate learning behaviors and eliminate the impacts of switching rate mismatch in memristors. Synapses can be used with STDP-based on-chip learning to support spiking neural networks.

The rapid progress of brain-inspired computing and the inefficiencies in CMOS implementation of neuromorphic systems have led to the creation of effective hardware replicating the functional parts of the brain (i.e., neurons and synapses). However, a lot of progress has been made in the electrical field, with potential connecting losses, switching speed, and packing density constraints in large integrated systems. As a result, neuromorphic engineering in the field of photonics has drawn a lot of attention. Phase change materials have energy restrictions, but an Integrate-and-Fire Spiking Neuron with solely photonic operation has been proposed to alleviate these restrictions (PCM) (Schuecker et al., 2017).

CYBORG, BRAIN-INSPIRED ROBOTICS, AND BRAIN-COMPUTER INTERFACE

Brain-computer interfaces (BCIs) reflect the thoughts and intentions of the user by converting electrical signals from brain activity into understandable information without the use of neuromuscular control. Depending on whether a surgery is performed, BCI technology can be classified as either invasive or non-invasive. The EEG-based BCI speller has been employed in non-invasive BCIs for paralyzed patients due to its low cost, high time-resolution, external electrode safety, and wide range of applications (Sayyaparaju et al., 2018) (Bing et al., 2018).

A new technology called brain-machine interface (BMI) combines advanced technologies (such as signal processing, wireless communication, robot control, and neural electrodes) to progress the creation of artificial limbs and novel input devices. The ability of neural electrodes to record a variety of quick impulses released by neurons makes them a crucial part of the BMI.

To produce accurate, stable, and consistent signals, electrodes are created utilizing a variety of templates and materials. The electrode size can be decreased using micromachining techniques and micro electro mechanical systems (MEMS). Many selective and low-noise signals can be recorded using a variety of designs and materials. Three types of electrodes have been used to study neuronal signals: non-penetrating electrodes, which record signals from on or below the scalp, penetrating electrodes, which measure signals in vivo, particularly in the brain, and microelectrode array (MEA) electrodes, which record neuronal signals in vitro (Song et al., 2018)(Song et al., 2016)-24].

The computation of spiking-neural-networks (SNNs) considerably benefits from parallel processing. Each presynaptic neuron does not have to provide a weight value to a spiking neuron at each calculation step. In an SNN, just a small number of neurons are active at any given moment, eliminating the traditional message-passing bottleneck. In SNN parallel operation as opposed to classic ANNs, communication time and computation cost are better balanced. SNNs have shown considerable promise in achieving sophisticated robotic intelligence in terms of processing power, speed, and energy efficiency by emulating the brain function. Table 2 provides a list of some of the available platforms. The absence of a widely used training method, like backpropagation in conventional ANNs, is a major obstacle for control tasks based on SNNs (Bing et al., 2018).

Robots that can interact with a dynamic environment and have brain-inspired cognitive capacities, such as memory and learning, are the focus of cognitive developmental robotics (CDR). Through the use of an SNNs-based controller, CDR can react to a changing environment. It is essential that emotional cognition creates robots with anthropomorphic and diverse emotions have organic communication

Table 2. Robot control platforms using SNN

Platform Names	Methods
Musculoskeletal Robots	Integrating Myorobotics with SpiNNaker the proof of principle of a system.
Neurorobotics Platform	Design, import, and simulate various robot bodies and diverse brain models in a rich environment.
Retina Simulation	The platform is integrated in the Neurorobotics Platform (NRP).
AnimatLab	Provide functions (e.g., robot modeling), two neural models, and plugins used for importing other models.
iSpike	Interface between the iCub humanoid robot and SNN simulators
Neural Self-driving Vehicle Simulation Framework	A visual encoder from camera images to spikes inspired by the silicon retina, and a steering-wheel decoder.

with humans and environment in order to produce neuro-robots. Intelligent robots that are inspired by the brain may result from the fusion of neuroscience and robotics (Chakraborty et al., 2018)(Kim et al., 2019)-27].

Cyborg microrobots, which combine artificial and organic components, have provided a promising path for the development of microrobots in the future, particularly for their use in biomedicine. A cybernetic organism (cyborg) is an organism with expanded capabilities or restored functions as a result of the integration of artificial parts and technology (Bing et al., 2018).

Applications for cyborg microrobots include the administration of tailored drugs, cancer treatment, and water filtration. Microrobots utilized for targeted medicine delivery can regulate the drug release's timing and location to improve efficacy and lessen negative effects (Li et al., 2019).

Using an architecture for quantum robotics based on three main components—sensory units, a quantum controller/actuator, and multi quantum computing units—the efficiency of a quantum robot over a conventional robot was addressed. Quantum robots are artificially intelligent measurement systems that can measure target quantum systems and act on targets based on measured results. As a result, they can be used to manage quantum physical systems, which results in adaptive dynamics and rapid optimization of the target quantum systems. There is now a link between quantum artificial life (ALife) research, quantum robotics, and nanotechnology (Wei et al., 2019).

The development of quantum cyber-physical-cognitive (CPC) systems within the framework of quantum nanotechnology, including the potential for interaction and nanoscale management of quantum systems, is particularly pertinent to this. More recent research included machine learning and quantum robots (Gonçalves, 2018).

The ability to create cyborgs (human-machine hybrids) with higher capabilities is made possible by the development of neural implants for improving people's memories. Individuals' ethical evaluations of memory implants reveal disparities in their intents to use them, but they do not mitigate the impact of positive and negative emotions, effort and performance expectations, or social pressure (Reinares-Lara et al., 2018).

CONCLUSION

Because it is based on computing units with the co-location of memory and processing, brain-inspired computing considerably improves the efficiency of information processing and computation and saves energy. This is crucial for building a powerful AI, particularly for Big Data analytics.

The power efficiency and power consumption of neuromorphic computing systems are both improved by neuromorphic processors. Additionally, enhancing the hardware-aware algorithm increases device performance and reduces energy consumption.

Based on graph theories, brain association graphs quantify the topological characteristics and properties of complex brain networks. The brainnetome has been a crucial tool for understanding the brain in health and disease. Brain association networks, the brainnetome, and neuroimage processing are crucial tools for understanding how the brain's structure and function interact.

The development of artificial limbs and novel input devices is made possible by brain-computer interfaces, which convert electrical impulses from brain activity into understandable information. Spiking neural networks hold considerable promise for developing highly developed robotic intelligence. Target quantum systems can be measured and managed by quantum robots. The creation of memory-improving brain implants aids in the creation of powerful cyborgs.

REFERENCES

Amunts, K., Ebell, C., Muller, J., Telefont, M., Knoll, A., & Lippert, T. (2016). The human brain project: Creating a European research infrastructure to decode the human brain. *Neuron*, *92*(3), 574–581. doi:10.1016/j.neuron.2016.10.046 PMID:27809997

Bing, Z., Meschede, C., Röhrbein, F., Huang, K., & Knoll, A. C. (2018). A survey of robotics control based on learning-inspired spiking neural networks. *Frontiers in Neurorobotics*, *12*, 35. doi:10.3389/fnbot.2018.00035 PMID:30034334

Chakraborty, I., Saha, G., Sengupta, A., & Roy, K. (2018). Toward fast neural computing using all-photonic phase change spiking neurons. *Scientific Reports*, *8*(1), 12980. doi:10.103841598-018-31365-x PMID:30154507

Eördegh, G., Őze, A., Bodosi, B., Puszta, A., Pertich, Á., Rosu, A., Godó, G., & Nagy, A. (2019). Multisensory guided associative learning in healthy humans. *PLoS One*, *14*(3), 0213094. doi:10.1371/journal.pone.0213094 PMID:30861023

Gonçalves, C. P. (2018). *Quantum Robotics, Neural Networks and the Quantum Force Interpretation*. Neural Networks and the Quantum Force Interpretation. doi:10.2139srn.3244327

Hasan, M. S., Schuman, C. D., Najem, J. S., Weiss, R., Skuda, N. D., Belianinov, A., Collier, C. P., Sarles, S. A., & Rose, G. S. (2018). Biomimetic, Soft-Material Synapse for Neuromorphic Computing: from Device to Network. *IEEE 13th Dallas Circuits and Systems Conference (DCAS)*, 1-6.

Ho, T. C., Dennis, E. L., Thompson, P. M., & Gotlib, I. H. (2018). Network-based approaches to examining stress in the adolescent brain. *Neurobiology of Stress*, *8*, 147–157. doi:10.1016/j.ynstr.2018.05.002 PMID:29888310

Ielmini, D. (2018). Brain-inspired computing with resistive switching memory (RRAM): Devices, synapses and neural networks. *Microelectronic Engineering*, *190*, 44–53. doi:10.1016/j.mee.2018.01.009

Indiveri, G., & Liu, S. C. (2015). Memory and information processing in neuromorphic systems. *Proceedings of the IEEE*, *103*(8), 1379–1397. doi:10.1109/JPROC.2015.2444094

Jin, H., Hou, L. J., & Wang, Z. G. (2018). Military Brain Science–How to influence future wars. *Chinese Journal of Traumatology*, *21*(5), 277–280. doi:10.1016/j.cjtee.2018.01.006 PMID:30279039

Kang, W. M., Kim, C. H., Lee, S., Woo, S. Y., Bae, J. H., Park, B. G., & Lee, J. H. (2019). A Spiking Neural Network with a Global Self-Controller for Unsupervised Learning Based on Spike-Timing-Dependent Plasticity Using Flash Memory Synaptic Devices. *International Joint Conference on Neural Networks (IJCNN)*, 1-7. 10.1109/IJCNN.2019.8851744

Kim, D., Byun, W., Ku, Y., & Kim, J. H. (2019). High-Speed Visual Target Identification for Low-Cost Wearable Brain-Computer Interfaces. *IEEE Access: Practical Innovations, Open Solutions, 7,* 55169–55179. doi:10.1109/ACCESS.2019.2912997

Kim, G. H., Kim, K., Lee, E., An, T., Choi, W., Lim, G., & Shin, J. H. (2018). Recent progress on microelectrodes in neural interfaces. *Materials (Basel), 11*(10), 1995. doi:10.3390/ma11101995 PMID:30332782

Koelmans, W. W., Sebastian, A., Jonnalagadda, V. P., Krebs, D., Dellmann, L., & Eleftheriou, E. (2015). Projected phase-change memory devices. *Nature Communications, 6*(1), 8181. doi:10.1038/ncomms9181 PMID:26333363

Kopetzky, S., & Butz-Ostendorf, M. (2018). From matrices to knowledge: Using semantic networks to annotate the connectome. *Frontiers in Neuroanatomy, 12,* 111. doi:10.3389/fnana.2018.00111 PMID:30581382

Li, J., Li, Z., Chen, F., Bicchi, A., Sun, Y., & Fukuda, T. (2019). Combined Sensing, Cognition, Learning and Control to Developing Future Neuro-Robotics Systems: A Survey. *IEEE Transactions on Cognitive and Developmental Systems.*

Liu, Y., & Zheng, F. B. (2017). Object-oriented and multi-scale target classification and recognition based on hierarchical ensemble learning. *Computers & Electrical Engineering, 62,* 538–554. doi:10.1016/j.compeleceng.2016.12.026

Lu, K., Li, Y., He, W. F., Chen, J., Zhou, Y. X., Duan, N., Jin, M. M., Gu, W., Xue, K. H., Sun, H. J., & Miao, X. S. (2018). Diverse spike-timing- dependent plasticity based on multilevel HfO x memristor for neuromorphic computing. *Applied Physics. A, Materials Science & Processing, 124*(6), 438. doi:10.100700339-018-1847-3

Montagna, F., Rahimi, A., Benatti, S., Rossi, D., & Benini, L. (2018). Accelerating brain-inspired high-dimensional computing on a parallel ultra-low power platform. In *Proceedings of the 55th Annual Design Automation Conference 111.* ACM. 10.1145/3195970.3196096

Nazempour, R., Liu, C., Chen, Y., Ma, C., & Sheng, X. (2019). Performance evaluation of an implantable sensor for deep brain imaging: An analytical investigation. *Optical Materials Express, 9*(9), 3729–3737. doi:10.1364/OME.9.003729

Reinares-Lara, E., Olarte-Pascual, C., & Pelegrín-Borondo, J. (2018). Do you want to be a cyborg? The moderating effect of ethics on neural implant acceptance. *Computers in Human Behavior, 85,* 43–53. doi:10.1016/j.chb.2018.03.032

Sayyaparaju, S., Amer, S., & Rose, G. S. (2018). A bi-memristor synapse with spike-timing-dependent plasticity for on-chip learning in memristive neuromorphic systems. *19th International Symposium on Quality Electronic Design (ISQED)*, 69-74. 10.1109/ISQED.2018.8357267

Schuecker, J., Schmidt, M., van Albada, S. J., Diesmann, M., & Helias, M. (2017). Fundamental activity constraints lead to specific interpretations of the connectome. *PLoS Computational Biology*, *13*(2), e1005179. doi:10.1371/journal.pcbi.1005179 PMID:28146554

Shamsi, J., Shokouhi, S. B., & Mohammadi, K. (2018). On the capacity of Columnar Organized Memory (COM). *IEEE 61st International Midwest Symposium on Circuits and Systems (MWSCAS)*, 65-68.

Smith, S. M., Vidaurre, D., Alfaro-Almagro, F., Nichols, T. E., & Miller, K. L. (2019). Estimation of brain age delta from brain imaging. *NeuroImage*, *200*, 528–539. doi:10.1016/j.neuroimage.2019.06.017 PMID:31201988

Song, C., Liu, B., Liu, C., Li, H., & Chen, Y. (2016). Design techniques of eNVM-enabled neuromorphic computing systems. *2016 IEEE 34th International Conference on Computer Design (ICCD)*, 674-677. 10.1109/ICCD.2016.7753356

Song, M., Zhang, Y., Cui, Y., Yang, Y., & Jiang, T. (2018). Brain network studies in chronic disorders of consciousness: Advances and perspectives. *Neuroscience Bulletin*, *34*(4), 592–604. doi:10.100712264-018-0243-5 PMID:29916113

Sun, Y., Xu, H., Liu, S., Song, B., Liu, H., Liu, Q., & Li, Q. (2018). Short-term and long-term plasticity mimicked in low-voltage Ag/GeSe/TiN electronic synapse. *IEEE Electron Device Letters*, *39*(4), 492–495. doi:10.1109/LED.2018.2809784

Tadić, B., Andjelković, M., & Melnik, R. (2019, August 19). functional Geometry of Human connectomes. *Scientific Reports*, *9*(1), 1–2. doi:10.103841598-019-48568-5 PMID:31427676

Wei, F., Yin, C., Zheng, J., Zhan, Z., & Yao, L. (2019). Rise of cyborg microrobot: Different story for different configuration. *IET Nanobiotechnology / IET*, *13*(7), 651–664. doi:10.1049/iet-nbt.2018.5374 PMID:31573533

Yin, D., Chen, X., Zeljic, K., Zhan, Y., Shen, X., Yan, G., & Wang, Z. (2019). A graph representation of functional diversity of brain regions. *Brain and Behavior*, *9*(9). Advance online publication. doi:10.1002/brb3.1358 PMID:31350830

Zhong, N., Yau, S. S., Ma, J., Shimojo, S., Just, M., Hu, B., Wang, G., Oiwa, K., & Anzai, Y. (2015). Brain informatics-based big data and the wisdom web of things. *IEEE Intelligent Systems*, *30*(5), 2–7. doi:10.1109/MIS.2015.83

Chapter 8
Knowledge Representation– Based Hemispheric Specialization of the Brain

Bikram Pratim Bhuyan
University of Petroleum and Energy Studies, India

ABSTRACT

Knowledge is an essential ingredient for the development of the majority of human cognitive skills. The subject of how to define knowledge is a challenging one. Knowledge is an organised collection of information that may be acquired by learning, perception, or the application of reasoning. This chapter focuses on human brains and computer knowledge models. Concepts and categories are offered as a paradigm for storing information, followed by semantic networks and a description of how individuals store and interpret information. The authors also explore artificial methods to store and retrieve information and make quick judgments, as well as biological features. After studying how information is stored and accessed in artificial and human systems, they analyse hemisphere specialisation. This chapter reviews trials that have advanced research in this area and examines if they interpret information differently.

INTRODUCTION

Knowledge is a familiarity, understanding, or comprehension of someone or something, such as the facts, information, descriptions, or skills of that person or thing (Zagzebski, 2017). Knowledge may be acquired by perception, discovery, or study. As it serves as the foundation or medium for most of our cognitive functions,

DOI: 10.4018/978-1-6684-6980-4.ch008

we refer to it as knowledge. How do different people navigate their environments? How do people come up with answers to problems, how do they get an awareness of their surroundings, and what criteria do they use to draw conclusions and make decisions? The expansion of one's horizons, the acquisition of new knowledge, and the development of one's mental picture of the world are both components of the answer to all of these issues (Leonard, 1995).

Because they are in close contact with the world around them, people with knowledge are considered to be in a very desirable mental state. Therefore, there is a link between the two. One side of a connection consists of a knower and some component of reality with which they are connected or otherwise associated. Even though directness is a relative concept, it is common practice to regard knowledge of things as being more direct than knowledge about things (Bhuyan et al., 2021). Knowledge of the former is typically referred to as "knowledge by acquaintance," given that the subject has direct personal experience with the component of reality that is known. Knowledge of the latter is referred to as "propositional knowledge," given that the subject's knowledge is a genuine proposition about the universe. Knowing Roger personally falls under the category of "knowledge by acquaintance," while comprehending that Roger is a philosopher falls under the category of "knowledge by the proposition." The concept of familiarity involves factual information about the world and myself, and the inner workings of my body. It is a commonly held belief that the most directly knowable element of reality is the one that pertains to the knower's mental state (Ji et al., 2021).

The neural networks in our minds are compared to those in our computer models in this chapter, and we discuss the similarities and contrasts between the two sets of networks (Chakraborty et al., 2019). An attempt is made to explain how people organize and keep track of information. The first step in doing so is to provide ideas and categories as a model for storing and sorting data, which is then followed by the presentation of semantic networks. In addition to the biological aspect, we will also go over the representation of knowledge in artificial systems, which may be helpful tools for storing and retrieving information and making snap decisions.

After analyzing the similarities and differences between how the human brain and artificial systems store and retrieve information, the next topic of discussion will be the specialized functions of the human brain's hemispheres (Bartolomeo et al., 2019). This notion is significant not only to the chapter on knowledge representation but also to a wide variety of other chapters within this book due to the fact that the two hemispheres of the brain store distinct types of information. Where in the brain are different processes like memory, emotion, and motivation carried out, for example? In this part of the discussion, we will examine the fundamental differences that exist between the two hemispheres. We discuss the likelihood that they process information differently, as well as related topics, and present an overview of experiments that have advanced the field.

KNOWLEDGE

The majority of epistemological attention has been directed on the subject side of the relationship between a conscious subject and some component of reality, with the understanding that a valid proposition mediates knowledge. Someone who is in the state of knowledge has a relationship to a true statement while they are in this condition. The phrase "state of belief" refers to the connection between the person who knows something and the known proposition (Hogan et al., 2021). This relationship is often characterized by the fact that the person accepts the proposition as true. Because epistemology operates on the presumption that the knowing state is a subspecies of the believing state, one of the most common ways to describe knowledge is as the combination of sincere belief and something else. However, this viewpoint needs to be revised due to the fact that the development of epistemic ideas demonstrates that belief and knowledge were, at times, considered incompatible epistemic states. Consequently, this viewpoint needs to be more conclusive. This was done for one of two reasons: either it was thought that knowledge and belief are aimed at separate things, or it was viewed as fitting to restrict belief to epistemic states judged "lesser" than knowledge (Phillips et al., 2021). Both of these justifications led to the same action being taken. The first concern has been alleviated to the satisfaction of almost all contemporary epistemologists, and it has been shown that the same proposition can be either known or believed. This general notion that propositions are the objects of belief as well as of knowledge and that the same proposition can be either known or believed has led to the satisfaction of almost all contemporary epistemologists. It is possible that by doing so, a person would learn the truth about something that he just had a hunch about the day before, such as whether or not his team will win the game. In the event that this is the case, the contention that knowledge is a subset of belief cannot be challenged owing to the dissimilarities between the two concepts' respective topics (Gou et al., 2021).

The alleviation of the second problem is made possible by Augustine's definition of belief as "thinking with permission." According to the Augustinian definition of belief (Klein, 2018), knowing may be seen as a subset of belief. This is due to the fact that it is self-evident that to know propositionally is to accept a proposition to be accurate, and to agree to a bid merely is to believe it to be true.

Therefore, it makes sense to say that knowledge is a type of belief (Bird, 2019); however, this does not necessarily help in the search for a definition of knowledge because the concept of belief needs defining and, according to some philosophers, has outlived its usefulness. This does not mean, however, that saying knowledge is a type of belief is useless in the search for a definition of knowledge. Nevertheless, it is often acknowledged that the notion of belief, as opposed to the idea of knowledge, is more open to interpretation and presents fewer points of contention. The widely held practice of defining knowledge as some belief must be correct for it to be illuminating and true.

Any attempt to establish an accurate definition of knowledge is going to run into difficulties as a result of the fact that the concept of knowledge has been interpreted in a wide variety of different ways over the course of the history of philosophy at various different eras. Is there a point of contention that is shared by more than one of these papers, or do they each just focus on a different subject? When we take into consideration how many schools of thought have defined knowledge and how severe their requirements are, this topic takes on a far more exciting quality. In some schools of thought, having knowledge necessitates adhering to stringent and narrow standards, whereas in others, having knowledge necessitates adhering to expansive and lax standards. Although contemporary philosophy is developing on a path that is anti-rigorist, philosophical tradition is more on the side of the rigorist position (Verburgt, 2020).

It is a widely held belief in today's society that even the simplest interactions of vision and memory may result in the acquisition of knowledge and that even very young newborns and perhaps animals are capable of acquiring information in this way. It is essential to emphasize how very different this is from the rigorist tales that have gone before it, starting with Plato's Phaedo and Republic (Betegh, 2020). Because of the differences between Plato's rigorous perspective of knowledge and the more lenient one that is prevalent today, we could be prompted to question whether or not it is even possible to provide a definitive definition of what it is to know something. The various kinds of knowledge representation techniques are shown in Figure 1.

REPRESENTING KNOWLEDGE OF THE BRAIN

Concepts are fundamental for many different mental functions. Ideas are mental representations that assist with a variety of cognitive processes, including learning, problem-solving, and communication. One of the many functions that concepts provide is to facilitate the organization of a large amount of knowledge that has been gathered via study (Bhuyan et al., 2018). The remainder of this chapter will be devoted to discussing the function that ideas serve in society.

Imagine that the moment you open your eyes each morning, you are instantly drawn to learn more about everything that you have never encountered before.

Figure 1. Different types of knowledge representation techniques

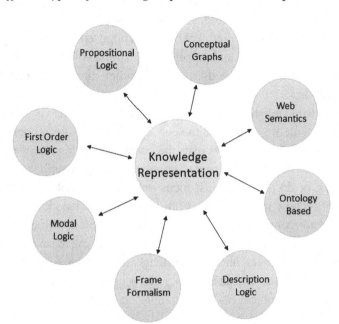

Imagine how you would feel if you came home one day to find a strange bike parked in front of your house. In spite of the fact that you have seen millions of autos throughout your life, you are unable to explain why this particular automobile is located in this location. Given that we can derive a cause, we need to investigate how we can generalize from the knowledge we already possess and why we do not need to begin from the very beginning if we come across a somewhat different case. The easiest way to explain it is by saying that we categorize information. When we speak about ordering anything, we are referring to the process of putting different things into distinct categories.

We also refer to categories as "Knowledge Pointers." One way to see a category is as a container that holds items that are similar to one another and contains labels that describe the characteristics that the items share, in addition to providing an overall summary of the category's contents (Bhuyan et al., 2022). Memory for groups of things contains both specific examples of objects that fall into a category as well as general qualities that those things share and that define the category. Memory for groups of items is referred to as group memory. Suppose we continue to use motorbike bikes as an illustration in Figure 2. In that case, this suggests that our brains not only store the details of how your vehicle, your neighbor's vehicle, and your friends' vehicle look but also provide us with the general information that most bikes have two wheels, need fuel, and so on. Because it enables us to instantly acquire a fundamental perspective of a scene by recognizing new elements as members of a category, categorization helps us save time and reduces the amount of work we have to put in. Our capacity to glean useful information from our surroundings and arrive at correct inferences is bolstered as a result of this skill. Imagine that you are standing by the side of a road waiting for anything to happen. This should help you grasp this point more clearly. A bike is moving closer and closer to driving on the left side of the road. The only thing you need to know about this vehicle is what is conveyed by the category it belongs in, which is that it will run you over if you don't get out of its path. You are not concerned with the color of the automobile, the number of indicators, or anything else of the kind. You would be hit because, rather than taking a step back to examine the situation, you would be consumed with attempting to find out what sort of bike it was. This would prevent you from stepping back and assessing the situation. As a consequence of this, the capacity to categorize objects has been shown to be essential to human survival over the course of evolutionary history. This skill makes it possible for us to travel between diverse settings swiftly and easily.

Figure 2. Different types of a motorcycle with varying properties like shape and color

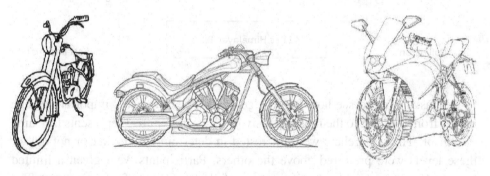

Why do we believe that we have such a firm grasp of these things? A single term can be used to describe all of these different types of cars. What is the total number of wheels for each one? False; in some families, there are just three children. Is there no other kind of fuel that can be used in automobiles than gasoline? This is different from the situation with every car. It would seem that we will need more than reaching a consensus on a definition. The oversimplification that was required in order to arrive at a definition that could be used effectively is to blame. Perhaps for geometric forms, but not at all for anything that exists in the natural world. It may be challenging to define them since they are distinct from one another and have no similarities. However, people who belong to the same broad category have some qualities; how should we make sense of this fact? It is said that the famous philosopher and linguist Ludwig Wittgenstein asked himself this question and said that he knew the solution to it. He was the one who first put up the idea that we all have a common genetic background. That is to imply that individuals who belong to the same group have a lot of characteristics in common. Automobiles may differ in size, color, shape, and a variety of other qualities, but they all have some traits in common. The following two strategies both utilize similarities between the objects to determine how they should be grouped.

Figure 3. Relationship between object cluster size and information obtained

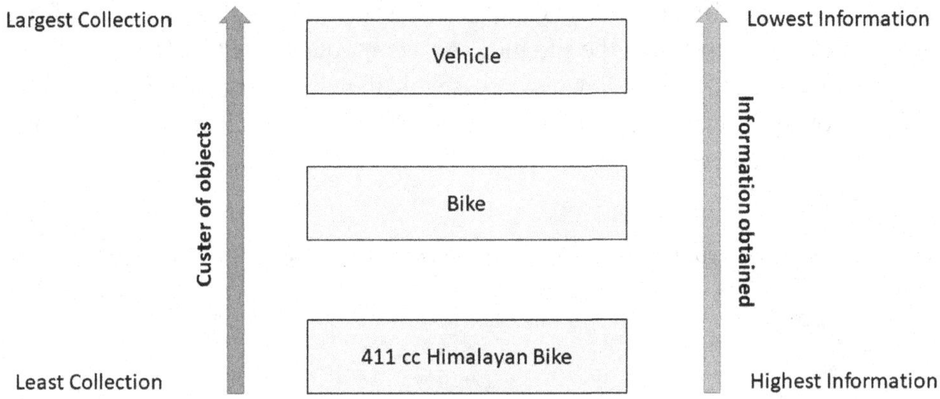

It's fascinating to see how knowledge quickly becomes less important as one moves from the least to the most extensive collection. Figure 3 represents the same statement. The researchers were interested in determining whether or not any of these levels were preferred above the others. Participants were given a limited amount of time to quickly identify a group of objects as part of an assignment. The participants preferred the version of the term that was the most efficient, which was the one at the most basic level. It is for this reason that an image of a Himalayan Bike that resembles a Bajaj Pulsar bike would be referred to as a "Bike" rather than a "vehicle" or "pulsar" It is essential to keep in mind that everyone's levels are different, depending on factors such as their experiences and the way they were raised.

The very nature of knowledge is one of the factors that contribute to the formation of the categories that we make use of. When compared to the typical individual, professionals in a certain subject pay far greater attention to minute details. For instance, persons who are experts in fish are more likely to use a particular name ("rohu," "Katla," etc.) after being shown photos of fish than those who are not fish experts. In a given area of study, an expert's admission barrier is lower than it is for a non-specialist. Consequently, people's skills to categorize are affected by the prior information and experiences they have gained throughout their lives.

Culture is another very essential factor. Imagine a group of people who are more knowledgeable about the plants and animals in their local environment than, for example, students in India are about the natural world around them. When asked what they perceive in nature, those who live in more rural locations are more likely to refer to the trees they see by their particular species names, such as a "banyan tree," than those who reside in urban areas.

Although it is plausible that the brain contains specialized circuitry for some kinds of information, it is very doubtful that each sort of information has its very own devoted brain area. Studies in neurophysiology have shown that there is a dual distinction that may be made between living and nonliving substances. Research using fMRI has revealed evidence that they are, in fact, represented in separate brain areas. However, it is important to point out that despite this, there is a significant amount of consistency in the manner in which different parts of the brain are engaged depending on the kinds of activities that are being carried out. In addition, when one gets closer to the actual site, there is a relationship that is established between mental categories and the location. Neurons, also known as "concept-specific neurons," seem to exist and exhibit an amplified reaction to things that belong to a certain category. These neurons react not only to a single stimulus but rather to an entire category of stimuli. This shows that a vast number of neurons may be involved in the identification of a particular item and that the item might be represented by the patterns that are created by the activities of the neurons working together as a group.

CONCEPT REPRESENTATION IN THE BRAIN

Studies in monkeys using neurophysiology, neuropsychology, and functional brain imaging have accumulated evidence indicating that the ventral occipitotemporal processing stream is necessary for object recognition. In addition, the occipitotemporal cortex is not a unified object-processing system; rather, it possesses a fine-grained structure that appears to be connected to object categories, as demonstrated by functional brain imaging investigations of object recognition. This information was gleaned from studies of object recognition (Hayat et al., 2022). Extensive study has been conducted on a variety of subjects, including human faces, buildings, animals, and objects (Sukanya et al., 2016). When comparing several kinds of items through direct comparison, patterns of behavior that are similar to one another have been shown to cluster together.

In addition, pattern analysis techniques have found discrete patterns of behavior associated with object categories, which may discriminate between many distinct

Figure 4. Lateral view of the brain (Left Hemisphere)
IPS: intraparietal sulcus, LO: lateral occipital cortex, pMTG: posterior middle temporal gyrus,
VPMC: ventral premotor cortex

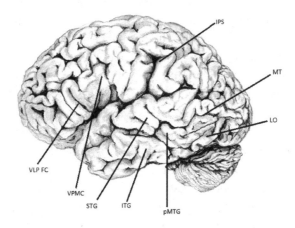

kinds of objects (Jain et al., 2000). These patterns in the occipitotemporal cortex that are linked with certain item categories are ubiquitous, stable from one person to the next, and identifiable even when individuals are studying sophisticated pictures at their own discretion (Fan et al., 2020). Clusters of activity in the occipitotemporal cortex associated with categories are not just noticeable when individuals view pictures of items; they are also present when they take a verbal, conceptual processing test. Perceptual processing was evaluated through passive viewing and delayed match-to-sample with images of animals, tools, faces, and houses. Conceptual processing was assessed through silent picture naming and a property verification task that probed knowledge of animals and tools denoted by written names. Direct head-to-head comparisons of several different kinds of animals revealed modest differences across the groups. Viewing pictures of animals evoked a far greater level of involvement from participants than did gazing at images of human faces. This makes perfect sense when one considers the significant visual similarities that can be seen across different types of human faces. In addition, the stimuli that are used to represent animals are comprised of multiple exemplars, each of which is given a unique name at the most fundamental level, while faces only symbolize a single concept at this level. When it came to processing faces and animals, however, the lateral portion of the fusiform gyrus was more active than when it came to processing artificial objects. Accordingly, despite the fact that each concept of an object must have its own specific representation in the brain, it would seem that the lateral and medial regions of the fusiform gyrus are responsible for distinguishing between real actors and artificial entities that may be manipulated. The recent finding of human body representations close to face representations in the lateral fusiform gyrus lends credence to this notion.

Variations in both category and attribute have been connected to the process of differentiation that takes place in the ventral and lateral temporal cortices (Benarroch, 2019). Figure 4 shows the lateral view of the brain for the left hemisphere. After adding motion to images of tools and people, there was not much of a change in the responses related to categories in the fusiform gyrus; however, there was a considerable rise in the responses from the lateral temporal cortex. The removal of form and color from moving stimuli (point-light displays) had no effect on the category-related reactions in lateral temporal regions; however, the response was dramatically reduced in the ventral temporal cortex. According to these findings, putative substrates for category-related effects include differences in object form (ventral temporal cortex) and motion (lateral temporal cortex). Lateral temporal sulcus (pSTS) neurons responded most favorably to the fully articulated, flexible motion of living beings. In contrast, pMTG neurons reacted primarily to the rigid, unarticulated move of inanimate objects (Patel et al., 2019). This difference in response preference can be explained by the fact that pSTS neurons are located more profoundly in the brain (Ramezanpour et al., 2021).

Increased activity in the left inferior prefrontal cortex has been associated with judging the similarity of two objects based on their manipulation (for example, are a keyboard and a piano performed similarly?). In contrast to similarity based on more vocally mediated functional information (do a cigarette lighter and a match fulfill the same function?), similarity based on morphological similarities has been shown to be more predictive of future behavior (Ong et al., 2019).

According to the findings of other studies (Arioli et al., 2019), the left inferior prefrontal cortex (IPS) and ventromedial prefrontal cortex (VPMC) are more active when considering and imagining the grasping of common tools than when considering and imagining the grasping of the novel, graspable objects; holding manipulable, but not non-manipulatable, things in working memory. These findings suggest that regions of the brain that become active during the actual use of an object are also involved throughout the process of retrieving information about that object's function (Mow et al., 2020). Additionally, this data is automatically obtained when these things are recognized, regardless of the stimulus modality (visual, auditory, etc.) or format, which is compatible with the study of object categories that was addressed earlier in this article (verbal, nonverbal).

The "Semantic Network method" holds that one's mental concepts may be organized into networks, which can be thought of as a functional database for the "meanings" of words (Sarica et al., 2021). Figure 5 represents a knowledge graph of the semantic network method. The concept of a semantic net naturally leaves a lot of wiggle area for further development. Discrete nodes in a graphical depiction of a semantic net stand in for individual pieces of knowledge about the world, much as the ideas in our mental dictionary do. This allows the representation to be more easily understood. The characteristics of a concept can be "stored" close to the node representing the idea. The connections between the nodes are symbolic of the ties that bind the items together. One possible indication of the nature of the relationship being exhibited is the length of the links between the nodes in the graph. On the web, every concept is dynamically linked to others, some of which may have archetypal characteristics or roles in common with one another (Luo et al., 2020).

The logical structure of the network reveals that the network's distances coincide with the amount of time it takes to retrieve a thought (Kang et al., 2020). This fact lends credibility to the argument that the network presents. The relationship may be seen clearly from the sentence-verification analysis. Participants in the experiment were given a series of conceptual knowledge-testing statements to which they were instructed to reply "1" or "0" When the nodes holding the ideas were farther away, it took a longer amount of time for the system to say "1".

The term "spreading activation" describes the process through which thoughts that are relatively adjacent to one another in space are likewise activated (Heo et al., 2019). These notions are considerably simpler to summon to the mind as a direct result of this priming. The research was carried out in this field by early researchers utilizing a lexical choice task (Meyer et al., 1971), and the results of their investigation were validated by the data (Kurdi et al., 2019). The probands were tasked with determining whether or not a particular set of words formed a word when put together. The degree to which the concepts represented by two words were located in close proximity to one another in the intended network determined how quickly they were able to discover actual word pairs. Although the model contains a number of flaws, it is nevertheless capable of solving many difficulties. One such example is the bias toward typical behavior. According to a popular proverb, "reaction times for more typical members of a category are faster than for less typical individuals" According to Collins' and Quillian's Model (MITECS) (Collins et al., 1970), which maintains that the distance in the net impacts reaction time, this contradicts their assumptions. The validity of the cognitive economy is now being called into question as a result of empirical evidence which demonstrates that certain characteristics are stored at particular nodes. In addition, there have been instances in which faster idea retrieval was accomplished despite the presence of higher network distances.

Research by (Sahu et al., 2020) made an effort to resolve these problems by using links of varied lengths, which were determined according to the degree of relatedness and connectedness between concepts that had not been formally linked in the past. A structure that is more analogous to that of an individual has been put in place in lieu of the hierarchical structure that was there before. In order to provide a condensed summary of some of the improvements. The new model (Siew et al.,

Figure 5. Knowledge Graph for a Semantic Network

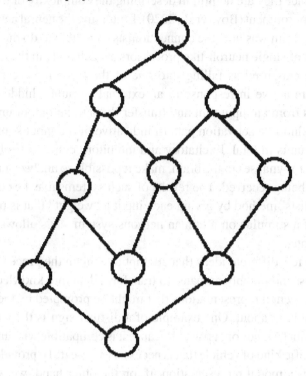

2019), which can be seen on the right, takes into consideration unique qualities, including those that a person has picked up over the course of their life. They may be observed, for instance, in the way thoughts that are connected to one another are organized, as well as in the different lengths of the linkages that connect them.

As an example, the words "bike," "car," and "bus" are all linked to the concept of "vehicle" by intermediate connections. Still, the terms "fire engine" and "ambulance" are connected to the concept through more extensive linkages. As a consequence of these modifications, the model has become so extensive that it has been challenged by a number of experts for being too flexible. They say that since there is no way to demonstrate that their model is incorrect, it can no longer be deemed a scientific hypothesis. In addition to that, we need to be made aware of the length of time that these bonds have been attached to our bodies. If they were to be measured, how precisely ought they to be measured, and are they even capable of being measured?

Every idea in a semantic net is dynamically associated with other notions, some of which may have traits or functions that are prototypically equivalent to those of the others (Zheng et al., 2021). The neuronal networks in the brain have a consistent organizational pattern. In addition, the characteristics of "spreading activation" and "parallel distributed activity" are beneficial to include in a concept of such a semantic net since they are helpful in describing the complexity of the exceedingly complicated environment (Bova et al., 2020). Emulating the neural networks that can be found in the brain was how the connectionists were able to do this. The network model consists of single neuron-like processors at each node in the network. These things may be classified as falling into one of the three main categories: Input units, which are active in response to an external stimulus; hidden units, which receive signals from an input unit and transfer them to an output unit; and output units, which exhibit an activation pattern indicative of the input stimuli. There are three kinds of units in total. Excitatory and inhibitory connections between units, which are akin to synapses in the brain, make it possible to analyze and evaluate the "input" that is being received. The results of such systems may be computed using the connectionists' method by giving each input a "weight" that is proportional to the strength of a stimulus on a human nervous system. This allows the results to be more accurate.

There are a few different ideas that attempt to explain the processes that enable living creatures, and notably humans, to transform data into knowledge. There are many different mental representations that might be prompted by the same subject that we are thinking about. One example of a distinct sign is the letter "b" in the word "bike," which stands on its own. Because it is compatible with any automotive, there is no specific kind of vehicle that is necessary to use it. To provide more clarity, we can call this a modal representation. If, on the other hand, we were presented with a picture of a bike, the scenario would be quite different. It's possible that the offender was driving a red sports car. Now we're talking about a symbol that isn't binary, a mental picture that only matches specific autos because they look similar enough to it. Using the Propositional Approach (De Houwer, 2018), it is possible to create a simulation that mimics human mental representations. This approach makes use of discrete symbols that have strong links between them. When working with discrete symbols, you need to have crystal-clear definitions of each symbol, as well as knowledge of the syntactic rules and context dependencies associated with the circumstances in which the symbols may be employed. Only those who are proficient in English and have really experienced being in the presence of a bike in the real world would be able to comprehend the "vehicle" sign. The Propositional Approach offers a straightforward structure that may be used to understand better the idea of mental representation (Sant'Anna, 2018).

Propositions continue to be problematic notions, with meanings that differ from discipline to discipline and often contradict one another. It is possible to communicate a single idea using almost an unlimited number of different expressions. However, "Concepts" are more atomic than "Propositions" themselves since they serve as the building blocks from which "Propositions" may be dismantled. In addition, mental propositions investigate the ways in which the human brain organizes, retrieves, and connects previously acquired information. There is much debate as to whether or not propositions are the primary tool that the brain uses for organizing and storing information or if the brain uses a different mechanism, or perhaps several mechanisms, to convert information into knowledge. This topic has been the subject of much discussion in recent years (Aberšek, 2018).

KNOWLEDGE REPRESENTATION AS A FORMAL MODEL

The reasoning is an internal process, whereas the vast majority of the things a sentient being seeks to reason about can only be found in its external environment. This is a crucial and unavoidable truth that any sentient being that seeks to claim about its environment must face, as it is a truth that cannot be avoided. Even if the components of a bicycle can only be found in the physical world, a piece of software (or a person) building a bike may need to reason about things like as wheels, chains, sprockets, handlebars, and other similar parts.

One of the most fundamental responsibilities of a representation is to fulfill the role of a stand-in for the real world that exists outside the realm of the reasoner. Instead of engaging directly with the surrounding world, we may execute activities on and with representations of that environment instead. If we are unable to take action in the world, or if we do not want to, we may at least make an effort to make sense of it via our thoughts.

Taking into account symbols as alternatives raise two very important questions. When it comes to choosing a surrogate, the first consideration should be what the surrogate will be employed. This relationship between the surrogate and its worldly referent is the representation's semantics, and it is required that they have a specified link (Cheng et al., 2022).

The second issue that must be addressed is the degree to which the surrogate resembles the original. How well does it recreate the attributes of the original while also making any necessary adjustments clear? In either theory or practice, reaching the goal of absolute loyalty may be challenging (Meles et al., 2022). It is technically impossible since everything else than the item itself is essentially separate from the thing itself (in location if nothing else). To put it another way, the object itself is the only depiction of an item that is entirely accurate. Every other representation needs to be revised due to the fact that it oversimplifies the assumptions on which it is based and may even include artifacts.

This idea of representations functioning as replacements is developed further by adding two more specifics. To begin, it seems to function as effectively for non-material objects, such as thoughts, as it does for material things, such as gears: It is possible for an entity to define abstract ideas like as actions, processes, beliefs, causes, categories, and so on by using representations in order to make it possible to reason about these concepts. Second, the machine is capable of hosting formal objects with a precision of one hundred percent (Karer et al., 2020). For instance, as a case in point, mathematical entities are able to be recorded precisely due to the fact that they are formal objects. Due to the necessity to deal with both natural objects (those encountered in the real world) and ceremonial objects, faulty surrogates are inescapable in nearly every reasoning task. This is because of the practical problem of defective surrogates being unavoidable.

To restate this notion in a different manner, the concept of linking triggers and procedures to frames is more of a description of a beneficial approach to organizing information than it is a declaration about what processes to write down. For instance, we might attach to each frame information on how to utilize the frame, what to do if expectations are not verified, etc. This is analogous to how the grouping of frames according to taxonomic order both shows and encourages taxonomic thinking (as in structured inheritance networks) (Feng et al., 2021).

Instructions of a similar kind may be derived from many images. Traditional semantic nets enable bidirectional propagation because they have an appropriate set of links (Wu et al., 2020). Despite the fact that designers of representations have tried to find solutions to the issue of wasteful utilization, the industry as a whole has had a conflicted perspective on the matter in the past. Despite the fact that early recognition of the concept of heuristic adequacy demonstrates that researchers appreciated the significance of the computational properties of a representation, the tone of much later work in logic suggested that epistemology (knowledge content) alone mattered and defined computational efficiency out of the agenda. This was despite the fact that the notion of heuristic adequacy demonstrated that researchers appreciated the significance of the computational properties of a representation. It goes without saying that epistemology is essential, and it could be in your best interest to study it without the potential distraction of time restraints. However, at some point in the process of computing, we will be required to employ our representations.

The majority of applications of computational knowledge representation do not use it as a model of cognition but rather as an extension of database technology to facilitate the discovery and use of large amounts of information (Mikhailov, 2019). This is because it is easier to find and use large amounts of information with this technology. In this particular situation, overarching concepts and models are optional in any capacity. It is now feasible, as a result of ever-improving data storage capacity, to create factual databases that are both comprehensive and succinct. The data is preserved using a medium known as "sentential knowledge," which may be understood as information that is retained in the form of sentences and is comparable to propositions and computer code. Rather than acting as a basis for a theory of cognition, knowledge is considered as a repository of facts and figures. The development of memory technology has made it possible to use representations that are considered to be "compute intensive." Instead of providing overarching concepts, these representations list all of the particular facts that have been uncovered. These allow statistical procedures to be used, such as the Markov simulation, but they seem to give up any pretense of psychological realism in the process (Cai et al., 2018).

Hemispheric Knowledge Representation

Now that we've covered how the brain stores information, we can move on to the topic of whether or not the brain is specialized, and if it is, which functions are housed in which hemispheres, as well as which kinds of knowledge are present in each. If the brain is specialized, then we can move on to the topic of which functions are housed in which hemispheres, as well as which types of knowledge are present in each. These lines of inquiry may be categorized under the overarching idea of "hemispheric specialization" or "lateralization of processing," which investigates the ways in which the left and right lobes of the human brain differ in their respective functional capabilities (Wang et al., 2021).

Around 3.5 million years ago, the two hemispheres started moving in different directions. The existence of australopithecine fossils provides evidence of this (which is an ancient ancestor of homo sapiens). Differences that have lasted during the course of evolution and the application of selection pressure must, in some way, contribute to the way in which our minds work (Michel, 2021).

The primary connection between the two hemispheres of the brain is made by the corpus callosum. There are about 250 million nerve fibers that make up the highway that connects the two halves of the brain, which may be compared to an autobahn for neural data. In point of fact, there are some tiny links between the hemispheres; nevertheless, these routes are minor (Kumarasinghe et al., 2020). It is necessary for information to pass through the corpus callosum prior to being transferred from one hemisphere to the other. The transmission time of ERP may be measured in milliseconds.

Even though studies were designed in a variety of different ways (Park et al., 2019), they all shared the essential premise that the hemisphere of the brain that is opposite the side of the body from where the sensory input originated is responsible for processing it. In one experiment, participants were instructed to identify various objects by using just one hand to touch them while also wearing blindfolds. Next, the patients attempted to identify the object that they felt, and it was noticed that they were unable to do so while using their left hands, which are connected to the left hemisphere of the brain. It was concluded that this was due to the fact that the left hemisphere was affected. The question of whether or if this inability was brought on by the right hemisphere's putative function as a "spare tire" or by some other source gave rise to a dispute that arose.

Through the use of a variety of experiments, more study on hemisphere specialization has been carried out (Yin et al., 2022). Patients who have epilepsy who were scheduled to have surgery in which a section of one of their brain hemispheres would be removed were among those who participated. It was essential to determine which hemisphere of the patient's brain was dominant before commencing surgery in order to safeguard that hemisphere from injury. The Wada method, in which a barbiturate is injected directly into a major cerebral artery (Trébuchon et al., 2020), was the one that was employed for this procedure. When one side of the body is injected, it nearly instantly induces paralysis on the opposing side of the body. Because this individual is able to keep talking, we may deduce that the hemisphere of their brain that was affected by the chemical is not the one responsible for speech. There are considerable drawbacks to doing research on individuals who have had brain lesions or even a commissurotomy performed on them. In most cases, epileptic seizures are the primary reason why a patient requires this particular kind of surgery. This suggests that their brains may not be typical or that the treatment may have caused damage to other portions of their brains. In addition, the statistical reliability of this research may be inadequate as a result of the small sample sizes.

The following significant conclusions may be drawn from the trials that have been discussed so far: As a general rule, the right hemisphere of the brain is superior when it comes to non-verbal activities such as face recognition or spatial abilities such as line alignment, whereas the left hemisphere of the brain is superior when it comes to verbal tasks such as speech processing, speech production, and letter recognition. This indicates that the idea of cerebral dominance is false, according to which the right hemisphere of the brain plays the function of a "spare tire." The removal of one hemisphere would have a significant impact on mental function due to the fact that each hemisphere is specialized for a particular sort of job. Even while each hemisphere is highly specialized in its own area of operation, it is only partly prepared to tackle responsibilities that are generally done by the other hemisphere. This is the case even though each hemisphere is highly specialized in its own field of operation. The list of capabilities that are the purview of each hemisphere of the brain is shown above in outline form.

The corpus callosum facilitates communication in both directions between different parts of the brain. The performance of the whole brain is measured by first determining how well each of the brain's hemispheres performs on its own and then contrasting those results with one another. As a consequence of this, the overall performance could be either as good or just as bad as the performance of one of the solo hemispheres, depending on the task that has to be completed. A scenario in which dual-hemispheric processing is inferior to unilateral activity is provided by the surprising possibility that the hemisphere that dominates may actually be the one with the lower level of specialization. Together, the two hemispheres of the brain are responsible for the brain's overall processing capacity, which is calculated as the average of the two hemispheres' individual capacities. The third and perhaps most surprising way in which the hemispheres could interact is by demonstrating behaviors that are wholly different from one another when they are working together on a task. This is related to how people behave in social settings, when their behavior may differ from that which is shown when they are operating alone in the context of the circumstance.

CONCLUSION

However, despite the fact that the two hemispheres seem to be reflections of each other at first glance, this is different. When you look at the two halves of the brain more attentively, you'll see that they have entirely different functions and structures from one another. Both hemispheres of the brain are capable of performing all of the basic cognitive tasks, despite the fact that there is no specific function that can only be performed by one hemisphere of the brain. The right hemisphere of the brain is often superior at doing non-verbal tasks, while the left hemisphere is typically superior at performing verbal tasks. Even though the left and right sides of the brain are responsible for separate functions, they are nevertheless able to communicate with one another because of a structure called the corpus callosum.

The research that Sperry conducted on split-brain patients used this discovery (Thiebaut de Schotten et al., 2021). They were the first people to invalidate the hemisphere dominance theory, and as a result, they were given the Nobel Prize in Medicine and Physiology. This makes them stand out from other tests that evaluate perceptual asymmetries since they were the first to do so.

REFERENCES

Aberšek, B. (2018). *Problem-based learning and proprioception.* Cambridge Scholars Publishing.

Arioli, M., & Canessa, N. (2019). Neural processing of social interaction: Coordinate-based meta-analytic evidence from human neuroimaging studies. *Human Brain Mapping, 40*(13), 3712–3737. doi:10.1002/hbm.24627 PMID:31077492

Bartolomeo, P., & Malkinson, T. S. (2019). Hemispheric lateralization of attention processes in the human brain. *Current Opinion in Psychology*, *29*, 90–96. doi:10.1016/j.copsyc.2018.12.023 PMID:30711910

Benarroch, E. E. (2019). Insular cortex: Functional complexity and clinical correlations. *Neurology*, *93*(21), 932–938. doi:10.1212/WNL.0000000000008525 PMID:31645470

Betegh, G. (2020). Plato on Illness in the Phaedo, the Republic, and the Timaeus. In Plato's Timaeus (pp. 228-258). Brill. doi:10.1163/9789004437081_013

Bhuyan, B. P., Karmakar, A., & Hazarika, S. M. (2018). Bounding stability in formal concept analysis. In *Advanced Computational and Communication Paradigms* (pp. 545–552). Springer. doi:10.1007/978-981-10-8237-5_53

Bhuyan, B. P., Tomar, R., & Cherif, A. R. (2022). A Systematic Review of Knowledge Representation Techniques in Smart Agriculture (Urban). *Sustainability*, *14*(22), 15249. doi:10.3390u142215249

Bhuyan, B. P., Tomar, R., Gupta, M., & Ramdane-Cherif, A. (2021, December). An Ontological Knowledge Representation for Smart Agriculture. *In 2021 IEEE International Conference on Big Data (Big Data)* (pp. 3400-3406). IEEE. 10.1109/BigData52589.2021.9672020

Bhuyan, B. P., Um, J. S., Singh, T. P., & Choudhury, T. (2022). Decision Intelligence Analytics: Making Decisions Through Data Pattern and Segmented Analytics. In *Decision Intelligence Analytics and the Implementation of Strategic Business Management* (pp. 99–107). Springer. doi:10.1007/978-3-030-82763-2_9

Bird, A. (2019). Group belief and knowledge. In *The Routledge handbook of social epistemology* (pp. 274–283). Routledge. doi:10.4324/9781315717937-27

Bova, V. V., Kravchenko, Y. A., Rodzin, S. I., & Kuliev, E. V. (2020, October). Simulation of the Semantic Network of Knowledge Representation in Intelligent Assistant Systems Based on Ontological Approach. In *International Conference on Futuristic Trends in Networks and Computing Technologies* (pp. 241-252). Springer.

Cai, B., Kong, X., Liu, Y., Lin, J., Yuan, X., Xu, H., & Ji, R. (2018). Application of Bayesian networks in reliability evaluation. *IEEE Transactions on Industrial Informatics*, *15*(4), 2146–2157. doi:10.1109/TII.2018.2858281

Chakraborty, N., Lukovnikov, D., Maheshwari, G., Trivedi, P., Lehmann, J., & Fischer, A. (2019). *Introduction to neural network based approaches for question answering over knowledge graphs*. arXiv preprint arXiv:1907.09361.

Cheng, M., Dang, C., Frangopol, D. M., Beer, M., & Yuan, X. X. (2022). Transfer prior knowledge from surrogate modelling: A meta-learning approach. *Computers & Structures*, *260*, 106719. doi:10.1016/j.compstruc.2021.106719

Collins, A. M., & Quillian, M. R. (1970). Facilitating retrieval from semantic memory: The effect of repeating part of an inference. *Acta Psychologica*, *33*, 304–314. doi:10.1016/0001-6918(70)90142-3

De Houwer, J. (2018). Propositional models of evaluative conditioning. *Social Psychological Bulletin*, *13*(3), 1–21. doi:10.5964pb.v13i3.28046

Fan, X., Wang, F., Shao, H., Zhang, P., & He, S. (2020). The bottom-up and top-down processing of faces in the human occipitotemporal cortex. *eLife*, *9*, e48764. doi:10.7554/eLife.48764 PMID:31934855

Feng, Y., Sun, X., Diao, W., Li, J., Gao, X., & Fu, K. (2021). Continual learning with structured inheritance for semantic segmentation in aerial imagery. *IEEE Transactions on Geoscience and Remote Sensing*, *60*, 1–17.

Gou, J., Yu, B., Maybank, S. J., & Tao, D. (2021). Knowledge distillation: A survey. *International Journal of Computer Vision*, *129*(6), 1789–1819. doi:10.100711263-021-01453-z

Hayat, A., Morgado-Dias, F., Bhuyan, B. P., & Tomar, R. (2022). Human Activity Recognition for Elderly People Using Machine and Deep Learning Approaches. *Information*, *13*(6), 275. doi:10.3390/info13060275

Heo, B., Lee, M., Yun, S., & Choi, J. Y. (2019, July). Knowledge transfer via distillation of activation boundaries formed by hidden neurons. *Proceedings of the AAAI Conference on Artificial Intelligence*, *33*(01), 3779–3787. doi:10.1609/aaai.v33i01.33013779

Hogan, A., Blomqvist, E., Cochez, M., d'Amato, C., Melo, G. D., Gutierrez, C., Kirrane, S., Gayo, J. E. L., Navigli, R., Neumaier, S., Ngomo, A.-C. N., Polleres, A., Rashid, S. M., Rula, A., Schmelzeisen, L., Sequeda, J., Staab, S., & Zimmermann, A. (2021). Knowledge graphs. *ACM Computing Surveys*, *54*(4), 1–37. doi:10.1145/3447772

Jain, A. K., Duin, R. P. W., & Mao, J. (2000). Statistical pattern recognition: A review. *IEEE Transactions on Pattern Analysis and Machine Intelligence*, *22*(1), 4–37. doi:10.1109/34.824819

Ji, S., Pan, S., Cambria, E., Marttinen, P., & Philip, S. Y. (2021). A survey on knowledge graphs: Representation, acquisition, and applications. *IEEE Transactions on Neural Networks and Learning Systems*, *33*(2), 494–514. doi:10.1109/TNNLS.2021.3070843 PMID:33900922

Kang, C., Yu, X., Wang, S. H., Guttery, D. S., Pandey, H. M., Tian, Y., & Zhang, Y. D. (2020). A heuristic neural network structure relying on fuzzy logic for images scoring. *IEEE Transactions on Fuzzy Systems*, *29*(1), 34–45. doi:10.1109/TFUZZ.2020.2966163 PMID:33408453

Karer, B., Scheler, I., Hagen, H., & Leitte, H. (2020, September). Conceptgraph: A formal model for interpretation and reasoning during visual analysis. *Computer Graphics Forum*, *39*(6), 5–18. doi:10.1111/cgf.13899

Klein, E. (2018). *Augustine's theology of angels*. Cambridge University Press. doi:10.1017/9781108335652

Kumarasinghe, K., Kasabov, N., & Taylor, D. (2020). Deep learning and deep knowledge representation in Spiking Neural Networks for Brain-Computer Interfaces. *Neural Networks*, *121*, 169–185. doi:10.1016/j.neunet.2019.08.029 PMID:31568895

Kurdi, B., Seitchik, A. E., Axt, J. R., Carroll, T. J., Karapetyan, A., Kaushik, N., Tomezsko, D., Greenwald, A. G., & Banaji, M. R. (2019). Relationship between the Implicit Association Test and intergroup behavior: A meta-analysis. *The American Psychologist*, *74*(5), 569–586. doi:10.1037/amp0000364 PMID:30550298

Leonard, D. (1995). *Wellsprings of knowledge*. Harvard Business School Press.

Luo, X., Wu, J., Zhou, C., Zhang, X., & Wang, Y. (2020, November). Deep Semantic Network Representation. In *2020 IEEE International Conference on Data Mining (ICDM)* (pp. 1154-1159). IEEE. 10.1109/ICDM50108.2020.00141

Meles, G. A., Linde, N., & Marelli, S. (2022). Bayesian tomography with prior-knowledge-based parametrization and surrogate modeling. *Geophysical Journal International*, *231*(1), 673–691. doi:10.1093/gji/ggac214

Meyer, D. E., & Schvaneveldt, R. W. (1971). Facilitation in recognizing pairs of words: Evidence of a dependence between retrieval operations. *Journal of Experimental Psychology*, *90*(2), 227–234. doi:10.1037/h0031564 PMID:5134329

Michel, G. F. (2021). Handedness development: A model for investigating the development of hemispheric specialization and interhemispheric coordination. *Symmetry*, *13*(6), 992. doi:10.3390ym13060992

Mikhailov, I. F. (2019). Computational Knowledge Representation in Cognitive Science. *Epistemology & Philosophy of Science, 56*(3), 138–152. doi:10.5840/eps201956355

Mow, J. L., Gandhi, A., & Fulford, D. (2020). Imaging the "social brain" in schizophrenia: A systematic review of neuroimaging studies of social reward and punishment. *Neuroscience and Biobehavioral Reviews, 118*, 704–722. doi:10.1016/j.neubiorev.2020.08.005 PMID:32841653

Ong, W. Y., Stohler, C. S., & Herr, D. R. (2019). Role of the prefrontal cortex in pain processing. *Molecular Neurobiology, 56*(2), 1137–1166. doi:10.100712035-018-1130-9 PMID:29876878

Park, S. A., Lee, A. Y., Park, H. G., & Lee, W. L. (2019). Benefits of gardening activities for cognitive function according to measurement of brain nerve growth factor levels. *International Journal of Environmental Research and Public Health, 16*(5), 760. doi:10.3390/ijerph16050760 PMID:30832372

Patel, G. H., Sestieri, C., & Corbetta, M. (2019). The evolution of the temporoparietal junction and posterior superior temporal sulcus. *Cortex, 118*, 38–50. doi:10.1016/j.cortex.2019.01.026 PMID:30808550

Phillips, J., Buckwalter, W., Cushman, F., Friedman, O., Martin, A., Turri, J., ... Knobe, J. (2021). Knowledge before belief. *Behavioral and Brain Sciences, 44*. PMID:32895070

Ramezanpour, H., Görner, M., & Thier, P. (2021). Variability of neuronal responses in the posterior superior temporal sulcus predicts choice behavior during social interactions. *Journal of Neurophysiology, 126*(6), 1925–1933. doi:10.1152/jn.00194.2021 PMID:34705592

Sahu, A. K., Padhy, R. K., & Dhir, A. (2020). Envisioning the future of behavioral decision-making: A systematic literature review of behavioral reasoning theory. *Australasian Marketing Journal, 28*(4), 145–159. doi:10.1016/j.ausmj.2020.05.001

Sant'Anna, A. (2018). Episodic memory as a propositional attitude: A critical perspective. *Frontiers in Psychology, 9*, 1220. doi:10.3389/fpsyg.2018.01220 PMID:30072933

Sarica, S., & Luo, J. (2021). Design knowledge representation with technology semantic network. *Proceedings of the Design Society, 1*, 1043–1052. doi:10.1017/pds.2021.104

Siew, C. S., Wulff, D. U., Beckage, N. M., Kenett, Y. N., & Meštrović, A. (2019). Cognitive network science: A review of research on cognition through the lens of network representations, processes, and dynamics. *Complexity*, *2019*, 2019. doi:10.1155/2019/2108423

Sukanya, C. M., Gokul, R., & Paul, V. (2016). A survey on object recognition methods. International Journal of Science. *Engineering and Computer Technology*, *6*(1), 48.

Thiebaut de Schotten, M., & Beckmann, C. F. (2021). Asymmetry of brain structure and function: 40 years after Sperry's Nobel Prize. *Brain Structure & Function*, 1–4. PMID:34779912

Trébuchon, A., Liégeois-Chauvel, C., Gonzalez-Martinez, J. A., & Alario, F. X. (2020). Contributions of electrophysiology for identifying cortical language systems in patients with epilepsy. *Epilepsy & Behavior*, *112*, 107407. doi:10.1016/j.yebeh.2020.107407 PMID:33181892

Verburgt, L. M. (2020). The history of knowledge and the future history of ignorance. *KNOW: A Journal on the Formation of Knowledge, 4*(1), 1-24.

Wang, Y., Zhan, G., Cai, Z., Jiao, B., Zhao, Y., Li, S., & Luo, A. (2021). Vagus nerve stimulation in brain diseases: Therapeutic applications and biological mechanisms. *Neuroscience and Biobehavioral Reviews*, *127*, 37–53. doi:10.1016/j.neubiorev.2021.04.018 PMID:33894241

Wu, Y., Zhang, G., Gao, Y., Deng, X., Gong, K., Liang, X., & Lin, L. (2020). Bidirectional graph reasoning network for panoptic segmentation. In *Proceedings of the IEEE/CVF Conference on Computer Vision and Pattern Recognition* (pp. 9080-9089). 10.1109/CVPR42600.2020.00910

Yin, Y., Wang, F., Yang, Y., Tian, M., Gao, L., & Liu, H. (2022). Abnormalities of hemispheric specialization in drug-naïve and drug-receiving self-limited epilepsy with centrotemporal spikes. *Epilepsy & Behavior*, *136*, 108940. doi:10.1016/j.yebeh.2022.108940 PMID:36228484

Zagzebski, L. (2017). What is knowledge? *The Blackwell guide to epistemology*, 92-116.

Zheng, W., Liu, X., Ni, X., Yin, L., & Yang, B. (2021). Improving visual reasoning through semantic representation. *IEEE Access: Practical Innovations, Open Solutions*, *9*, 91476–91486. doi:10.1109/ACCESS.2021.3074937

Chapter 9
Data Analysis Tools for Neural Data Cognitive Computing:
Neural-Inspired Algorithms

Shiddarth Srivastava
Ajay Kumar Garg Engineering College, India

Rashmi Sharma
Ajay Kumar Garg Engineering College, India

ABSTRACT

The ability to draw conclusions and take action from data hasn't altered all that much despite significant technological developments in recent years. Applications are still typically created to carry out predefined tasks or automate business procedures; therefore, the logic must be coded to account for all possible usage scenarios. They do not grow from their mistakes or adjust to changes in the data. Although they are cheaper and faster, computers aren't substantially smarter. Of course, people now aren't all that much brighter than they were in the past. For both humans and machines, that is about to change. The old notion of computing as process automation is being replaced by a new generation of information systems that offer a collaborative platform for discovery. These systems' initial wave has already improved human cognition in a number of areas.

INTRODUCTION

Cognitive computing is a technological strategy that facilitates human-machine collaboration. If cognitive computing is compared to the human brain, then all

DOI: 10.4018/978-1-6684-6980-4.ch009

forms of data must be analysed contextually, including structured data in databases and unstructured data in text, images, speech, sensors, and video. Because they evaluate and learn from this data, these machines work on a different level than conventional IT systems.

Cognitive computing is a technological progression that aims to make sense of a complex world awash with data of all sorts and sizes (L. Sanchez et al.,2014). You are entering a new era in computing that will fundamentally alter how humans collaborate with machines to generate meaningful insights. Technology advancements have revolutionized industries and the way people live their lives for decades. In the 1950s, transactional and operational processing applications significantly improved the efficiency of government and company processes. Organizations have standardized their business operations and controlled their corporate data more efficiently and precisely than they could be using manual approaches. As the volume and variety of data have expanded tremendously, however, many organizations are unable to convert it into useful knowledge. The amount of new information a person must comprehend or process to make sound decisions is overwhelming. The next generation of solutions combines certain old technology strategies with innovations to help businesses address difficult issues. Cognitive computing is in its infancy of development. The techniques covered in this book will be included in the majority of future systems over time. This book focuses on a new approach to computing that can provide systems with enhanced problem-solving capabilities.

Big Data describes a situation in which data sets have grown so large that traditional technologies can no longer effectively manage their size, scale, or growth. Cognitive computing is the use of reasoning, language processing, machine learning, and human capabilities to improve problem-solving and data-analysis capabilities. A cognitive assistant can provide students with personalized tutorials, guide them through their courses, and aid them in comprehending key topics at their own pace. It can also assist students in choosing courses based on their interests and serve as a career advisor.

Cognitive systems are still in their evolutionary infancy. In the coming decade, cognitive skills will be integrated into a variety of applications and systems. There will be new applications that focus on either horizontal issues (such as security) or industry-specific challenges (such as determining the best way to anticipate retail customer requirements and increase sales or diagnose an illness). Currently, the earliest use cases encompass both new frontiers and challenges that have plagued the industry for decades. For instance, tools are being developed that will enable city managers to forecast when weather-related traffic disruptions may occur and divert traffic to minimize difficulties. In the healthcare industry, cognitive systems are being developed that can be used in tandem with a hospital's electronic medical records to test for omissions and enhance precision. The cognitive system can aid in teaching medical best practices to new physicians and enhancing clinical decision-making. Also in other industries, cognitive systems can facilitate the transfer of information and best practices. In these use scenarios, a cognitive system is designed to establish a dialogue between humans and computers such that best practices are learned by the system rather than being pre-programmed.

In this chapter, we will investigate the characteristics of cognitive computing and how they align with big data, as well as the kind of relationship that both of these things have with one another. In addition, with regard to the varied fields in which cognitive computing can be applied, aspects of open-source software that can affect different aspects of data analysis.

WHAT IS BIG DATA?

Large data sets that are too big to manage and analyse using conventional data processing tools are frequently referred to as "big data." Looking for hints on the Web reveals an almost universal definition that most people supporting the Big Data ideology agree upon, which can be summed up as follows: Big Data describes a situation in which data sets have grown so large that traditional information technologies can no longer effectively manage their size, scale, or growth (T. Nam et al.,2011). In other words, the data set has gotten so big that managing it and extracting value from it are both challenging. The primary difficulties are the acquisition, storage, searching, sharing, analytics, and visualization of data A. P. Appel et al., 2017).

There is a lot more to be said regarding what Big Data is in reality. The idea has developed to now take into account both the size of the data set and the procedures used to leverage the data. Even other business concepts, like business intelligence, analytics, and data mining, have been equated with big data.

Paradoxically, Big Data is not that new. Although enormous data sets have only recently been produced, Big Data has its roots in the scientific and medical fields because these fields are where intricate data analysis is done.

WHAT IS COGNITIVE COMPUTING?

Cognitive computing refers to the use of reasoning, language processing, machine learning, and human capabilities to improve the problem-solving and data-analysis capabilities of traditional computing. By gaining intelligence and learning patterns and behaviors, a computer system can handle complex decision-making processes.

A cognitive computing technology platform uses machine learning and pattern recognition to adapt to and interpret data, including unstructured data such as natural speech. Cognitive computing typically provides the following characteristics, which were developed by the Cognitive Computing Consortium in 2014, to achieve these capabilities:

Adaptive Learning

Cognitive systems must accommodate an influx of rapidly altering information and data that contribute to the achievement of an evolving set of objectives. The platforms process dynamic data in real time and adapt to the environment and data requirements in the vicinity.

Interactive

Cognitive machines require human-computer interaction (HCI). Users interact with cognitive systems and set their parameters, even though these parameters are dynamic. The technology is compatible with other devices, processors, and cloud-based platforms.

Iterative and Stateful

If a fixed query is incomplete or ambiguous, cognitive computing systems identify problems by posing questions or pulling in supplementary data. This is made possible by the technology's ability to store information about related situations and potential scenarios.

Contextual

Cognitive computing systems must recognize, comprehend, and mine contextual data, such as time, syntax, domain, location, requirements, or a user's tasks, profile, and objectives. They may utilize multiple data sources, such as auditory, visual, or sensor data, as well as structured or unstructured data.

RELATIONSHIP BETWEEN COGNITIVE COMPUTING AND BIG DATA

A sufficient amount of data is required for a cognitive computing environment to identify patterns or anomalies within that data. Frequently, a large data set is required. It is crucial to have sufficient data within a cognitive system so that the results of analytics are reliable and consistent. A cognitive system necessitates the ingestion and mapping of data for the system to discover where there are connections between data sources and commence the discovery of insights. A cognitive system incorporates both structured and unstructured data to achieve the goal of gaining insights from data (J. Hurwitz et al.,2015). The creation of structured data, such as relational database data, for computer processing. Unstructured data, such as textual content, video, and images, is designed for human consumption and interpretation.

The management of large data sets is not a novel concept. In normal form database records, the content and structure are intended to reduce redundancy and preconfigure the relationships between fields. Consequently, a relational database is optimized for how systems interpret and interact with data. Initially, humans were intended to process the data within a cognitive system. These data range from journal articles and other documents to videos, audio, and images, as well as disparate streams of sensor and machine data. This type of data requires a level of processing that exceeds the capabilities of relational database systems, as the objective is to interpret the meaning and create data that is readable by humans. Managing terabytes of data, let alone petabytes, has been technically and financially challenging until the last few years. In the past, the best that most organizations could do was collect data samples and hope that the correct data was captured. When significant data elements were missing, however, the amount of analysis that could be performed was limited. In addition, the breadth of data required for a thorough comprehension of business and technical issues has expanded significantly. Companies want to see into the future and predict what will occur next, and then they want to comprehend the most effective course of action. Cognitive computing would not be nearly as beneficial without big data techniques.

DATA ANALYSIS TOOLS FOR NEURAL DATA COGNITIVE COMPUTING

The next technical miracle will be the creation of a computer model that can accurately simulate the functioning of the human brain. The foundation of cognitive computing is artificial intelligence, the branch of computer science that seeks to recreate human mental processes within a digital environment. These kinds of systems have the capability of continually gaining knowledge from the organized data that is provided to them, which is an efficient use of their resources. These kinds of technologies routinely get large amounts of data as input. This is done to improve such systems in terms of decision-making and forecast particular trends.

Spark Cognition

Failure to perform proper maintenance may undoubtedly affect the entire industrial supply chain. To address this maintenance mindset, Spark Cognition developed the analytical solution Spark Predict. It assisted in overcoming maintenance downtime and increased operating cost reductions overall. Spark Predict analyses both structured and unstructured data. The system then employs machine learning techniques to determine what behaviors are permitted at that moment. Using machine learning approaches, this tool can predict mistakes or patterns with sufficient accuracy.

TCS ignio™ Cheetah

In 2015, TCS ignio™ was introduced to combine three key pillars of technology. These included machine learning, artificial intelligence, and sophisticated software engineering. This platform's primary objective was to independently address issues whenever they arose. It is a cognitive automation software suite that specializes in accelerating deployments and customer value realization.TCS ignio™ Cheetah has added new features to its blueprinting and automation properties, including:

- Management of events with a higher priority.
- Attempting to anticipate the activities that require immediate attention.
- Reduce the number of erroneous alerts.
- Effective enough to deal with the incidents using the knowledge it has gained from its previous experience.

Not only does it understand real-time human actions, but it can also adapt to the technologies that are currently in use. This is what is meant by the term "adaptive property". Because of this property of ignio™ Cheetah, it is much simpler for a large number of the software's users to be able to extend the functional capacity of supporting new technologies.

Some of the features of ignio™ are:

- Support for deployments in the cloud.
- SaaS engagement models.
- The capability of managing larger quantities of data.

Iris by Apixio

Data accessibility is still a significant obstacle for many of the world's largest technology companies. The healthcare industry appears to be plagued with the vast majority of these problems. With federal agencies becoming increasingly stringent on healthcare organizations, robust measurements and better data are being requested of these organizations. As a result, there was a demand for a specialized product that could fulfil the same function. Iris, the cognitive computing platform developed by Apixio Inc., a company that specializes in AI for use in healthcare analytics, is helping to close this knowledge gap. Iris consults the patient's medical notes and records to gain new perspectives on the situation. Iris makes use of a machine learning model that is fed with data that has been extracted using data integration tools in addition to real-time data-providing tools. This data is fed into the machine learning model.

AlphaGo

AlphaGo, developed by Google, is a cognitive computing tool that was introduced into the field of playing board games. AlphaGo focuses on the game of Go. It accomplishes its tasks on the algorithms by employing a variety of methods, including machine learning, tree traversal, and deep neural network technology, among others. An additional bit of game-supportive functionality is applied to the input just before it is transmitted to the neural networks.

This cognitive computing tool requires a significant amount of training on both the part of humans and computers. During the early development stages, neural networks were constructed to study the actions taken by humans during gameplay. To make AlphaGo intelligent enough to defeat the grandmasters of the board game, it was also programmed to imitate the moves from historical games that had been recorded.

Aila by Enterra Solutions

The introduction of Aila was made by Enterra Solutions. It aims to answer questions that traditional data analytics cannot answer. It aims for minimal reliance on data or data specialists and the production of cost-effective insights. Aila combines artificial intelligence and sophisticated mathematics to solve human problems. Aila is unlike earlier enterprise software, which had predefined tasks when it comes to its functionality. Aila is a cognitive system that improvises based on experience and generates on-demand insights. Aila, unlike other tools, uses logic to distinguish between complex interactions between variables. It accesses information repositories containing knowledge about your business. Additionally, it circumvents the statistical barriers to deriving insights rapidly and on-demand.

IBM Watson

IBM Watson focuses primarily on healthcare data.

It was implemented to assist the healthcare industry in combating fraud and providing superior medical care. Additionally, it aids in strategic treatment decision-making. It uses the medical literature to determine the correlation between symptoms and its findings. IBM Watson searches through data libraries to find the answers to questions. Similar to other tools, its intelligence increases with each interaction and discovery. Thus, it can return pertinent responses to specific questions.

It generates hypotheses based on the vast amount of data and potential connections rather than any predefined rule. IBM Watson Explorer Engine is one of IBM Watson's offerings. It has the capability of transforming unstructured data into information.

It works in three stages:

- Data feeding
- Data indexing
- Linguistic processing

When data is fed, it is indexed, which enables developers to determine its cognitive characteristics. Watson then conducts position-based indexing. This type of indexing has additional benefits over the conventional method, which is almost universally used in open-source search systems. IBM Watson's application of positional indexing liberates the data from the traditional rigid document models. The linguistic process is performed when data is ready for indexing and again whenever a user makes a query. IBM Watson provides e-mail alerts, which is another of its many useful features.

APPLICATIONS OF COGNITIVE COMPUTING

Nearly every industry makes use of cognitive computing; however, we will only go through a few of those industries here:

Retail Industry

Cognitive Computing offers highly interesting applications in the retail industry. It enables the marketing team to collect more data, which can subsequently be analyzed to improve the efficiency and adaptability of shops. These enable businesses to increase sales and deliver customized recommendations to clients. E-commerce sites have effectively integrated cognitive computing; they take some basic information from clients about the product specifications they are seeking, analyze the vast amount of available data, and then recommend products to the customer. Cognitive computing has contributed to various industry developments. Cognitive computing has provided retailers with the means to construct more adaptable enterprises via demand forecasting, price optimization, and website design. In addition to e-commerce websites, cognition is also effective for in-store buying. It will enable retailers to provide customers with personalized products – what they want when they want it, and how they want to derive meaningful experiences. It will also provide opportunities to reduce wastage and losses by providing fresh products by anticipating demand, and by automating certain areas, it will reduce cycle time, and effort, and increase efficiency.

Logistics

The new frontier in the Transportation, Logistics, and Supply chain is cognition. It aids in each phase of logistics, including Warehouse Designing Decisions, Warehouse Management, Warehouse Automation, the Internet of Things, and Networking. In the process of warehousing, cognition facilitates the compilation of storage codes, while autonomous picking with an automated guided vehicle and the usage of warehouse robots will increase job efficiency (M. Chen et al.,2018). Logistics distribution networks employ cognition to plan the optimal route, increasing the recognition rate and saving a substantial amount of labor. IoT will improve warehouse infrastructure management, inventory optimization, and warehouse operations, and autonomous guided vehicles can be utilized for picking and putting. In addition to the Internet of Things, another significant technology is Wearable Devices, which convert all items into sensors and enhance human decision-making and warehouse operations (Z. Xiong 2012). From smartwatches, these devices have progressed to smart clothing, smart glasses, computing devices, exoskeletons, ring scanners, and speech recognition.

Healthcare

Healthcare applications of Cognitive Computing have been briefly considered. Recent advancements in cognitive computing have enabled medical personnel to make better treatment decisions, hence enhancing their efficiency and the results for their patients. It is a self-learning program that employs Machine learning algorithms, data mining techniques, image recognition, and natural language processing based on real-time patient data, medical transcripts, and other data. The technology processes a vast quantity of data instantaneously to provide answers to particular questions and intelligent recommendations. Cognitive computing in healthcare connects human and machine functions, where computers and the human brain genuinely intersect to enhance human decision-making (M. Chen et al.,2017). This will allow doctors and other medical professionals to diagnose and treat their patients more accurately, and it will also facilitate the creation of individualized therapy modules. Genome medicine is one such field that has evolved as a result of cognitive computing.

COVID (through chest X-ray anomaly detection), etc., has proven a significant influence. Therefore, if we work to integrate anomaly detection into every element of the clinical sector, we might be able to swiftly and accurately detect diseases and anomalies. Numerous additional neurally inspired algorithms are advancing numerous processes and benefiting society.

Healthcare professionals will benefit from cognitive computing because it will be simpler for them to extract the insights they want from various forms of data and information to act confidently and improve their decision-making. In the healthcare sector, there is a considerable danger of not identifying the appropriate linkages and patterns in the data. Patients may suffer long-term injury or even death in this field if crucial details are missed or misconstrued. Cognitive computing combines artificial intelligence, machine learning, and natural language processing to enable healthcare practitioners to learn from patterns and relationships found in data (L. Catarinucci et al.,2015). A best practices approach that enables healthcare companies to get more value out of data and solve difficult challenges is supported by the interaction between humans and machines that is inherent in cognitive systems.

Education

Cognitive computing will transform how the education industry operates. It has already initiated many alterations. It will transform how schools, colleges, and universities operate and assist in providing students with individualized study materials. Can you even conceive how quickly a cognitive system can search a digital library's periodicals and research papers?

A cognitive assistant can provide students with personalized tutorials, guide them through their courses, and aid them in comprehending key topics at their own pace. It can also assist students in choosing courses based on their interests. It can serve as a career advisor. Cognitive computing will aid not only students, but also teachers, support staff, and administrative personnel in providing better service, preparing student reports, and providing feedback.

Cyber Security

Cognitive Algorithms offer end-to-end security platforms that identify, assess, investigate, and eliminate threats. It will aid in preventing cyber-Attacks (or cognitive hacking), making clients less susceptible to manipulation and providing a technical way to detect any false data or disinformation.

Due to the increase in volumetric data, the rise in cyber attacks, and the lack of qualified cybersecurity experts, we require innovative technologies such as cognitive computing to combat cyber threats. Industry leaders in security have already implemented cognitive-based cyber threat detection and security analytics services. These cognitive systems not only detect threats, but also evaluate systems, scan for system vulnerabilities, and recommend actions. The flip side of the coin is that cognitive computing requires large volumes of data, therefore protecting the privacy of the data is of vital importance as well. To maximize the benefits of cognitive computing, we must construct a big database of information while maintaining its secrecy and preventing data leakage (Y. Zhang et al.,2017).

Impact of Open-Source Tools on Data Analytics

Open-source analytics tools have a significant impact on the expansion of predictive analytics in numerous organizations. R, an open-source programming environment and language, is quickly becoming one of the most important tools for data scientists, statisticians, and other enterprise users.

The language of choice for graduate students conducting research in advanced analytics and cognitive computing is R, which is designed for computational statistics and data visualization. This has resulted in a very active open-source community. Members of the community share information regarding models, algorithms, and best practices for coding. Users appreciate the adaptability afforded by a language and environment designed for the development of specialized applications. Flexibility and adaptability are two of R's many advantages. A version of the statistical programming language is called R.

S, which was created at Bell Laboratories as a more sophisticated alternative to FORTRAN statistical subroutines. Unless you are an experienced data scientist or statistician, R can be difficult to use. However, many vendors offer connections to R that make it easier to use. Preconfigured and ready-to-use algorithms are provided by vendors for model development. The open-source community has spawned and continues to support numerous projects that serve as the basis for advanced analytics applications. Cassandra (distributed database management system) and Spark are two important Apache Foundation projects, for instance (an analytics framework for cluster computing in the Hadoop space).

CREATING VALUE WITH ADVANCED ANALYTICS

The ultimate objective of deploying advanced analytics processes and cognitive computing is to enhance decision-making. Companies use analytics to differentiate themselves from the competition by listening to customers more attentively, anticipating their needs, and making highly targeted offers. Government agencies use analytics to distinguish their cities by making them safer, more responsive to the needs of citizens, and more environmentally friendly. Utilizing analytics, healthcare organizations improve physician training, eliminate unnecessary hospitalizations, and enhance the overall quality of care. Building the analytics models and cognitive computing environments that support these improvements in decision-making requires more data, more accurate data, more refined data, and the capacity to manage and interpret data from all input streams quickly.

NEURAL INSPIRED ALGORITHM: NLP'S ROLE IN COGNITIVE SYSTEMS

NLP is a set of techniques for determining the meaning of the text. These techniques determine the meaning of a word, phrase, sentence, or document by identifying the language's grammatical rules, or predictable patterns (K. Hwang et al.,2017). They use dictionaries, recurrent patterns of co-occurring words, and other contextual clues to determine the potential meaning. NLP uses the same established rules and patterns to infer the meaning of a text document. In addition, these techniques can identify and extract elements of meaning, such as proper names, locations, actions, and events, to determine their relationships across documents. These techniques can also be applied to the text within a database and have been used for more than a decade to find duplicate names and addresses in large customer databases or to analyze a comment or reason field.

NLP is responsible for translating unstructured content from a corpus of information into a meaningful knowledge base. Linguistic analysis dissects the text to determine its meaning. The text must be transformed so that the user can pose questions to the knowledge base and receive meaningful responses. Any system, be it a structured database, a query engine, or a knowledge base, necessitates techniques and tools that permit the user to interpret the data (M. Chan et al., 2009). The quality of the information is crucial for converting data into comprehension. NLP enables the interpretation of data and the relationships between words. It is essential to determine what information to retain and how to search for patterns in the information's structure to extract meaning and context. NLP makes it possible for cognitive systems to derive meaning from text. Phrases, sentences, and lengthy complex documents provide context for understanding the meaning of a word or term.

This context is essential for determining the actual significance of text-based data. To begin to comprehend the meaning and actual intent of communications, patterns, and relationships between words and phrases within the text must be identified. When humans read or hear natural language text, they automatically identify these patterns and form associations between words to determine the meaning and comprehend emotion. There is a great deal of ambiguity in language, and many words can have multiple meanings depending on the topic being discussed or how a word is used in a phrase, sentence, or paragraph. When human beings communicate information, context is assumed.

Consider a truck driver who desires to use a cognitive system to plan a trip. He needs to know the most efficient travel route. However, it would be even better if he knew the expected weather patterns for the week of his trip. He would also like to be aware of any major construction projects he should avoid. Additionally, it would be useful to know which routes prohibit trucks weighing more than 10 tons. The truck driver is permitted to collect these responses. Nonetheless, he would need to access multiple systems, search multiple databases, and formulate targeted questions. Even if the truck driver discovers all the answers, they are not correlated to provide the optimal travel route based on his needs at a given time. Two weeks later, the same truck driver will have entirely different questions. This time, the truck driver may be planning his return after delivering goods, and he wants to incorporate a vacation. The recipient (the truck driver) must provide context and comprehension for the fragmented information he is accumulating.

Consider the scenario of a lung cancer specialist reviewing an MRI. Although some MRIs provide precise diagnostic information, there are numerous shades of gray. The specialist may wish to compare the MRI results to those of other patients whose conditions appear to be comparable. The specialist has treated lung cancer patients for many years and has developed many hypotheses regarding the best treatments. However, a single specialist can't keep up with all the new research and treatments discussed in technical journals. This specialist must instruct the cognitive system to search for anomalies that appear in multiple MRIs. She may wish to inquire further about the experiences of other specialists who have treated the same type of lung cancer. She may wish to request evidence and engage in a conversation with the cognitive system to comprehend context and relationships.

These two instances highlight the difficulties in concluding text and language. History, definitions, and other background information that would help the reader better understand the context of the text are frequently left out of written texts. To better understand the meaning, each reader of a text brings a different level of experience. Humans, therefore, use their knowledge of the world to draw connections and provide context (M. Amiribesheli et.al, 2015). Of course, depending on the level of knowledge and the expertise required for the text, some text may not be understood without additional information or training. NLP tools rely on rules of language to determine the meaning and extract elements. NLP tools must function in a system where the data is dynamic by nature if they are to be combined with cognitive systems. This means that the system is designed to learn from examples or patterns; therefore, language has to be interpreted based on context.

CONCLUSION AND SUMMARY

We discovered in this chapter that cognitive computing plays an important part in advanced analytics when it is used in conjunction with large amounts of data. We discussed the potential applications of cognitive computing in a variety of fields, including cyber security, healthcare, and education, among others. We also gained an understanding of the various tools that are required for cognitive computing. The influence of open sources is also discussed in this article. The text is broken down into its parts to determine its meaning through linguistic analysis. Context is essential to gaining an understanding of a word or term, and it can be found in phrases, sentences, and lengthy, complex documents. The interpretation of data as well as the connections between words are both made possible by NLP. It is essential to decide what information should be retained and how to search for patterns in the structure of the information.

REFERENCES

Amiribesheli, M., Benmansour, A., & Bouchachia, A. (2015). A review of smart homes in healthcare. *Journal of Ambient Intelligence and Humanized Computing*, 6(4), 495–517. doi:10.100712652-015-0270-2

Appel, A. P., Candello, H., & Gandour, F. L. (2017). Cognitive computing: Where big data is driving us. Handbook of Big Data Technologies.

Armbrust, M. (2009). Above the clouds: A Berkeley view of cloud computing. Eecs Dept. Univ. California Berkeley, 53(4).

Botta, A., Donato, W. D., Persico, V., & Pescapé, A. E. (2014). On the integration of cloud computing and Internet of Things. *Proc. IEEE Int. Conf. Future Internet Things Cloud*. 10.1109/FiCloud.2014.14

Catarinucci. (2015). An IoT-aware architecture for smart healthcare systems. *IEEE Internet Things J., 2*(6).

Chan, M., Campo, E., Estéve, D., & Fourniols, J. Y. (2009). Smart homes—Current features and future perspectives. *Maturitas, 64*(2), 90–97. doi:10.1016/j.maturitas.2009.07.014 PMID:19729255

Charte, D., Charte, F., García, S., del Jesus, M. J., & Herrera, F. (2017, November). A practical tutorial on autoencoders for nonlinear feature fusion: Taxonomy, models, software and guidelines. *Information Fusion, 44.*

Chaturvedi, I., Cambria, E., Welsch, R. E., & Herrera, F. (2018, November). Distinguishing between facts and opinions for sentiment analysis: Survey and challenges. *Information Fusion, 44*, 65–77. doi:10.1016/j.inffus.2017.12.006

Chen, Shi, Zhang, Wu, & Mohsen. (2017). Deep features learning for medical image analysis with convolutional autoencoder neural network. *IEEE Trans. Big Data.* DOI: doi:10.1109/TBDATA.2017.2717439

Chen, L., Nugent, C. D., & Wang, H. (2012, June). A knowledge-driven approach to activity recognition in smart homes. *IEEE Transactions on Knowledge and Data Engineering, 24*(6), 961–974. doi:10.1109/TKDE.2011.51

Chen, M., Hao, Y., Hu, L., Huang, K., & Lau, V. (2017, December). Green and mobility-aware caching in 5G networks. *IEEE Transactions on Wireless Communications, 16*(12), 8347–8361. doi:10.1109/TWC.2017.2760830

Chen, M., Hao, Y., Kai, H., Wang, L., & Wang, L. (2017). Disease prediction by machine learning over big data from healthcare communities. *IEEE Access: Practical Innovations, Open Solutions, 5*(1), 8869–8879. doi:10.1109/ACCESS.2017.2694446

Chen, M., Mao, S., & Liu, Y. (2014, April). Big data: A survey. *Mobile Networks and Applications, 19*(2), 171–209. doi:10.100711036-013-0489-0

Chen, M., Miao, Y., Hao, Y., & Hwang, K. (2017). *Narrowband Internet of Things* (Vol. 5). IEEE Access.

Chen, M., Qian, Y., Hao, Y., Li, Y., & Song, J. (2018, February). Data-driven computing and caching in 5G networks: Architecture and delay analysis. *IEEE Wireless Communications, 25*(1), 70–75. doi:10.1109/MWC.2018.1700216

Chen, M., Tian, Y., Fortino, G., Zhang, J., & Humar, I. (2018). Cognitive Internet of vehicles. *Computer Communications, 120*, 58–70. Advance online publication. doi:10.1016/j.comcom.2018.02.006

Chen, M., Yang, J., Zhu, X., Wang, X., Liu, M., & Song, J. (2017, December). Smart home 2.0: Innovative smart home system powered by botanical IoT and emotion detection. *Mobile Networks and Applications*, *22*(6), 1159–1169. doi:10.100711036-017-0866-1

Chen, M., Zhou, P., & Fortino, G. (2017). *Emotion communication system* (Vol. 5). IEEE Access.

Fasel, B., & Luettin, J. (2003, January). Automatic facial expression analysis: A survey. *Pattern Recognition*, *36*(1), 259–275. doi:10.1016/S0031-3203(02)00052-3

Fernández, A. (2014). Big data with cloud computing: An insight on the computing environment, mapreduce, and programming frameworks. *Wiley Interdiscipl. Rev. Data Mining and Knowledge Discovery*, *4*(5).

Gudivada, V. N. (2016). *Cognitive computing: Concepts, architectures, systems, and Applications* (Vol. 35). Handbook Stat.

Han, D.-M., & Lim, J.-H. (2010, August). Smart home energy management system using IEEE 802.15.4 and ZigBee. *IEEE Transactions on Consumer Electronics*, *56*(3), 1403–1410. doi:10.1109/TCE.2010.5606276

Hao, Y., Chen, M., Hu, L., Song, J., Volk, M., & Humar, I. (2017). Wireless fractal ultra-dense cellular networks. *Sensors (Basel)*, *17*(4), 841. doi:10.339017040841 PMID:28417927

Hurwitz, Kaufman, & Bowles. (2015). Cognitive Computing and Big Data Analytics. Wiley.

Hwang, K., & Chen, M. (2017). *Big-Data Analytics for Cloud, IoT and Cognitive Learning*. Wiley.

Jin, Gubbi, Marusic, & Palaniswami. (2014). An information framework for creating a smart city through the Internet of Things. *IEEE IoT J.*, *1*(2).

Lake, B. M., Salakhutdinov, R., & Tenenbaum, J. B. (2015). Human-level concept learning through probabilistic program induction. *Science*, *350*(6266), 1332–1338. doi:10.1126cience.aab3050 PMID:26659050

Le, Q. V. (2013). Building high-level features using large scale unsupervised learning. *Proc. IEEE Int. Conf. Acoust., Speech Signal Process. (ICASSP)*. 10.1109/ICASSP.2013.6639343

Mundt, P. D. (2000). Why We Feel: The Science of Human Emotions (vol. 157). Academic Press.

Nam, T., & Pardo, T. A. (2011). Conceptualizing smart city with dimensions of technology, people, and institutions. *Proc. ACM Int. Digit. Government Res. Conf., Digit. Government Innov. Challenging Times.* 10.1145/2037556.2037602

Ogiela, L. (2010). Cognitive informatics in automatic pattern understanding and cognitive information systems. Advances in Cognitive Informatics and Cognitive Computing, 323.

Sanchez, L., Muñoz, L., Galache, J. A., Sotres, P., Santana, J. R., Gutierrez, V., Ramdhany, R., Gluhak, A., Krco, S., Theodoridis, E., & Pfisterer, D. (2014, March). SmartSantander: IoT experimentation over a smart city testbed. *Computer Networks*, *61*, 217–238. doi:10.1016/j.bjp.2013.12.020

Sheth, A. (2016, March). Internet of Things to smart IoT through semantic, cognitive, and perceptual computing. *IEEE Intelligent Systems*, *31*(2), 108–112. doi:10.1109/MIS.2016.34

Silver, D., Huang, A., Maddison, C. J., Guez, A., Sifre, L., van den Driessche, G., Schrittwieser, J., Antonoglou, I., Panneershelvam, V., Lanctot, M., Dieleman, S., Grewe, D., Nham, J., Kalchbrenner, N., Sutskever, I., Lillicrap, T., Leach, M., Kavukcuoglu, K., Graepel, T., & Hassabis, D. (2016). Mastering the game of go with deep neural networks and tree search. *Nature*, *529*(7587), 484–489. doi:10.1038/nature16961 PMID:26819042

Su, K., Li, J., & Fu, H. (2011). Smart city and the applications. *Proc. IEEE Int. Conf. Electron., Commun. Control (ICECC).* 10.1109/ICECC.2011.6066743

Tian, D., Zhou, J., & Sheng, Z. (2017, May). An adaptive fusion strategy for distributed information estimation over cooperative multi-agent networks. *IEEE Transactions on Information Theory*, *63*(5), 1. doi:10.1109/TIT.2017.2674678

Tian, D., Zhou, J., Sheng, Z., & Leung, V. (2016, June). Robust energy-efficient Mimo transmission for cognitive vehicular networks. *IEEE Transactions on Vehicular Technology*, *65*(6), 3845–3859. doi:10.1109/TVT.2016.2567062

Xiong, Z., Sheng, H., Rong, W. G., & Cooper, D. E. (2012). Intelligent transportation systems for smart cities: A progress review. *Science China*, *55*(12), 2908–2914. doi:10.100711432-012-4725-1

Zhang, Y., Chen, M., Guizani, N., Wu, D., & Leung, V. C. (2017). SOVCAN: Safety-oriented vehicular controller area network. *IEEE Communications Magazine*, *55*(8), 94–99. doi:10.1109/MCOM.2017.1601185

Zhang, Y., Qiu, M., Tsai, C.-W., Hassan, M. M., & Alamri, A. (2017, March). HealthCPS: Healthcare cyber-physical system assisted by cloud and big data. *IEEE Systems Journal, 11*(1), 88–95. doi:10.1109/JSYST.2015.2460747

Zhou. (n.d.). QoE-driven delay announcement for cloud mobile media. *IEEE Trans. Circuits Syst. Video Technol., 27*(1).

Zhou, L. (2016, May). On data-driven delay estimation for media cloud. *IEEE Transactions on Multimedia, 18*(5), 905–915. doi:10.1109/TMM.2016.2537782

Chapter 10
Performance Analysis of Pre-Trained Convolutional Models for Brain Tumor Classification

Rishabh Chauhan
Amity University, India

Garima Aggarwal
Amity University, India

ABSTRACT

Brain tumor is a common tumor and is damaging depending upon the type of tumor and the stage at which it is diagnosed. It is revealed by a doctor using magnetic resonance imaging of the brain. Analyzing these images is an exacting task, and human intervention might be a scope of error. Therefore, applying deep learning-based image classification systems can play a crucial role in classifying several tumors. This chapter aims to implement, analyze, and compare pre-trained convolutional neural network models and a proposed neural architecture to classify brain tumors. The dataset includes 7000 images classified into four classes of tumors: glioma, meningioma, no tumor, and pituitary. The proposed methodology involves cautious analysis of data and the development of a deep learning model. This has produced testing results with high accuracy of 99.0% and an error rate of 6.8%. According to the experimental findings, the proposed method for classifying brain tumors has a respectable level of accuracy and a low error rate, making it an appropriate tool for use in real-time applications.

DOI: 10.4018/978-1-6684-6980-4.ch010

INTRODUCTION

Deep Learning is a blooming field of machine learning that is used almost everywhere, from speech recognition and facial recognition to self-driving cars. It aims at mimicking the functioning and decision-making ability of the human brain. One of its prominent applications is in healthcare. Its ability to solve highly exacting and extremely complex problems makes it a significant asset to the healthcare and medical industry. An example of such a complex and high accuracy demanding problem is the detection and classification of brain tumors. Because they can press on or spread into healthy areas of the brain, brain tumors are harmful. Additionally, some brain tumors have the potential to develop into cancer (Zülch, K. J., 2013).

They may be problematic if they obstruct fluid movement around the brain since this may raise the pressure inside the skull. Certain malignancies have the potential to travel through the spinal fluid to distant regions of the brain or spine. Any portion of the brain or skull can develop a brain tumor, including the brain's protective coating, the base of the head, the brainstem, the sinuses, the nasal cavity, and many other places. Depending on the tissue from which they originate, the brain can develop any one of more than 120 distinct tumor forms. Generally, tumors are of two types malignant (cancerous) and benign (non-cancerous) tumors, and for this chapter, we will discuss only the primary three brain tumors: glioma, meningioma, and pituitary. Inside the brain and certain areas of spinal cord, a peculiar kind of glioma is observed. Meningioma develops from the meninges, the membranes that cover the brain and spinal cord. It is included in this group even if it is not strictly a brain tumor since it might compress or pressure the nearby brain, nerves, or blood vessels (Lanktree, C., & Briere, J., 1991).

Diagnoses of the tumor generally consist of a neurological exam and image testing. A neurological exam is a basic test in which a doctor checks a patient's abilities like hearing, vision, coordination, and strength; any problem in these abilities gives the doctor a clue of which kind of tumor it may be (Alqudah, A. M., et al., 2020). Brain cancers are frequently diagnosed using brain images with magnetic resonance imaging (MRI). MRI gives a detailed and greyscale image of the internal organs of the human body. A doctor analyses the brain MRI scans and diagnoses whether a patient has a tumor or not. This procedure may seem easy theoretically, but it is a highly complex task when performed practically, as there is a vast scope of human errors. This pool of errors was considered and was attempted to eliminate with the help of machine learning (ML) and deep learning (DL) techniques. Deep learning is a sub-field of machine learning which works on algorithms and models that mimic the human brain. That can be achieved with the help of neural networks with three or more layers, which aim to solve extremely abstruse problems (Alzubaidi, L., et al., 2021).

Convolutional Neural Network (CNN) is a trendy, state-of-the-art neural network widely used in the medical industry to diagnose diseases using CT and MRI scans. It is a robust image recognition algorithm that can extract features from an image and convert them into low dimensions without losing their features. Its architecture generally consists of an input layer (input image), a convolutional layer responsible for extracting features from the picture, a pooling layer that aims to reduce computational costs, and a fully connected layer used to join neurons in two different layers (Aggarwal, G. et al, 2020). Machine learning approaches to classify brain tumors through image recognition are made possible due to advancements in technology and algorithms. The use of Support vector machines (SVM) and decision trees yielded results that were not promising enough. Applying deep learning and neural networks like CNN for brain tumor categorization produced fascinating results (Bharati, P., et al., 2020).

A machine learning technique called transfer learning allows a model that has been trained for one task to be optimized for another, related activity. Because the knowledge gained from the original work can serve as a solid foundation for learning the new assignment, this enables the model to use its current knowledge and improve performance on the new task. In deep learning applications, transfer learning is frequently used to optimize huge, previously trained models for tasks like image classification or natural language processing. With less data and processing resources required, it can train more efficient models thanks to transfer learning.

Machine learning models that have already been trained on a sizable dataset and are prepared to be utilized for making predictions on new data are known as pre-trained models. These models are often created by sizable organizations, such as tech businesses or research institutes, and made accessible for usage by others, either for free or at a cost.

Pre-trained models have various advantages over models created from the ground up. First off, since they have already been trained on a sizable dataset, they can already generate good predictions without the user having to collect and classify a lot of training data.

This chapter's key contribution is reproducing the work on brain tumor classification by introducing a neural architecture along with the aid of pre-trained CNN models. It also suggests an automated, deep learning-based smart healthcare system that may be effectively used by doctors and other healthcare professionals to classify brain tumors accurately. A deep artificial neural network model that can accurately classify brain cancers will be presented in this study. A comparative analysis of several pre-trained models, including VGG-16, EfficientNetB0, EfficientNetB7, ResNet50, and InceptionV3, on a dataset of 7000 MRI scans gathered from an online open-source repository is another addition of this chapter.

This chapter briefly discusses various assessment metrics of the model being utilized and their accompanying significances to better evaluate and comprehend the presented models. The minimal comparative computation and low error rate of the pre-trained model used in the proposed study are further important contributions.

LITERATURE REVIEW

Some pertinent pre-existing research pertaining to the classification and segmentation of brain tumors has been covered in this section. Using a modified version of AlexNet CNN, Khawaldeh, Saed, et al. suggested a technique for non-invasive grading of glioma brain tumors. The categorization was performed using whole-brain MRI scans, and the labels were applied at the picture level rather than the pixel level. The experimental findings revealed that the approach performed relatively well, with an accuracy of 91.16% (Khawaldeh, Saed, et al., 2017).

According to the data, they attain an accuracy rate of 96.97% and a sensitivity rate of 97.0%, Mohsen, Heba, and colleagues offer a system that combines DWT characteristics with identifying brain cancers using the fuzzy c-mean approach to segment the brain tumor. For each detected lesion, the DWT was used to extract the features, which were then given into the principal component analysis (PCA) for feature dimension reduction before being fed to deep neural networks (DNN) (Mohsen, H., et al., 2018).

Cheng, Jun, et al. improved the effectiveness of the brain tumor classification procedure by using augmentation (ROI) as well as precise RF (ring-form) partitioning. These improvements were applied on respective feature extraction methods where the feature vectors are used as an input to the classifier. The testing findings revealed that the accuracy of the intensity histogram, GLCM, and BoW increased from 71.39% to 78.18%, 83.54% to 87.54%, and 89.72% to 91.28%, respectively (Cheng, J., et al., 2015).

J.Seetha, et al. developed a system for diagnosing and grading brain tumor. This technique uses fuzzy C-means to partition the brain. Texture and form characteristics were retrieved from these segmented areas before being fed into SVM and DNN classifiers. The findings indicated that the system has a 97.5% accuracy rate (Seetha, J., & Raja, S. S., 2018).

Ali Mohammad Alqudah, et al. presented a paper on brain tumor classification in which they used their proposed CNN architecture to compare cropped, uncropped, and segmented lesion images, their architecture consists of 18 neural layers to achieve an overall accuracy of 98% (Alqudah, A. M., et al., 2020). Table 1. Summarizes the results of the models used by respective authors.

Table 1. Literature Summary

Author	Classifier	Accuracy (%)
Khawaldeh, Saed, et al., 2017	AlexNet CNN	91.16
Mohsen, H., et al., 2018	DNN	96.97
Cheng, J., et al., 2015	Intensity Histogram GLCM BoW	78.18 83.54 91.28
Seetha, J., & Raja, S. S., 2018	SVM and DNN	97.5
Alqudah, A. M., et al., 2020	CNN	98

MATERIALS AND METHODOLOGY

Dataset

The dataset for developing a deep learning model for brain tumor classification is the foundation for this comparative study. This dataset is acquired from Kaggle, an online community for data scientists and a subsidiary of Google LLC. There are in total 7,023 comprehensive human brain MRI images that are classified into four categories: glioma, meningioma, pituitary, and no tumor. These images are captured from two views, top, and bottom, to bring some variability to the data.

Table 2. Summary of the dataset

Category	Count of images
Glioma	1,621
Meningioma	1,645
Pituitary	1,757
No tumor	2,000
Total	7.023

The Table 2 above represents a quick summary of the dataset. There are almost 1600-2000 images in each class labeled Glioma, Meningioma, Pituitary, no tumor.

Figure 1 given below shows the MRI scans of different classes of tumors that are present in the dataset, there are 4 images (a), (b), (c), and (d) showing Glioma tumor, Meningioma tumor, pituitary tumor, and no tumor respectively.

Figure 1. Magnetic Resonance Imaging of human brain

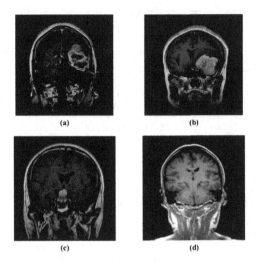

Pre-Trained Models and Transfer Learning

Pre-trained models are used to achieve the objective of this paper. These are simply the models trained on a similar input type to solve a similar problem. It is essential to choose the correct pre-trained model. The most significant benefit of a pre-trained model is that it produces better results and accuracy while being efficient and less time-consuming. The weight and architecture retrieved from the pre-trained model are directly applied to solving other problems. By using the labeled data that has already been collected for a task that is similar to another problem, transfer learning enables us to handle them (You, K., Liu, et al., 2021). An effort can be made to keep this information learned from completing the original assignment in the original domain and apply it to the situation. The main reason for using transfer learning is to reduce the computational power and eliminate model creation from scratch. A part and a task are notions that are involved in transfer learning (Liu, B., et al, 2021). A feature space X and a marginal probability distribution P(X) over the feature space make up a domain D, where:

$$X = x_1, \ldots, x_n \in X \tag{1}$$

X is the space containing all document representations, x_i is the i-th term vector corresponding to a specific copy, and X is the training sample of documents when categorizing documents using a bag-of-words representation (Aggarwal, G. et al, 2022). Task T comprises a label space Y, and a conditional probability distribution

P(X|Y) that is commonly acquired through training data made up of pairings of $x_i \in X$, and $y_i \in Y$. Task T is given a domain (Samma, H., &Suandi, S. A., 2020),

$$D=\{X,P(X)\}y \qquad (2)$$

There are many advantages to using transfer learning and pre-trained models. One of the main benefits is that it can save time and computational resources. Training a machine learning model from scratch can be time consuming and computationally intensive, especially when dealing large datasets. Much of this work has already been done using a pre-trained model, and the model can be fine-tuned for the new task relatively quickly.

Another advantage of transfer learning is that it can improve the model's performance on the new task. Because the pre-trained model has already learned to recognize a wide variety of features, it can provide a good starting point for the new task. This can help the model learn more quickly and perform better than if trained from scratch on the new task.

Additionally, transfer learning addresses the problem of limited data availability. In many cases, there may be a requirement for more data available to train a machine-learning model from scratch. In these situations, transfer learning can be a helpful approach, as it allows the model to leverage the knowledge gained from a larger dataset in order to perform well on the new task.

There are primarily two applications for transfer learning. The pre-trained model serves as a fixed feature extractor in the first method. In this instance, just the final classification layer is trained on the new dataset; the weights of the pre-trained model are left unchanged. This enables the model to draw on the pre-trained model's understanding of broad features while also learning task-specific features from the fresh data. The weights of the entire model are adjusted on the fresh dataset using the pre-trained model as a starting point in the second method. This enables the model to retain part of the knowledge from the pre-trained model while still being able to adapt to the specific peculiarities of the incoming data.

Transfer learning, where pre-trained models are frequently utilized as the foundation for new models, makes use of transfer learning particularly well. These pre-trained models, like the well-known ImageNet model, were trained on substantial datasets and can serve as a solid starting point for learning new jobs. With less data and processing resources, it is possible to train more efficient models via transfer learning.

Figure 2. The architecture of VGG-16

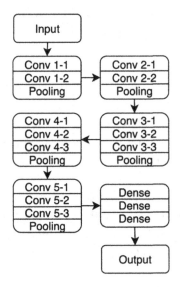

VGG-16

A ConvNet is another convolutional neural network, which is a type of artificial neural network. A convolutional neural network comprises of an input layer, an output layer, and a variety of hidden layers. VGG-16 pre-trained model consists of 16 weighted layers. Also, there are 13 convolutional layers, 5 max pooling layers, and 3 dense layers making up a total of 21-layer VGG-16. (Figure 2). Still, only 16 are weight layers, also known as learnable parameters layers (Ghosh, S., et al., 2021). VGG-16 puts more emphasis on having neural layers of 3x3 filter with stride 1 rather instead of a lot of hyper-parameters. Stride 2 always employs the same padding and maximum pool layer of a 2x2 filter. The max pool and convolution layers are arranged consistently throughout the architecture. A stack of convolutional layers is followed by three Fully Connected (FC) layers, the third of which conducts 1000-way ILSVRC classification and has 1000 channels (Qassim, H., et al., 2018). Figure 2 is the general architecture of the VGG-16 model representing the arrangement of different types of convolutional layer, pooling layer, and dense layer, etc.

In addition to its simplicity and depth, the VGG-16 model also uses a large amount of data for training. The model was trained on the ImageNet dataset, which consists of over 1 million images. This large dataset allows the model to learn rich and robust features from the data, which helps to improve its performance on the classification task. Overall, the VGG-16 model is a robust convolutional neural network that has achieved state-of-the-art performance on the ImageNet classification task. It's simple and uniform architecture and its use of a large dataset for training have allowed it to achieve impressive results.

The VGG-16 model achieved state-of-the-art performance on the ImageNet classification task when it was first introduced in 2014. This impressive performance demonstrates the effectiveness of the model's architecture and training data. The VGG-16 model can be used as a starting point for other image classification tasks. The pre-trained model can be fine-tuned on a new dataset, allowing the model to learn new features that are specific to the new task. This can save time and resources compared to training a new model from scratch.

EfficientNet

EfficientNet is a family of convolutional neural network models that were developed by Google Research. These models were designed to produce high performance on a variety of tasks, while using significantly fewer parameters and FLOPS (floating-point operations) than other state-of-the-art models. This makes EfficientNet models more efficient in terms of both memory and computational resources, while still achieving excellent performance. It is the latest and most advanced pre-trained model producing comparatively best accuracies for classification tasks.

EfficientNet is a CNN design and sizing method which scales resolution dimensions by incorporating a specific coefficient. In contrast to traditional practices, which scales breadth, resolution, etc. randomly, EfficientNet scaling method uses a set of predetermined scaling coefficients to uniformly scale the mentioned variables. Network width, depth, and resolution are all uniformly scaled by EfficientNet using a compound Coefficient ϕ (Tan, M., et al., 2019).

The rationale behind the compound scaling method is that larger input images necessitate more channels and layers in the network to catch more fine-grained patterns on the larger image. The earlier models, like ResNet, adopt the traditional strategy of arbitrary scaling of the dimensions and layer addition. The approach in EfficientNet states that if a fixed amount uniformly scales the dimensions, better performance is achieved. Two types of EfficientNet were used, namely, EfficientNetN0 and EfficientNetB7. Table 3 gives a detailed architecture of EfficientNetB0 showing its different convolution layers their resolutions, channels, and layers.

This network's primary structural component is MBConv, into which squeeze-and-excitation optimization is incorporated. The inverted residual blocks used in Mobile-Net v2 are comparable to MB Conv which provide a direct link from the beginning to the end of the CNN block. 1x1 convolutions are initially used to enlarge the input activation maps that improves the depth of the expected maps. Following this, 3x3 Depth-wise and Point-wise convolutions are used to cut down on the number of channels in the resulting feature map. The broader layers are

Table 3. Summary of EfficientNetB0 architecture

Stage	Operator	Resolution	Channels	Layers
1	Conv 3x3	224224	32	1
2	MBConv1,k3x3	112112	16	1
3	MBConv6,k3x3	112112	24	2
4	MBConv6,k5x5	5656	40	2
5	MBConv6,k3x3	2828	80	3
6	MBConv6,k5x5	1414	112	3
7	MBConv6,k5x5	1414	192	4
8	MBConv6,k3x3	77	320	1
9	Conv1x1 & Pooling & FC	77	1280	1

between the skip connections, while the short-cut connections link the light levels. This structure aids in reducing both the total number of operations needed and the model's size (Nayak, D. R., et al., 2022). The resolutions remain the same in both B0 and B7, but the number of layers is drastically increased from B0 to B7. Hence B7 takes more computational time than B0.

ResNet50

The building block of ResNets, referred to as a residual block, is based on the idea of "skip-connections" and extensively uses batch-normalization to train hundreds of layers over time without degrading speed successfully (Theckedath, D., et al., 2020). Skip Connection was first introduced by ResNet it is also depicted in figure 3. The different CNN layers are put on top of each other in the figure at the left, whereas figure on the right is incorporating a skip connection by using the initial input at the output of the CNN layers.

This allows models to form an identity function that ensures that the topmost layer will perform equivalent or even better than the bottom layer. With more neural layers, ResNet increases the effectiveness of deep neural networks while reducing the error rate. The Resnet-34 was the first ResNet architecture, and it included inserting short-cut connections to transform a plain network into an equivalent residual network. ResNets, however, are more straightforward and contain fewer filters than VGGNets (Rezende, E., et al., 2017).

This primary network now has short-cut connections. The identity short-cuts were employed directly even though the input and out-put dimensions were the same. There were two possibilities to consider as the size increased. The first was that the short-cut would still perform identity mapping while additional zero entries would be padded to account for growing dimensions. The projection short-cut to matching dimensions was the alternative.

Figure 3. Skip connection flow diagram

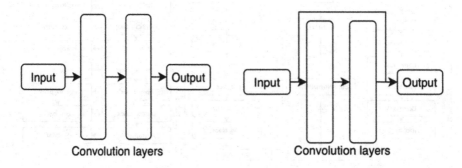

Figure 4. Detailed skip connection

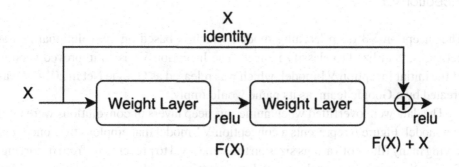

Figure 4 is representing a detailed diagram of skip connection along with weight layer and use of RELU activation functions. Resnet50 architecture is based on the concept mentioned above. However, there is one significant distinction. Due to worries about the time required to train the layers, the building block was changed into a bottleneck design in this instance. Instead of the preceding two layers, this utilized a stack of 3 (Mukti, I. Z., & Biswas, D., 2019).

Figure 5 is representing a complete architecture of ResNet50. The input image is processed through 6 neural layers, 7 iterations of identity block containing 3 sets of convolutions, batch normalization, and activation layers, and 4 iteration of convolution block containing similar arrangement of neural layers as identity block.

Figure 5. The architecture of ResNet50

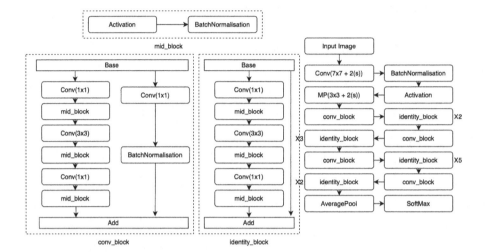

InceptionV3

The Inception V3 deep learning model, which is based on convolutional neural networks, is utilized to classify images. The Inception V3 is an improved version of the initial Inception V1 model, which was released as Google Net in 2014. It was created by a Google team, as its name would imply.

The data were overfitted when numerous deep layers of convolutions were used in a model. Figure 6 represents a conception V1 model that employs the concept of having many filters of various sizes on the same level to prevent this from occurring. Thus, in the inception models, parallel layers are used in place of deep layers, making the model larger rather than deeper (Szegedy, C., et al., 2016).

The Inception V1 model has simply been upgraded and improved into the Inception V3 model. It used a variety of techniques to optimize the network for better model adaptation. In comparison to the Inception V1 and V2 models, it is more efficient, has a deeper network but maintains the same speed, costs less to calculate, and uses auxiliary Classifiers as a regularize. The number of layers in V3 is a bit higher than the previous inception V1 and V2 models (Szegedy, C., et al., 2015). However, the efficiency of this model is awe-inspiring. The table 4 given below represents the architecture of inceptionv3.

The Inception V1 model has simply been upgraded and improved into the Inception V3 model. It used a variety of techniques to optimize the network for better model adaptation. In comparison to the Inception V1 and V2 models, it is more efficient, has a deeper network but maintains the same speed, costs less to calculate, and uses

Figure 6. Modified Neural architecture of inceptionV1

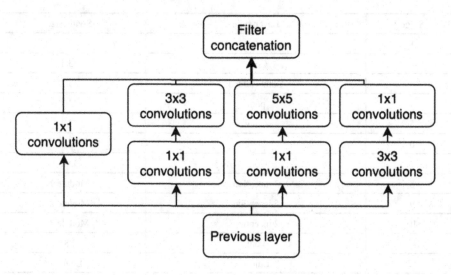

auxiliary Classifiers as a regularize. The number of layers in V3 is a bit higher than the previous inception V1 and V2 models (Szegedy, C., et al., 2015). However, the efficiency of this model is awe-inspiring. The table 4 given below represents the architecture of inceptionv3. The network of the InceptionV3 architecture is made up of several inception modules stacked on top of one another. The input image's resolution is decreased, and low-level characteristics are extracted from it by a series of convolutional and pooling layers in the network's first layer, known as the stem layer. Several block-organized inception modules are placed after the stem layer. Each block is made up of some inception modules that are linked to one another via parallel branches. These branches capture various facets of the input data at various scales, including spatial details, textures, and patterns. Each block's output is subsequently routed via a pooling layer, which lowers its spatial resolution and increases its translation invariance.

As a result, the network can pick up on more ethereal aspects that are not dependent on the precise placement of objects in the input image. The classification layer, the top layer of the network, creates a probability distribution over the classes in the training dataset using a softmax activation function. The network is trained to reduce the cross-entropy loss between the accurate distribution of the classes in the training data and the predicted probability distribution. Overall, it has been demonstrated that the InceptionV3 architecture achieves state-of-the-art performance on many benchmarks, making it a strong and effective model for picture categorization. Applications in computer vision, such as object detection, and recognition, are particularly well-suited to it.

Table 4. Summary of InceptionV3 architecture

Stage	Layer type	Stride size
1	Conv	33/2
2	Conv	33/1
3	Conv Padded	33/1
4	pool	33/2
5	Conv	33/1
6	Conv	33/2
7	Conv	33/1
8	3 inception	Module 1
9	5 inception	Module 2
10	2 inception	Module 3
11	Pool	88
12	Linear	Logits
13	Soft-max	Classifier

Proposed Architecture

This section contains a comprehensive study of the proposed neural architecture for improved brain tumor classification and the methodology followed to receive a successful model development. A new CNN architecture is proposed and implemented. This architecture consists of 7 layers that are common for all pre-trained models. It is necessary to keep in mind that all the implemented pre-trained models have their own set of neural layers. For example, VGG-16 already consists of 16 layers, and incep-tionv3 consists of 42 layers. So, the number of neural layers in the pre-trained models is variable, but all have seven common external layers. Two dense layers with rectified linear unit (RELU) activation function and final dense layers with four units (4 classes) with a Soft-max activation. There is a set of pooling and a dropout layer after the RELU activation dense layer. First set consists of a Max2D pooling layer with a dropout layer having rate of 0.25. The next set consists of a GlobalAverage2D pooling layer and a dropout rate of 0.5 (Sharma, S., et al., 2017).

Dropout layer is employed in proposed architecture to avoid overfitting. This is accomplished by a predefined number of neurons being randomly dropped out or ignored while training. In order to avoid overfitting, this requires the network to learn numerous distinct representations of the data rather than leaning too heavily on any one neuron. Dropout is a powerful regularization method that can greatly enhance the functionality of your neural network. It is a straightforward yet effective

Table 5. Summary of proposed architecture

Layer	Type	Output Shape	Parameters
dense	Dense (64)	(None, 5, 5, 64)	81984
max_pooling2d	MaxPooling2D	(None, 2, 2, 64)	0
dropout	Dropout (0.25)	(None, 2, 2, 64)	0
dense_1	Dense (64)	(None, 2, 2, 64)	4160
Global_average_pooling_2d	GlobalAveragePooling	(None, 64)	0
dropout_1	Dropout (0.5)	(None, 64)	0
dense_2	Dense (4)	(None, 4)	260

method for lowering overfitting and enhancing the generalizability of your model. Table 5 shows the different neural layers used to develop the model. It also shows the output shape and parameters at each layer.

Softmax is a generalization of the logistic function, frequently used to handle many classes in binary classification problems. The softmax activation function takes a vector of real-valued inputs and outputs a vector of values between 0 and 1 that sum to 1. This output can be interpreted as a probability distribution over the classes; the predicted class has the highest probability. The critical property of the softmax function is that it squashes the inputs to the range [0, 1] and normalizes them so that they sum to 1. This makes it possible to interpret the outputs as probabilities and allows the network to make predictions based on the class with the highest probability.

The rectified linear unit (ReLU) activation function is a standard function. Its formula is $f(x) = \max(0, x)$, where x is the activation function's input. Compared to other activation functions like the sigmoid or "tanh" functions, the ReLU activation function provides some advantages. Its simplicity and ease of computation make it effective in a neural network, which is one advantage. Another benefit is that it is non-saturating, which means that, unlike the sigmoid and "tanh" functions, its output does not become flat for significant inputs. This can assist in preventing the vanishing gradients issue, which makes it challenging for a network to learn. Additionally non-linear, the ReLU activation function is required for a neural network to model complex data. Additionally, the function is zero for negative inputs, which might provide sparsity to the network and enhance its performance.

Convolutional neural networks frequently employ intermediate layers and global average pooling (CNNs). By reducing the input's spatial dimensions, both layers can help the network run more efficiently and with less computing complexity. A particular kind of pooling layer called average pooling computes the average value for each zone after dividing the input into several non-overlapping parts. Substituting a single value for each region in the input lowers the spatial dimensions of the input, which can help the network run more efficiently and with fewer parameters.

On the other hand, global average pooling determines the average value of all input values, independent of their spatial locations. This lowers the input's spatial dimensions to a single value, which helps streamline the network and increase its effectiveness. In the last layers of a CNN, following the convolutional and pooling layers, average pooling and global average pooling can both be used to minimize the spatial dimensions of the output and make it simpler to use the output for classification or other tasks.

The model is not trained on default arguments. The validation split is 10%, and the entire dataset is passed forward and backward through the neural network 30 times (epoch=30). The callback "Reduce learning rate on plateau" helps the model by lowering its learning rate by a certain amount. This callback keeps track of a specific quantity, and the learning rate is decreased if the amount doesn't improve after a certain number of epochs.

Figure 7. Proposed architecture

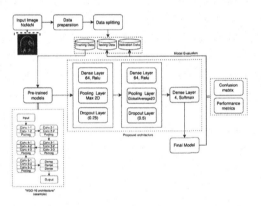

Performance Evaluation

To evaluate the performance of the proposed architecture and the pre-trained models on the dataset, performance metrics like accuracy, precision, loss, and f1-score are calculated. A Confusion matrix is generated for all trained models which is necessary to calculate the performance metrics.

The classification model's efficacy is evaluated using a N*N matrix, where N is the overall number of target classes, in this case four. Compare the actual goal values in the matrix to what the deep learning model predicted.

Figure 8. Elements of confusion matrix

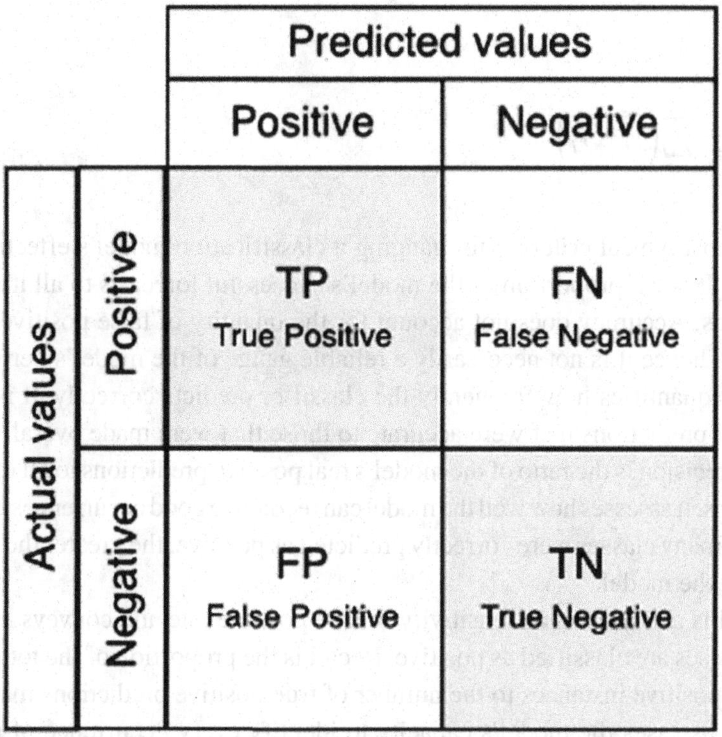

Figure 8 represents a confusion matrix that is generated from a set of actual values and a set of predicted values. There are four statistical indices in the matrix, 'True Positive' (TP), 'True Negative' (TN), 'False Positive' (FP), and 'False Negative' (FN). These indices are used to calculate the metrics like.

$$Accuracy = \frac{TP + TN}{TP + TN + FN + FP} \tag{3}$$

$$Recall = \frac{TP}{TP + FN} \tag{4}$$

$$Precision = \frac{TP}{TP + FP} \tag{5}$$

$$F1\,score = 2 \times \left(\frac{Precision \times Recall}{Precision + Recall} \right) \tag{6}$$

$$MSE = \frac{1}{N} \sum_{i=1}^{N} \left(\widehat{y}_i - \widehat{y}_i \right)^2 \tag{7}$$

The most typical criterion for gauging a classification model's effectiveness is accuracy. It is the proportion of the model's successful forecasts to all its previous predictions. Accuracy does not account for the quantity of false positives or false negatives; hence it is not necessarily a reliable gauge of the model's performance. Accuracy quantifies how frequently the classifier predicts correctly. It is the proportion of predictions that were accurate to those that were made overall.

The precision is the ratio of the model's real positive predictions to all its positive predictions. It assesses how well the model can recognize good occurrences. Precision tells how many classes were correctly predicted as positive, the greater the precision the better the model.

Recall is also known as sensitivity or true positive rate and conveys how many actual classes are classified as positive. Recall is the proportion of the total number of actual positive instances to the number of true positive predictions made by the model. It assesses the model's capacity to identify every occurrence of positivity included in the data. It is recommended to be higher.

F1-score is the harmonic mean of precision and recall and is better when close to 1. Mean square error (MSE) is the average squared loss of the model over the entire dataset. It is important that loss should be minimum for the better results of the model (Novaković, J. D., et al., 2017).

RESULTS

This section presents the results generated after following the methodology explained in the previous section. The use of pre-trained models and proposed neural architecture for classifying brain tumors has shown to be a promising approach. These models can effectively learn and identify complex patterns in medical imaging data, leading to improved accuracy in tumor classification. Additionally, the use of transfer learning techniques can further fine-tune the models for specific tasks, such as identifying the type and location of a tumor.

All the models were trained on the given dataset under the same circumstances on the google Collaboratory research platform using the TensorFlow graphic processing unit for fast computation. The dataset was divided into three sections, training, testing, and evaluation with percentages of 80%, 10%, and 10% respectively. The training set is utilized to fit the model, the validation set is used to fine-tune the model's hyperparameters, and the test set is used to assess the model's effectiveness. The model is fitted using the training data, which entails changing the model's weights to reduce the difference between the anticipated and actual values. The model's hyperparameters, such as the learning rate and the number of hidden units, are tuned using the validation set. This is significant because the hyperparameters' selection can significantly impact the model's performance.

As mentioned previously the entire dataset was passed forward and backward through the models 30 times. Performance metrics like accuracy, loss, precision, f1-score, and sensitivity (recall) are calculated using the confusion matrix, generated from VGG-16, Resnet50, EfficientNetB0, EfficientNetB7, and InceptionV3. Figure 9 represents the confusion matrices of the implemented pre-trained models, where (a), (b), (c), (d), (e) represents the confusion matrices of VGG-16, EfficientNetB0, ResNet50, EfficientNetB7, InceptionV3 respectively.

COMPARATIVE ANALYSIS

This section provides an in-depth comparison and analysis of the results produced by the used pre-trained CNN models. Comparative analysis of classification models aims to assess the performance of various models on a specific classification job and identify the optimal model for the given data and use case. The first stage in comparing categorization models is to decide which models will be examined. Order to assess the effectiveness of each model type, this may entail choosing a variety of alternative model types, such as decision trees, support vector machines, or neural networks.

The chosen models are then trained on identical data and assessed using the same criteria. The performance of classification models is frequently assessed using measures including accuracy, precision, recall, and f1-score, which can be one of these metrics.

The analytical results are compared after the models have been trained and evaluated to decide which model performs the best on the given classification job. It may be necessary to compare each model's precision and recall for various classes and its overall accuracy.

Finally, a choice can be made on which model is the best for the specific classification task at hand based on the comparative study findings. The accuracy, precision, and recall of each model, the computational difficulty, and other elements pertinent to the particular use case may all impact this choice. VGG-16 had an accuracy

Figure 9. Confusion matrices generated from models

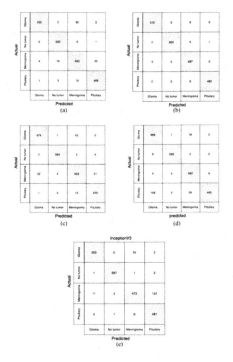

of 92 percent, loss (MSE) of 0.3, being 92 percent precise, f1-score of 92 percent, and a sensitivity of 92 percent as well. InceptionV3 had an accuracy of 98 percent, a loss of 0.1, a precision of 97 percent, an f1-score of 97 percent, and a sensitivity of 97 percent as well. ResNet50 had an accuracy, precision, f1-score, a sensitivity of 94 percent, and a loss of 0.1. EfficientNetB7 had an accuracy, precision, and f1-score of 96 percent, a loss of 0.18, and a sensitivity of 95 percent. EfficientNetB0 had the highest accuracy of 99 percent with a loss of 0.06. EfficientNetB0 had a precision, an f1-score of 99 percent, and a sensitivity of 98 percent. Table 6 shows a tabulated summary of the pre-trained models and their respective performance metrics

CONCLUSION

In this work, the proposed neural network alongside the advanced pre-trained models have been successfully implemented and compared to classify brain tumors as Glioma, Meningioma, Pituitary, and no tumor. The dataset had 7,023 images for training, testing, and validation.

Table 6. Performance metrics of the models

Pre-trained model	F1-score	Sensitivity	Precision	Loss	Accuracy (%)
EfficientNetB0	0.99	0.98	0.99	0.068	99.0
InceptionV3	0.97	0.97	0.97	0.114	97.57
EfficientNetB7	0.96	0.95	0.96	0.187	96.10
VGG-16	0.92	0.92	0.92	0.316	92.16
ResNet50	0.94	0.94	0.94	0.133	94.58

The results have clearly shown that deep learning has an unremarkable application for classification purposes which can be utilized in the field of medical image classification. This work successfully provides an automated, deep learning-based smart healthcare system that may be effectively used by doctors and other healthcare professionals to classify brain tumors accurately. It also provides a better understanding of different pretrained CNN models.

The proposed architecture works extremely well with the pre-trained models giving an accuracy of above 90 percent in all models. The activation function RELU and softmax were used during the training phase of the model. The confusion matrix created clearly indicates that the number of true positives is the largest in EfficientNetB0.

With the proposed neural layer architecture and combining it with the pre-trained models EfficientNetB0 turns out to have the highest accuracy of 99.0 percent, a loss of 6.0 percent. 99 percent of classes were correctly predicted. EfficientNetB0 had a true positive rate of 99 percent. The model also had a macro and weighted average of 99 percent. It also showed a validation accuracy of 98 percent. Thus, the proposed model successfully gives a superior and novel strategy for classifying brain tumors.

ACKNOWLEDGMENT

Authors are thankful to the reviewers who have given their valuable suggestions to improve the quality of the paper.

REFERENCES

Abd-Ellah, M. K., Awad, A. I., Khalaf, A. A., & Hamed, H. F. (2019). A review on brain tumor diagnosis from MRI images: Practical implications, key achievements, and lessons learned. *Magnetic Resonance Imaging*, *61*, 300–318. doi:10.1016/j.mri.2019.05.028 PMID:31173851

Alqudah, A. M., Alquraan, H., Qasmieh, I. A., Alqudah, A., & Al-Sharu, W. (2020). *Brain tumor classification using deep learning technique--a comparison between cropped, un-cropped, and segmented lesion images with different sizes.* arXiv preprint ar-Xiv:2001.08844.

Alzubaidi, L., Zhang, J., Humaidi, A. J., Al-Dujaili, A., Duan, Y., Al-Shamma, O., Santamaría, J., Fadhel, M. A., Al-Amidie, M., & Farhan, L. (2021). Review of deep learning: Concepts, CNN architectures, challenges, ap-plications, future directions. *Journal of Big Data*, *8*(1), 1–74. doi:10.118640537-021-00444-8 PMID:33425651

Bharati, P., &Pramanik, A. (2020). Deep learning techniques—R-CNN to mask R-CNN: a survey. *Computational Intelligence in Pattern Recognition*, 657-668.

Cheng, J., Huang, W., Cao, S., Yang, R., Yang, W., Yun, Z., Wang, Z., & Feng, Q. (2015). Enhanced performance of brain tumor classification via tumor region augmentation and partition. *PLoS One*, *10*(10), e0140381. doi:10.1371/journal.pone.0140381 PMID:26447861

Dhall, I., Vashisth, S., & Aggarwal, G. (2020, January). Automated hand gesture recognition using a deep convolutional neural network model. In *2020 10th International Conference on Cloud Computing, Data Science & Engineering (Confluence)* (pp. 811-816). IEEE. 10.1109/Confluence47617.2020.9057853

Ghosh, S., Chaki, A., & Santosh, K. C. (2021). Improved U-Net architecture with VGG-16 for brain tumor segmentation. *Physical and Engineering Sciences in Medicine*, *44*(3), 703–712. doi:10.100713246-021-01019-w PMID:34047928

Khawaldeh, S., Pervaiz, U., Rafiq, A., & Alkhawaldeh, R. S. (2017). Noninvasive grading of glioma tumor using magnetic resonance imaging with convolutional neural networks. *Applied Sciences (Basel, Switzerland)*, *8*(1), 27. doi:10.3390/app8010027

Lanktree, C., & Briere, J. (1991, January). *Early data on the trauma symptom checklist for children (TSC-C)*. Paper presented at the meeting of the American Professional Society on the Abuse of Children, San Diego, CA.

Liu, B., Cai, Y., Guo, Y., & Chen, X. (2021, May). TransTailor: Pruning the pre-trained model for improved transfer learning. *Proceedings of the AAAI Conference on Artificial Intelligence*, *35*(10), 8627–8634. doi:10.1609/aaai.v35i10.17046

Mohsen, H., El-Dahshan, E. S. A., El-Horbaty, E. S. M., & Salem, A. B. M. (2018). Classification using deep learning neural networks for brain tumors. *Future Computing and Informatics Journal*, *3*(1), 68–71. doi:10.1016/j.fcij.2017.12.001

Mukti, I. Z., & Biswas, D. (2019, December). Transfer learning based plant diseases detec-tion using ResNet50. In *2019 4th International conference on electrical information and communication technology (EICT)* (pp. 1-6). IEEE.

Nayak, D. R., Padhy, N., Mallick, P. K., Zymbler, M., & Kumar, S. (2022). Brain Tumor Classification Using Dense Efficient-Net. *Axioms*, *11*(1), 34. doi:10.3390/axioms11010034

Novaković, J. D., Veljović, A., Ilić, S. S., Papić, Ž., & Milica, T. (2017). Evaluation of classification models in machine learning. *Theory and Applications of Mathematics & Computer Science*, *7*(1), 39–46.

Optimized Deep Convolutional Neural Networks for Identification of Macular Diseases from Optical Coherence Tomography Images - Scientific Figure on ResearchGate. (n.d.). Available from: https://www.researchgate.net/figure/Left-ResNet50-architectu re-Blocks-with-dotted-line-represents-modules-that-might-be_ fig3_331364877

Qassim, H., Verma, A., & Feinzimer, D. (2018, January). Compressed residual-VGG16 CNN model for big data places image recognition. In *2018 IEEE 8th annual computing and communication workshop and conference (CCWC)* (pp. 169-175). IEEE. 10.1109/CCWC.2018.8301729

Rezende, E., Ruppert, G., Carvalho, T., Ramos, F., & De Geus, P. (2017, December). Ma-licious software classification using transfer learning of resnet-50 deep neural network. In *2017 16th IEEE International Conference on Machine Learning and Applications (ICMLA)* (pp. 1011-1014). IEEE.

Roy, M. K., Aggarwal, G., Bansal, A., & Juneja, D. (2022, January). Open domain Conversational Model using transfer learning. In *2022 12th International Conference on Cloud Computing, Data Science & Engineering (Confluence)* (pp. 280-284). IEEE. 10.1109/Confluence52989.2022.9734155

Samma, H., & Suandi, S. A. (2020). Transfer Learning of Pre-Trained CNN Models for Fingerprint Liveness Detection. In Biometric Systems. IntechOpen. doi:10.5772/intechopen.93473

Seetha, J., & Raja, S. S. (2018). Brain tumor classification using convolutional neural networks. *Biomedical & Pharmacology Journal, 11*(3), 1457–1461. doi:10.13005/bpj/1511

Sharma, S., Sharma, S., &Athaiya, A. (2017). Activation functions in neural networks. *Towards Data Science, 6*(12), 310-316.]

Smirniotopoulos, J. G. (1999). The new WHO classification of brain tumors. *Neuroimaging Clinics of North America, 9*(4), 595–613. PMID:10517936

Szegedy, C., Liu, W., Jia, Y., Sermanet, P., Reed, S., Anguelov, D., ... Rabinovich, A. (2015). Going deeper with convolutions. In *Proceedings of the IEEE conference on com-puter vision and pattern recognition* (pp. 1-9). IEEE.

Szegedy, C., Vanhoucke, V., Ioffe, S., Shlens, J., & Wojna, Z. (2016). Rethinking the in-ception architecture for computer vision. In *Proceedings of the IEEE conference on computer vision and pattern recognition* (pp. 2818-2826). IEEE.

Tan, M., & Le, Q. (2019, May). Efficientnet: Rethinking model scaling for convolutional neural networks. In *International conference on machine learning* (pp. 6105-6114). PMLR.

Theckedath, D., & Sedamkar, R. R. (2020). Detecting affect states using VGG16, ResNet50 and SE-ResNet50 networks. *SN Computer Science, 1*(2), 1–7. doi:10.100742979-020-0114-9

You, K., Liu, Y., Wang, J., & Long, M. (2021, July). Logme: Practical assessment of pre-trained models for transfer learning. In *International Conference on Machine Learning* (pp. 12133-12143). PMLR.

Zülch, K. J. (2013). *Brain tumors: Their biology and pathology*. Springer-Verlag.

Compilation of References

Abd-Ellah, M. K., Awad, A. I., Khalaf, A. A., & Hamed, H. F. (2019). A review on brain tumor diagnosis from MRI images: Practical implications, key achievements, and lessons learned. Magnetic Resonance Imaging, 61, 300–318. doi:10.1016/j.mri.2019.05.028 PMID:31173851

Aberšek, B. (2018). Problem-based learning and proprioception. Cambridge Scholars Publishing.

Abramovich, F., & Grinshtein, V. (2016). Model Selection and Minimax Estimation in Generalized Linear Models. IEEE Transactions on Information Theory, 62(6), 3721–3730. doi:10.1109/TIT.2016.2555812

Adutwum, L. A., & Harynuk, J. J. (2014). Unique ion filter: A data reduction tool for GC/MS data preprocessing prior to chemometric analysis. Analytical Chemistry, 86(15), 7726–7733. doi:10.1021/ac501660a PMID:25002039

Ahamed, F., Shahrestani, S., & Cheung, H. (2020). Internet of things and machine learning for healthy ageing: Identifying the early signs of dementia. Sensors (Basel), 20(21), 6031. doi:10.3390/s20216031 PMID:33114070

Akinduko, A. A., Mirkes, E. M., & Gorban, A. N. (2016). SOM: Stochastic initialization versus principal components. Inf. Sci., 364, 213–221. doi:10.1016/j.ins.2015.10.013

Al-Shaqi, R., Mourshed, M., & Rezgui, Y. (2016). Progress in ambient assisted systems for independent living by the elderly. SpringerPlus, 5(1), 1–20. doi:10.1186/40064-016-2272-8 PMID:27330890

Allen, J., Ferguson, G., Blaylock, N., Byron, D., Chambers, N., Dzikovska, M., Galescu, L., & Swift, M. (2006). Chester: Towards a personal medication advisor. Journal of Biomedical Informatics, 39(5), 500–513. doi:10.1016/j.jbi.2006.02.004 PMID:16545620

Alqudah, A. M., Alquraan, H., Qasmieh, I. A., Alqudah, A., & Al-Sharu, W. (2020). Brain tumor classification using deep learning technique--a comparison between cropped, un-cropped, and segmented lesion images with different sizes. arXiv preprint ar-Xiv:2001.08844.

Alzheimer's Disease Facts and Figures. (2010). Rep (Vol. 6). Alzheimer's Association.

Alzubaidi, L., Zhang, J., *Humaid*i, *A. J.*, Al-Dujaili, A., Duan, Y., Al-Shamma, O., Santamaría, J., Fadhel, M. A., Al-Amidie, M., & Farhan, L. (2021). Review of deep learning: *Concepts, CNN architectures, challenges, a*p-*pl*ications, future directions. Journal of Big Data, 8(1), 1–74. doi:10.118640537-021-*00444-8 PMID:33425651*

*Amiribesheli, M., Benmansour, A., & Bouchachia, A. (2015). A review of smart homes in healthcare. Journal of Ambient Intelligence and Humanize*d Computing, 6(4), 495–517. doi:10.100712652-015-0270-2

Amunts, K., Ebell, C., Muller, J., Telefont, M., Knoll, A., & Lippert, T. (2016). The human brai*n project: Creatin*g *a* European research infrastructure to decode the human brain. Neuron, 92(3), 574–581. doi:10.1016/j.neuron.2016.10.046 PMID:27809997

Appel, A. P., Candello, H., & Gandour, F. L. (2017). Cognitive computing: *Where big data is drivi*ng us. Handbook of Big Data Technologies.

Arioli, M., & Canessa, N. (2019). Neural processing of social interaction: Coordinate-based meta-analytic evidence from human neuroimaging studies. Human Brain Mapping, 40(13*), 3712–3737. do*i:10.1002/hbm.24627 PMID:31077492

Armbrust, M. (2009). Above the clouds: A Berkeley view of cloud computing. Eecs Dept. Univ. California Berkeley, 53(4).

Arul*kumaran, K., Deisenroth, M. P.*, Brundage, M., & Bharath, A. A. (2017). Deep reinforcement learning: A bri*ef survey. IEEE Signal Processing Magazine, 34(6), 26–38. doi:10.1109/ MSP.2017.2743240*

Bal, M., Shen, W., Hao, Q., & Xue, H. (2011, June). Collaborative smart home technologies for *senior independent living: a review. In Proceedings of the 2011 15th In*ternational Conference on Computer Supported Cooperative Work in Design (CSCWD) (pp. 481-488). IEEE. 10.1109/ *CSCWD.2011.5960116*

Bartolomeo, P., & Malkinson, T. S. (2019). Hemispheric lateralization of attention processes in the human brain. Current Opinion in Psychology, 29, 90–96. doi:10.1016/j.*copsyc.2018.12.023 PMID:30711910*

Bauer, Z., Escalona, F., Cruz, E., Cazorla, M., & Gomez-Donoso, F. (2018, November). Improving the 3D perception of the pepper robot using depth prediction from monocular frames. In Workshop of Physical A*g*ents (pp. 132–146). Spri*nger.*

Benarroch, E. E. (2019). Insular cortex: Functional complexity and clinical correlations. Neurology, 93(21), 932–938. doi:10.1212/WNL.0000000000008525 PMID:31645470

Best-Rowden, L., Han*, H., Otto, C., Klare,* B. F., & Jain, A. K. (2014). Unconstrained face recognition: Identifying a person of interest from a media collection. IEEE Transactions on Information Forensics and Security, 9(12), 2144–2157. doi:10.1109/TIFS.2014.2359577

Betegh, G. (2020). Plato on Illnes*s in the Phaedo, the Republic, and the Timaeus. In Plato'*s Timaeus (pp. 228-258). Brill. doi:10.1163/9789004437081_013

Bharati, P., &Pramanik, A. (2020). Deep learning techniques—R-CNN to mask R-CNN: a survey. Computational Intelligence in Pattern Recognition, *657-668.*

*Bhuyan, B. P., Karmakar, A., & Haza*rika, S. M. (2018). Bounding stability in formal concept analysis. In Advanced Computational and Communication Paradigms (pp. 545–552). Springer. doi:10.1007/978-981-10-8237-5_53

Bhuy*an, B. P., Toma*r, R., & Cherif, A. R. (2022). A Systematic Review of Knowledge Representation Techniques in Smart Agriculture (Urban). Sustainability, 14(22), 15249. doi:10.3390u142215249

Bhuyan, B. P., Tomar, R., Gupta, M., & Ramdane-Cheri*f, A. (2021, December). A*n Ontological Knowledge Representation for Smart Agriculture. In 2021 IEEE International Conference on Big Data (Big Data) (pp. 3400-3406). IEEE. 10.1109/BigData52589.2021.9672020

Bhuyan, B. P., Um, J. S., Singh, T. P., & Choudhury, T. (2022). Decision Intelligence Analytics*: Making Decisions Through Data Pattern and Segmented Analy*tics. In Decision Intelligence Analytics and the Implementation of Strategic Business Management *(pp. 99–107). Springer.* doi:10.1007/978-3-030-82763-2_9

Bing, Z., Meschede, C., Röhrbein, F., Huang, K., & Knoll, A. C. (2018). A survey of robotics control based on learning-inspired spiking neural networks. *Frontiers in Neurorobo*tics, 12, 35. doi:10.3389/fnbot.2018.00035 PMID:30034334

Bird, A. (2019). Group belief and knowledge. In The Routledge handbook of social epistemology (pp. 274–283). Routledge. doi*:10.4324/9781315717937-27*

Bishop, C. M., & Lasserre, J. (2007). Generative or discriminative? Getting the best of both worlds. Bayesian Statist., 8, 3–24.

Block, V. A., Pitsch, E., Tahir, P., Cree, B. A., Allen, D. D., & Gelfand, J. M. (2016). Remote Physical Activity Monitoring in Neuro*logical Disease: A Systematic Revi*ew. PLoS One, 11(4), e0154335. doi:10.1371/journal.pone.0154335 PMID:27124611

Bobinski, M., de Leon, M. J., Convit, A., De Santi, S., Wegiel, J., Tarshish, C. Y., Saint Louis, L. A., & Wisniewski, H. M. (1999). MRI of entorhinal corte*x in mild Alzheimer's disease. Lancet, 353(9146), 38–40. doi:10.1*016/S0140-6736(05)74869-8 PMID:10023955

Botta, A., Donato, W. D., Persico, V., & Pescapé, A. E. (2014). On the integration of *cloud computing and Internet of Things.* Proc. IEEE Int. Conf. Future Internet Things Cloud. 10.1109/FiCloud.2014.14

Bova, V. V., Kravchenko, Y. A., Rodzin, S. I., & Kuliev, E. V. (2020, O*ctober). Simulatio*n of the Semantic Network of Knowledge Representation in Intelligent Assistant Systems Based on Ontological Approach. In International Conference on Futuristic Trends in Networks and Computing Technologies *(pp. 241-252). Springer.*

Buhmann, M. D. (2003). Ra*d*ial Basis Functions. Cambridge Univ. Press. doi:10.1017/CBO9780511543241

Cai, B., Kong, X., Liu, Y., Lin, J., Yuan, X., Xu, H., & Ji, R. (2018). Application of Bayesian networks in reliability evaluation. *IEEE Transactions on Industrial* Informatics, 15(4), 2146–2157. doi:10.1109/TII.2018.2858281

*Cao, Z., Simon, T., Wei, S. E., & Sheikh, Y. (2017). Realtime multi-person 2d pose estimation using part affinity f*ields. In Proceedings of the IEEE conference on computer vision and pattern recognition (pp. 7291-7299). IEEE.

Catarinucci. *(2015). An IoT-aware architecture for smart healthcare systems. IEEE I*nternet Things J., 2(6).

Chakraborty, I., Saha, G., Sengupta, A., & Roy, K. (2018). Toward fast neural computing using all-photonic phase change spiking neurons. Scientif*ic Reports, 8(1),* 12980. doi:10.103841598-018-31365-x PMID:30154507

Chakraborty, N., Lukovnikov, D., Maheshwari, G., Trivedi, P., Lehmann, J., & Fischer, A. (2019). Introduction to neural network based approaches for questi*on answering over knowledg*e g*r*aphs. arXiv preprint arXiv:1907.09361.

Chan, M., Campo, E., Estéve, D., & Fourniols, J. Y. (2009). Smart homes— Current features and future perspectives. Maturitas, 64(2), 90–97. doi:10.1016/j.maturitas.*2009.07.014 PMID:19729255*

Chang, C. H., Lin, C. H., & Lane, H. Y. (2021). Machine Learning and Novel Biomarkers for the Diagnosis of Alzheimer's Disease. Int J Mol Sci., 22(5), 2761. doi:10.3390/ijms22052761 PMID:33803217

Chang, *P. H., & Tan, A. H. (2017). Encoding and recall of spat*io-temporal episodic memory in real time. Academic Press.

Charte, D., Charte, F., García, S., del Jesus, M. J., & Herrera, F. (2017, November). A practical tutorial on autoencoders for no*nlinear feature fus*ion: Taxonomy, models, software and guidelines. Information Fusion, 44.

Chaturvedi, I., Cambria, E., Welsch, R. E., & Herrera, F. (2018, November). Distinguishing between facts and opinions for sentimen*t analysis: Survey and challenges. I*nformation Fusion, 44, 65–77. doi:10.1016/j.inffus.2017.12.006

Chen, K. (2015). Deep and modular neural networks" in Springer Handbook of Computational Intelligence. S*pringer.*

*Chen, L., Nugent, C. D., & Wa*ng, H. (2012, June). A knowledge-driven approach to activity recognition in smart homes. IEEE Transactions on Knowledge and Data Engineering, 24(6), 961–974. doi:10.1109/TKDE.2011.51

Chen, M., *Hao, Y., Hu, L., Huang, K., & Lau*, V. (2017, December). Green and mobility-aware caching in 5G networks. IEEE Transactions on Wireless Communications, 16(12), 8347–8361. doi:10.1109/TWC.2017.2760830

Chen, M., *Hao, Y., Kai, H., Wang, L.*, & Wang, L. (2017). Disease prediction by machine learning over big data from healthcare *communities. IEEE Access: Practical Innovations, Open Solutions, 5(1)*, 8869–8879. doi:10.1109/ACCESS.2017.2694446

Chen, M., Mao, S., & Liu, Y. (2014, April). Big data: A survey. Mobile Networks and Applications, 19(2), 171–209. doi:*10.100711036-013-0489-0*

Chen, M., Miao, Y., Hao, Y., & Hwang, K. (2017). Narrowband Internet of Things (Vol. 5). IEEE Access.

Chen, M., Qian, Y., Hao, Y., Li, Y., & Song, J. (2018, February). Data-driven computing and caching *in 5G networks: Architecture and delay analysis. IEEE Wireless* Communications, 25(1), 70–75. doi:10.1109/MWC.2018.1700216

Chen, M., Tian, Y., Fortino, G., Zhang, J., & Humar, I. (2018). Cognitive Internet of vehicles. Computer Communications, 120, 58–70. Advance online publication. *doi:10.1016/j. comcom.2018.02.006*

Chen, M., Yang, J., Zhu, X., Wang, X., Liu, M., & Song, J. (2017, December). Smart home 2.0: Innovative smart home system powered by botanical IoT *and emotion detection. Mobile Networks and Appli*cations, 22(6), 1159–1169. doi:10.100711036-017-0866-1

Chen, M., Zhou, P., & Fortino, G. (2017). Emotion communication system (Vol. 5). IEEE Access.

Chen, Shi, Zhang, *Wu, & Mohse*n. (2017). Deep features learning for medical image analysis with convolutional autoencoder neural network. IEEE Trans. Big Data. Doi:10.1109/TBDATA.2017.2717439

*Chen, Y. (2018). Brain MRI super re*solution using 3D deep densely connected neural networks. In 2018 IEEE 15th International Symposium on Biomedical Imaging (ISBI 2018). IEEE. 10.1109/ISBI.2018.8363679

Cheng, J., Huang, W., *Cao, S., Yang, R., Yang, W., Yun,* Z., Wang, Z., & Feng, Q. (2015). Enhanced performance of brain tumor classification via tumor region augmentation and partition. PLoS One, 10(10), e0140381. doi:10.1371/journal.pone.0140381 PMID:26447861

Che*ng, M., Dang, C., Fr*angopol, D. M., Beer, M., & Yuan, X. X. (2022). Transfer prior knowledge from surrogate modelling: A meta-learning approach. Computers & Structures, *260, 106719. doi:10.1016/j.com*pstruc.2021.106719

Cho, J., Lee, K., Shin, E., Choy, G., & Do, S. (2015). How much data is needed to train a medical image deep learning system to achieve necessary high accuracy. arXiv. 20151511.06348

*Choo, I. H., Chong, A., Chung, J. Y., & Kim, H. (2019). As*sociation of Subjective Memory Complaints with the Left Parahippocampal Amyloid Burden in Mild Cognitive Impairment. Journal of Alzheimer's Disease, 7(Nov), 1261–1268. doi:10.323*3/JAD-190816 PMID:31707367*

Collins, A. M., & Quillian, M. R. (1970). Facilitating retrieval from semantic memory: The effect of repeating part of an inference. *Acta Psychologica, 33,* 304–314. doi:10.1016/0001-6918(70)90142-3

Cruz, E., Escalona, F., Bauer, Z., Cazorla, M., Garcia-Rodriguez, J., Martinez-Martin, E., ... Gomez-Donoso, F. (2018). Geoffrey: An automated schedule system on a social robot for the intellectually challenged. Computational Intelligence and Neuroscience.

Cummings, J. L., & Benson, D. F. (1992). Dementia: A clinical approach. Butterworth-Heinemann.

Cybenko, G. (1989). Approximation by super positions of a sigmoidal function. Mathematics of Control, Signals, and Systems, 2(4), 303–314. doi:10.1007/BF02551274

Deardorff & Grossberg. (2019). A fixed-dose combination of memantine extended-release and donepezil in the treatment of moderate-to-severe Alzheimer's disease. Drug Des Devel Ther., *10, 3267-3279.*

*De Houwer, J. (2018). Propositi*onal models of evaluative conditioning. Social Psychological Bulletin, 13(3), 1–21. doi:10.5964pb.v13i3.28046

Demirel, H., & Anbarjafari, G. (2010). Image resolution *enhancement by using discrete and stati*onary wavelet decomposition. IEEE Transactions on Image Processing, 20(5), 1458–1460. doi:10.1109/TIP.2010.2087767 PMID:20959267

Deshpande, A., & Patavardhan, P. P. (2019). Survey o*f super resolution techniq*ues. ICTACT Journal on Image & Video Processing, 9(3).

Dhall, I., Vashisth, S., & Aggarwal, G. (2020, January). *Automated hand gesture recognition using a deep convolutional neural netwo*rk model. In 2020 10th International Conference on Cloud Computing, Data Science & Engineering (Confluence) (pp. 811-816). IEEE. 10.1109/Confluence47617.2020.9057853

Diamantas, S. C., Oikonom*idis, A., & Crowder, R. M.* (20*10,* July). Depth estimation for autonomous robot navigation: A comparative ap*proach. In 2010 IEEE International Confer*ence on Imaging Systems and Techniques (pp. 426-430). IEEE.

Du, J., Wang, L., Liu, Y., Zhou, Z., He, Z., & Jia, Y. (2020). Brain MRI super-reso*lution using 3D dilated Convolutional e*ncod*e*r–decoder network. IEEE Access: Practical Innovations, Open Solutions, 8, 18938–18950. doi:10.1109/ACCESS.2020.2968395

Duchi, J., Hazan, E., & Singer, Y. (2011). Adaptive subgradient met*hods for online lear*ning and stochastic optimization. Journal of Machine Learning Research, 12, 2121–2159.

El-Khamy, S. E. (2005). Regularized super-resolution reconstruction of images using wavelet fusion. Optical Engineering, *44(9).*

*El Houb*y, *E.* M. F. (2018). Framework of Computer Aided Diagnosis Systems for Cancer Classification Based on Medical Images. Journal of Medical Systems, 42(8), 157. doi:10.100*710916-018-1010-*x PMID:29995204

Emilien, G. R. (2004). Alzheimer Disease: Neuropsychology and Pharmacology. Birkhauser. doi:10.1007/978-3-0348-7842-5

Encarnação, P. (2013). Episodic memory visualization in robot companions providing a memory prosthesis for elderly users. Assistive Technology: From Research to Practice, 33, 120.

Escalante, H. J., Montes, M., & Sucar, L. E. (2009). Particle *swarm model selection. Journal of Machine Learning Research, 10, 405–440.*

*Esteva. (2017). Dermatologist-level classification of skin cancer with d*eep neural networks. Academic Press.

Etemad-Sajadi, R., & Dos Santos, G. G. (2019). Senior citizens' acceptance of connected health technologies in their homes. *International* Journal of Health Care Quality Assurance, 32(8), 1162–1174. Advance online publication. doi:10.1108/IJHCQA-10-2018-0240 PMID:31566513

Eördegh, G., Őze, A., Bodosi, B., Puszta, A., Pertich, Á., Rosu, A., Godó, G., & Nagy, A. (2019). Multisensory guided associative learning in healthy humans. PLoS One, 14(3), 0213094. doi:10.1371/journal.pone.0213094 PMID:30861023

Fan, J., Fang, L., Wu, J., *Guo, Y., & Dai, Q.* (2020). From brain science to artificial intelligence. Engineering, 6(3), 248–252. doi:10.1016/j.eng.2019.11.012

Fan, X., Wang, F., Shao, H., Zhang, P., & *He, S. (2020). The bottom-up and top-down processing* of faces in the human occipitotemporal cortex. eLife, 9, e48764. doi:10.7554/eLife.48764 PMID:31934855

Fasel, B., & Luettin, J. (2003, January). Automatic facial expression analysis: A survey. Pattern Recognition, 36(1), 259–275. doi:10.1016/S0031-3203(02)00052-3

Fathi, S., Ahmadi, M., & Dehnad, A. (2022, July). Early diagnosis of *Alzheimer's disea*se ba*s*ed on deep learning: A systematic review. Computers in Biology and Medicine, 146, 105634. doi:10.1016/j.compbiomed.2022.105634 PMID:35605488

Fei, B. (2017). Computer-aided diagnosis of prostate cancer with MRI. Curr Opin Biomed Eng., 3, 20–27. doi:10.1016/j.cobme.2017.09.009 PMID:29732440

Fe*ng, Y., Sun, X., Diao, W., Li,* J., Gao, X., & Fu, K. (2021). Continual learning with structured inheritance for semantic segmentation in aerial imagery. IEEE Transactions on Geoscience and Remote Sensing, 60, 1–*17.*

Fernández, A. (2014). Big data with cloud computing: An insight on the computing environment, mapreduce, and programming frameworks. Wiley Interdiscipl. Rev. Data Mining and Knowledge Discovery, 4(5).

Fukami, K., Fukagata, K., & Taira, K. (2021). Machine-learning-bas*ed spatial-temporal super resolu*tion reconstruction of turbulent flows. Journal of Fluid Mechanics, 909.

Gavin. (2016). The Levenberg-Marquardt method for nonlinear least squares curve-fitting problems. Academic Press.

Genitha, C. H., & Vani, K. (2010). Super resolution *mapping of satellite image*s using hopfield neural networks. In Recent Advances in Space Technology Services and Climate Change 2010 (RSTS & CC-*2010*). *IEEE.*

Gheisari, M., Wang, G., & Bhuiyan, M. Z. A. (2017). A survey on deep learning in big data. Proc. IEEE Int. Conf. Computing. Sci. Eng. (CSE), 173-180. 10.1109/CSE-EUC.2017.215

Ghosh, S., Chaki, A., & Santosh, K. C. (2021). *Improved U-Net architecture with VGG-16 for brain tumor* segmentation. Physical and Engineering Sciences in Medicine, 44(3), 703–712. doi:10.100713246-021-01019-w PMID:34047928

Glorot, X., & Bengio, Y. (2010). Understanding the difficulty of training deep feed forward neural networks. Proc. 13th Int. Conf. Artif. Intell. Statist., 249-256.

Goldberg, *D. E. (2013). The Design of Innovation: Lessons* from and for Competent Genetic Algorithms. Springer.

Gomez-Donoso, F., Escalona, F., Rivas, F. M., Cañas, J. M., & Cazorla, M. (2019). Enhancing the a*mbient assisted living capabilities with a mobile robot. Com*putational Intelligence and Neuroscience.

Gonçalves, C. P. (2018). Quantum Robotics, Neural Networks and the Quantum Force Interpretation. Neural Networks and the *Quantum Force Interpretation. doi:10.2139srn.3244327*

Goodfellow, I., Bengio, Y., & Courville, A. (2016). Deep learning. In Adaptive Computation And Machine Learning. MIT Press.

Gosche, K. M., Mortimer, J. A., Smith, C. D., Markesbery, W. R., & Sno*wdon, A. D. (2002)*. Hippocampal Volume as an Index of Alzheimer Neuropathology: Findings from the Nun Study. Neurology, 58(10), 1476–1482. doi:10.1212/WNL.58.10.1476 PMID:12034782

Gou, J., Yu, B., Maybank, S. J., & T*ao, D. (2021). Knowledge distillation: A survey. International Journal of Computer Visio*n, 129(6), 1789–1819. doi:10.100711263-021-01453-z

Greenspan, H. (2009). Super-resolution in medical ima*ging. The Computer Journal, 52(1), 43–63. doi*:10.1093/comjnl/bxm075

Guan, S., Zhao, K., & Yang, S. (2019). Motor imagery EEG classification based on decision tree framework and Riemannian geometry. Comp*utational Intellige*nce and Neuroscience.

Gudivada, V. N. (2016). Cognitive computing: Concepts, architectures, systems, and Applications (Vol. 35). Handbook Stat.

Guo, Y., Cai, Q., Samuels, D. C., Ye, F., Long, J., Li, C.-I., Winther, J. F., Tawn, E. J., Stovall, M., Lähteenmäki, P., Malila, N., Levy, S., Shaffer, C., Shyr, Y., Shu, X., & Boice, J. D. Jr. (2012). The use of next generation sequencing technology to study the effect of radiation therapy on mitochondrial DNA mutation. Mutation Research/Genetic Toxicology and Environmental Mutagenesis, 744(2), 154–160. doi:10.1016/j.mrgentox.2012.02.006 PMID:22387842

Hadsell, R., Chopra, S., & LeCun, Y. (2006). *Dimensionality reduction by learning an inva*riant mapping. Proc. IEEE Comput. Soc. Conf. Computing Vis. Pattern Recognition (CVPR), 1735-1742. 10.1109/CVPR.2006.100

Hamdi, Bourouis, Rastislav, & Mohmed. (2022, February 7). Evaluation of Neuro Images for the Diagnosis of Alzheimer*'s Disease Using Deep Learning Neural Network. Frontiers in Public Health, 10, 8340*32. doi:10.3389/fpubh.2022.834032 PMID:35198526

Han, *D.-M., & Lim, J.-H.* (2010, August). Smart home energy management system using IEEE 802.15.4 and ZigBee. IEEE Transactions on Consumer Electronics, 56(3), 1403–1410. doi:10.1109/TCE.2010.5606276

Hao, Y., Ch*en, M., Hu, L., Song, J., Volk, M., & Humar, I.* (2017). Wireless fractal ultra-dense cellular networks. Sensors (Basel), 17(4), 841. doi:10.339017040841 PMID:28417927

Hasan, M. S., Schuman, C. D., Najem, J. S., Weiss, *R., Skuda, N. D., Belianinov, A., Collier, C. P., Sarles, S. A., & Rose, G.* S. (2018). Biomimetic, Soft-Material Synapse for Neuromorphic Computing: from Device to Network. IEEE *13th Dallas Circuits and S*ystems Conference (DCAS), 1-6.

Hassabis, D., Kumaran, D., Summerfield, C., & Botvinick, M. (2017). Neu*roscience-inspired artificial intelligence. Neuron, 95(2), 245–258. doi:10.1016/j.neuron.2017.*06.011 PMID:28728020

Hayat, A., Morgado-Dias, F., Bhuyan, B. P., & T*omar, R. (2022). Human Activity Recognition for Elderly People Usin*g Machine and Deep Learning Approaches. Information, 13(6), 275. doi:10.3390/info13060275

He, H., Li, Y., & Tan, J. (2018). Relative motion estima*tion using visual–*inertial optical flow. Autonomous Robots, 42(3), 615–629.

He, K., Zhang, X., Ren, S., & Sun, J. (2016). Deep residual learning for image recognition. Proc. IEEE Conf. *Comput. V*is. Pattern Recognit. (CVPR), 770-778. 10.1109/CVPR.2016.90

Heo, B., Lee, M., Yun, S., & Choi, J. Y. (2019, July). Knowledge transfer via distillation of activation boundaries formed by hidden neurons. Proceedings of the AAAI Conference on Artificial Intellige*nce, 33(01), 3779–3787.* doi:10.1609/aaai.v33i01.33013779

Hinton, G. E. (2007). Learning multiple layers of representation. Trends in Cognitive Sciences, 11(10), 428–434. doi:10.1016/j.tics.*2007.09.004 PMID:17921042*

Hinton, G. E., & Salakhutdinov, R. R. (2006). Reducing the dimensionality of data with neural networks. Science, 313(5786), 504–507. doi:10.1126cience.1127647 PMID:16873662

Hintzman, D. L. (1984). MINERVA 2: A simulation model of human memory. Behavior Research Methods, Instruments, & Computers, 16(2), 96–101.

Ho, T. C., Dennis, E. L., Thompson, P. M., & Gotlib, I. H. (2018). Network-based approaches to examining stress in the adolescent brain. Neurobiology of Stress, 8, 147–157. doi:10.1016/j.ynstr.2018.05.002 PMID:29888310

Hogan, A., Blomqvist, E., Cochez, M., d'Amato, C., Melo, G. D., Gutierrez, C., Kirrane, S., Gayo, J. E. L., Navigli, R., Neumaier, S., Ngomo, A.-C. N., Polleres, A., Rashid, S. M., Rula, A., Schmelzeisen, L., Sequeda, J., Staab, S., & Zimmermann, A. (2021). Knowledge graphs. ACM Computing Surveys, 54(4), 1–37. doi:10.1145/3447772

Hornik, K. (1991). Approximation capabilities of multilayer feed forward networks. Neural Networks, 4(2), 251–257. doi:10.1016/0893-6080(91)90009-T

Hou, Y., & Chen, S. (2019). Distinguishing different emotions evoked by music via electroencephalographic signals. Computational Intelligence and Neuroscience.

Huang, B., Bates, M., & Zhuang, X. (2009). Super-resolution fluorescence microscopy. Annual Review of Biochemistry, 78(1), 993–1016. doi:10.1146/annurev.biochem.77.061906.092014 PMID:19489737

Huang, G.-B., Zhu, Q.-Y., & Siew, C.-K. (2006). Extreme learning machine: Theory and applications. Neurocomputing, 70(1-3), 489–501. doi:10.1016/j.neucom.2005.12.126

Huang, L., Joseph, A. D., Nelson, B., Rubinstein, B. I. P., & Tygar, J. D. (2011). Adversarial machine learning. 4th ACM Workshop Secur. Artif. Intell., 43-58.

Huang, S., Cai, N., Pacheco, P. P., Narrandes, S., Wang, Y., & Xu, W. (2018). Applications of Support Vector Machine (SVM) Learning in Cancer Genomics. Cancer Genomics & Proteomics, 15(1), 41–51. doi:10.21873/cgp.20063 PMID:29275361

Hurwitz, Kaufman, & Bowles. (2015). Cognitive Computing and Big Data Analytics. Wiley.

Hwang, K., & Chen, M. (2017). Big-Data Analytics for Cloud, IoT and Cognitive Learning. Wiley.

Ielmini, D. (2018). Brain-inspired computing with resistive switching memory (RRAM): Devices, synapses and neural networks. Microelectronic Engineering, 190, 44–53. doi:10.1016/j.mee.2018.01.009

Indiveri, G., & Liu, S. C. (2015). Memory and information processing in neuromorphic systems. Proceedings of the IEEE, 103(8), 1379–1397. doi:10.1109/JPROC.2015.2444094

İnçki, K., & Ari, I. (2018). Democratization of runtime verification for the internet of things. Computers & Electrical Engineering, 68, 570–580. doi:10.1016/j.compeleceng.2018.05.007

Ioffe & Szegedy. (2015). Batch normalization: Accelerating deep network training by reducing internal covariate shift. Academic Press.

Irani, M., & Peleg, S. (1991). Improving resolution by image registration. *CVGIP. Graph*ical Models and Image Processing, 53(3), 231–239. doi:10.1016/1049-9652(91)90045-L

Jain, A. K., Duin, R. P. W., & Mao, J. (2000). Statistical pattern recognition: A review. IEEE Transactions *on Pattern Analysi*s *a*nd Machine Intelligence, 22(1), 4–37. doi:10.1109/34.824819

Ji, S., Pan, S., Cambria, E., Marttinen, P., & Philip, S. Y. (2021). A survey on knowledge graphs: Representation, acquisition, and applications. IEEE Transactions on Neural Networks and Learning *Systems, 33(2), 494–514. doi:10.1109/TNNLS*.2021.3070843 PMID:33900922

Jin, Gubbi, Maru*sic, & Palaniswami. (2014). A*n information framework for creating a smart city through the Internet of Things. IEEE IoT J., 1(2).

*Jin, H., Hou, L. J., & Wang, Z. G. (2018). Mil*itary Brain Science–How to influence future wars. Chinese Journal of Traumatology, 21(5), 277–280. doi:10.1016/j.*cjtee.2018.01.006 PMID:30279039*

Jolliffe, I. T. (2022). Principal component analysis in Mathematics and Statistics. Springer.

Jordan, M. I., & Mitchell, T. M. (2015). Machine learning: Trends perspectives and prospects. Science, *349(6245), 255–260. doi*:10.1126cience.aaa8415 PMID:26185243

Julin, J., Kumar, K. R., & Mahendran, S. (2016). Optical flow-based velocity estimation for vision-based navigation of a*ircraft. International Journal of Applied Engineering Research, 11(6), 4402–4405.*

Juottonen, K., Laakso, M. P., Insausti, R., Lehtovirta, M., Pitkanen, A., Partanen, K., & Soininen, H. (1998). Volumes of the entorhinal and perirhinal cortices in Alzheimer's disease. Neurobiology of Aging, 19(1), *15–22. doi:10.1016/S0197-4580(98)00007-4 PMID:9562498*

Kang, C., Yu, X., Wang, S. H., Guttery, D. S., Pandey, H. M., Tian, Y., & Zhang, Y. D. (2020). A heuristic neural network structure relying on fuzzy logic f*or images scoring. IEEE Transactions o*n Fuzzy Systems, 29(1), 34–45. doi:10.1109/TFUZZ.2020.2966163 PMID:33408453

Kang, W. M., Kim, C. H., Lee, S., Woo, S. Y., Bae, J. H., Park, *B. G., & Lee, J. H. (2019). A* Spiking Neural Network with a Global Self-Controller for Unsupervised Learni*ng Based on Spike-Timing-Dependent Plasticity Usi*ng Flash Memory Synaptic Devices. International Joint Conference on Neural Networks (IJCNN), 1-7. 10.1109/IJCNN.2019.8851744

Kantarci, K., & Jack, C. R. (2004). Quanti*tative magnetic resonance techniques as surroga*te markers of Alzheimer's disease. NeuroRx, 1(2), 196–205. doi:10.1602/neurorx.1.2.196 PMID:15717*020*

*Karami, V., Nittari, G., & Amen*ta, F. (2019). Neuroimaging Compu*ter-Aided Diagnosis Systems for Alzheimer's Disease. International Journal* of Imaging Systems and Technology, 29(1), 83–94. doi:10.1002/ima.22300

Karami, V., Nittari, G., Traini, E., & Amenta, F. (2021). An Optimized *Decision Tree with Genetic Algorithm Rule-Based Appro*ach to Reveal the Brain's Changes During Alzheimer's Disease Dementia. Journal of Alzheimer's Disease, 84(4), 1–8. doi:10.3233/JAD-210626 PMID:34719494

Karer, B., Scheler, I., Hagen, H., & Leitte, H. (2020, September). Conceptgraph: A formal model for interpretation and reasoning during visual analysis. Computer Graphics Forum, 39(6), 5–18. doi:10.1111/cgf.13899

Kennedy, J. A., Israel, O., Frenkel, A., Bar-Shalom, R., & Azhari, H. (2007). Improved image fusion in PET/CT using hybrid image reconstruction and super-resolution. International *Journal of Biome*dical Imaging, 2007, 2007. doi:10.1155/2007/46846 PMID:18521180

Kennedy, J. A., Israel, O., Frenkel, A., Bar-Shalom, R., & Haim Azhari. (2006). Super-resolution in PET imaging. IEEE Transactions on Medical Imaging, 25(2), 137–147. doi:10.1109/TMI.2005.861705 PMID:16468448

Khawaldeh, S., Pervaiz, U., Rafiq, A., & Alkhawaldeh, R. S. (2017). Noninvasive grading of glioma tumor using magnetic resonance imaging with convolutional neural networks. Applied Sciences (Basel, Switzerland), 8(1), 27. doi:10.3390/app8010027

Khojaste-Sarakhsi, M., Haghighi, S. S., Ghomi, S. M. T. F., & Marchiori, E. (2022, August). Deep learning for Alzheimer's disease diagnosis: A survey. Artificial Intelligence in Medicine, 130, 102332. doi:10.1016/j.artmed.2022.102332 PMID:35809971

Killiany, R. J., Hyman, B. T., Gomez-Isla, T., Moss, M. B., Kikinis, R., Jolesz, F., Tanzi, R., Jones, K., & Albert, M. S. (2002). MRI measures of entorhinal cortex vs hippocampus in preclinical AD. Neurology, 58(8), 1188–1196. doi:10.1212/WNL.58.8.1188 PMID:11971085

Kim, D., Byun, W., Ku, Y., & Kim, J. H. (2019). High-Speed Visual Target Identification for Low-Cost Wearable Brain-Computer Interfaces. IEEE Access: Practical Innovations, Open Solutions, 7, 55169–55179. doi:10.1109/ACCESS.2019.2912997

Kim, G. H., Kim, K., Lee, E., An, T., Choi, W., Lim, G., & Shin, J. H. (2018). Recent progress on microelectrodes in neural interfaces. Materials (Basel), 11(10), 1995. doi:10.3390/ma11101995 PMID:30332782

Kingma & Ba. (2014). Adam: A method for stochastic optimization. Academic Press.

Kingma, D. P., & Welling, M. (2013). Auto-encoding variational Bayes. https://arxiv.org/abs/1312.6114

Klein, E. (2018). Augustine's theology of angels. Cambridge University Press. doi:10.1017/9781108335652

Knoefel, F., Emerson, V., & Schulman, B. (2005, March). TAFETA: an inclusive design for tele-health. Proceedings of the Technology and Persons with Disabilities Conference.

Koelmans, W. W., Sebastian, A., Jonnalagadda, V. P., Krebs, D., Dellmann, L., & Eleftheriou, E. (2015). Projected phase-change memory devices. Nature Communications, 6(1), 8181. doi:10.1038/ncomms9181 PMID:26333363

Kopetzky, S., & Butz-Ostendorf, M. (2018). From matrices to knowledge: Using semantic networks to annotate the connectome. Frontiers in Neuroanatomy, *12, 111. doi:10.3389/fnana.2018.00111* PMID:30581382

Kumar, N., & Sethi, A. (2016). Fast learning-based single image super-resolution. IEEE Transactions on Multimedia, 18(8), 1504–1515. doi:10.1109/TMM.2016.2571625

Kumarasinghe, K., Kasabov, N., & Taylor, D. *(2020). Deep learning and deep knowledge representation in Spiking Neural Networks for Brain-Compute*r Interfaces. Neural Networks, 121, 169–185. doi:10.1016/j.neunet.2019.08.029 PMID:31568895

Kuo, Hariharan, & Malik. (2015). Deep Box: Learning object ness with convolutional networks. Academic Press.

Kurdi, B., Seitchik, A. E., Axt, J. R., Carroll, T. J., Karapetyan, A., Kaushik, N., Tomezsko, D., Greenwald, A. G., & Banaji, M. R. (2019). Relationship between the Implicit Association Test and intergroup behavior: A meta-analysis. The American Psychologist, 74(5), 569–586. doi:10.1037/ amp0000364 PMID:30550298

Kussul, E., Baidyk, T., Kasatkina, L., & Lukovich, V. (2001, July). Rose*nblatt perceptrons for handwritten digit recognition. International Joi*nt Conference on Neural Networks. Proceedings, 2, 1516-1520. IEEE. 10.1109/IJCNN.2001.939589

Lake, B. M., Salakhutdinov, R., & Tenenbaum, J. B. (2015). Human-level concept learning through probabil*istic program induction. Sc*ience, 350(6266), 1332–1338. doi:10.1126cience. aab3050 PMID:26659050

Lanktree, C., & Briere, J. (1991, January). Early data on the trauma symptom checklist for child*ren (TSC-C). Paper presented at the meetin*g of the American Professional Society on the Abuse of Children, San Diego, CA.

Larrañaga, P., Kuijpers, C. M. H., Murga, R. H., Inza, I., & Dizdarevic, S. (1999). *Genetic algori*thms for the travelling salesman problem: A review of representations and operators. Artificial Intelligence Review, 13(2), 129–170. doi:10.1023/A:1006529012972

Le, *Q. V. (20*13). Building high-level features using large scale unsupervised learning. Proc. IEEE Int. Conf. Acoust., Speech Signal Process. (ICASSP). 10.1109/ICASSP.2013.6639343

LeCun, Y., & Bengio, Y. (1998). Convolutional n*etworks for im*ages speech and time series. In The Handbook of Brain Theory and Neural Networks. MIT Press.

LeCun, Y., Bengio, Y., & Hinton, G. *(2015). Deep learning. Nature, 521(7553), 436–444. doi:*10.1038/nature14539 PMID:26017442

LeCun, Y., Bottou, L., Bengio, Y., & Haffner, P. (1998). Gradient-based learning applied to do*cument recognitio*n. Proceedings of the IEEE, 86(11), 2278–2324. doi:10.1109/5.726791

Leonard, D. (1995). Wellsprings of knowledge. Harvard Business School Press.

Lerch, J. P., *Pruessner, J. C., Zijdenbos, A., Hampel, H., Teipel, S. J., &* Evans, A. C. (2005). Focal decline of cortical thickness in Alzheimer's disease identified by computational neuroanatomy. *Cerebral Cortex (New York, N.Y.)*, 15(7), 995–1001. doi:10.1093/cercor/bhh200 PMID:15537673

Letsche, T. A., & Berry, M. W. (1997). Large-scale information retrieval with latent semantic indexing. *Inf. Sci.*, 100(1-4), 105–137. doi:10.1016/S0020-0255(97)00044-3

Li, J., Li, Z., Chen, F., Bicchi, A., Sun, Y., & Fukuda, T. (2019). Combine*d Sensing, Cognition, Learning and Control to Devel*oping Future Neuro-Robotics Systems: A Survey. IEEE Transactions on Cognitive and Developmental Systems.

Li, L., Lee, C. C., Zhou, F. L., Molony, C., Doder, Z., Zalmover, E., Sharma, K., Juhaeri, J., & Wu, C. (2021). Performance assessment of different machine learning approaches in predictin*g diabetic ketoacidos*is *i*n adults with type 1 diabetes using electronic health records data. Pharmacoepidemiology and Drug Safety, 30(5), 6*10–618. doi:10.1*002/pds.5199 PMID:33480091

Li, M., & Nguyen, T. Q. (2008). Markov random field model-based edge-directed image interpolation. IEEE Transactions on Image Processing, *17(7), 1121–1128. doi:10.1109/ TIP.2008.924*289 PMID:18586620

Lin, C.-T., Prasad, M., & Saxena, A. (2015). An improved polynomial neural network classifier usin*g real-coded genetic algorithm. IEEE* Transactions on Systems, Man, and Cybernetics. Systems, 45(11), 1389–1401. doi:10.1109/TSMC.2015.2406855

Liu, *B., Cai, Y.,* Guo, Y., & Chen, X. (2021, May). TransTailor: Pruning the pre-trained model for improved transfer learning. Proceedings of the AAAI Conference on Artificial Intelligence, 35(10), 8627–8634. doi:10.1609/aaai.*v35i10.17046*

Liu, B., Guo, W., *&* Xin, C. (2020). Morphological Attribute Profile Cube and Deep Random Forest for Small Sample Classification of Hyperspectral Image. IEEE Access: Practical Innovation*s, Open Solutions, 8, 117096–117108. doi:10.1109/ACCESS.*2020.3004968

Liu, F., Shen, C., Lin, G., & Reid, I. (2015). Learning depth from single monocular images usin*g deep convolutional neural field*s. IEEE Transactions on Pattern Analysis and Machine Intelligence, 38(10), 2024*–2039.*

*Liu, Y., & Zheng, F. B. (2017). Object-oriented and multi-scale target classificati*on and recognition based on hierarchical ensemble learning. Computers & Electrical Engineering, 62, 538–554. *doi:10.1016/j.compeleceng.2016.12.026*

Lu, K., Li, Y., He, W. F., Chen, J., Zhou, Y. X., Duan, N., Jin, M. M., Gu, W., Xue, K. H., Sun, H. J., & Miao, X. S. (2018). Diverse spike-timing- dependent plasticity based on multilevel *HfO x memrist*or for neuromorphic computing. Applied Physics. A, Materials Science & Processing, 124(6), 438. doi:10.100700339-018-1847-3

Luo, X., Wu, J., Zhou, C., *Zhang, X., & Wang, Y. (2020, November). Deep Semantic Net*work Representation. In 2020 IEEE International Conference on Data Mining (ICDM) (pp. 11*54-1159). IEEE. 10.1109/ICDM50108.2020.00141*

Lutkevich, B. (n.d.). What is AI Winter? Definition, History and Timeline. Enterprise AI. https://www.techtarget.com/se*archent*erpriseai/definition/AI-winter

Mahandra, B. (1984). Dementia: A survey of the syndrome of dementia. MTP.

Malczewski, K., & Stasiński, R. (2009). Super resolution for multimedia, image, and *video processing applications. In Recent Advances in Mul*timedia Signal Processing and Communications (pp. 171–208). Springer. doi:10.1007/978-3-642-02900-4_8

Mancini, M., Costante, G., Valigi, P., & Ciarfuglia, T. A. (2016, October). Fast robust monocular de*pth estimation for obstac*le detection with fully convolutional networks. In 2016 IEEE/RSJ International Conference on Intelligent Robots and Systems (IROS) (pp. 4296-4303). IEEE.

Mane, V., Jadhav, S., & Lal, P. (2020). Image super-resolution for MRI Images us*ing 3D faster super-resolution con*volutional neural network architecture. ITM Web of Conferences, 32. 10.1051/itmconf/20203203044

Martens, J. (2010). Deep learning via Hessian-free optimization. Proc. 27th Int. Conf. In*t. Conf. M*ach. Learn., 735-742.

Mathis, Wang, Holt, Huang, Debnath, & Klunk. (2003). Synthesis and evaluation of 11C-labeled 6-substituted 2-arylbenzothiazoles as amyloid imaging agen*ts. Journal of Medicinal Chemistry, (46), 2740–2754.*

Meles, G. A., Linde, N., & Marelli, S. (2022). Bayesian tomography with prior-knowledge-based parametrization and surrogate modeling. Geophysical Journal International, 231(1), 673–691. doi:10.1093/gji/ggac214

Metz, C. (2019). Turing *Award Won by 3 Pioneers in Ar*tificial Intelligence. New York Times, p. B3.

Meyer, D. E., & Schvaneveldt, R. W. (1971). Facilitation in recognizing pairs of words: Evidence of a dependence between retrieval operations. Journal of Exper*imental Psychology, 90(2)*, 227–234. doi:10.1037/h0031564 PMID:5134329

Michel, G. F. (2021). Handedness development: A model for investigating the development of hemispheric specialization and interhemispheric coordination. Symmetry, *13(6), 992. doi:10.3390ym13060992*

*M*iikkulainen. (2017). Evolving deep neural networks. Academic Press.

Mikhailov, I. F. (2019). Computational Knowledge Representation in Cognitive Science. Epistemology & Philosophy of Scie*nce, 56(3), 138–152. doi:10.5840/ep*s201956355

Miocinovic, S., Somayajula, S., Chitnis, S., & Vitek, J. L. (2013). History, applications, and mechanisms of deep brain stimulation. JAMA Neurology, 70(2), 163–171. doi:10.1001/2013.jamaneurol.45 PMID:23407652

Mohsen, H., El-Dahshan, E. S. A., El-Ho*rbaty, E. S. M.,* & Salem, A. B. M. (2018). Classification using deep learning neural networ*ks for brain tumors. Future Computing and* Informatics Journal, 3(1), 68–71. doi:10.1016/j.fcij.201*7.12.001*

Montagna, F., Rahimi, A., Benatti, S., Rossi, D., & Benini, L. (2018). Acc*elerating brain-inspired high-*dimensional computing on a parallel ultra-low power platform. In Proceedings of the 55th Annual Design Automation Conference 111. ACM. 10.1145/3195970.3196096

*Mow, J. L., Gandhi, A., & Fulford, D. (2020). Imaging the "social br*ain" in schizophrenia: A systematic review of neuroimaging studies of social reward and punishment. Neuroscience and Biobehavioral Reviews, 118, 704–722. doi:10.*1016/j.neubiore*v.*2020.*08.005 PMID:32841653

Mukti, I. Z., & Biswas, D. (2019, December). Transfer learning based *plant diseases detec-tion using ResNet50. In 2019 4th Int*ernational conference on electrical information and communication technology (EICT) (pp. 1-6). IEEE.

Mundt, P. D. (2000). Why We Feel: The Science of Human Emotions (vol. 157). Academic Press.

Nagpal. (2018). Development and validation of a deep lear*ning algorithm for improvi*ng Gleason scoring of prostate cancer. Academic Press.

Najafabadi, M. M., Villanustre, F., Khoshgoftaar, T. M., Seliya, N., Wald, R., & Muharemagic, E. (2015). Deep learning applic*ations and challenges in big data analytics. Journal of Big Data,* 2(1), 1. doi:10.118640537-014-0007-7

Nam, T., & Pardo, T. A. (2011). Conceptualizing smart city with dimensions of technology, people, and institutions. Proc. ACM Int. Digit. *Governme*nt Res. Conf., Digit. Government Innov. Challenging Times. 10.1145/2037556.2037602

Naul, B., Bloom, J. S., *Pérez, F., & van der Walt, S. (2018). A recurrent neural networ*k for classification of unevenly sampled variable stars. Nature Astron., 2(2), 151–155. doi:10.103841550-017-0321-z

Nayak, D. R., Padhy, N., Mallick, P. K., Zymbler, M., & Kumar, S. (2022). Brain Tumor Classification Using Dense Efficient-Net. Axioms, 11(1), 34. doi:10.3390/axioms11010034

Na*ylor, S. (2003). Biomarkers: Cu*rren*t* perspectives and future prospects. Expert Review of Molecular Diagnostics, 3(5), 525–529. doi:10.1586/14737159.3.5.525 PMID:145*10173*

Nazempour, R., Liu, C., Chen, Y., Ma, C., & Sheng, X. (2019). Performance evaluation of an implantable sensor for deep *brain imaging: An analytical investigation. Optical Materials Express, 9(9), 3729–3737. doi:10.1364/OME.9.003*729

Nevo. (2019). ML for flood forecasting at scale. Academic Press.

Ng, *A. Y.,* & Jordan, M. I. (2001). On discriminative vs. generative classifiers: A comparison of logistic regression and naive Bayes. Proc. 14th Int. Conf. Neural Inf. Process. Syst., *841-848.*

Ng. (2019). Machine learning yearning: Technical strategy for ai engineers *in the era of deep learning*. Academic Press.

Noda, K. (2013). Multimodal integration learning of object manipulation behaviors using deep neural networks. Proc. IEEE/RSJ Int. Conf. Intell. Robots Syst., 1728-1733. 10.1109/IROS.2013.6696582

Novaković, J. D., *Veljović, A., Ilić, S. S., Papić, Ž.*, & Milica, T. (2017). Evaluation of classification models in machine learning. Theory and Applications of Mathematics & Computer Science, 7(1), 39–46.

Ogi*ela, L. (2010).* Cognitive informatics in automatic pattern understanding and cognitive information systems. Advances in Cognitive Informatics and Cognitive Computing, 323.

Ong, W. Y., Stohler, C. S., & Herr, D. R. (2019). Role of the prefrontal cortex in pain processing. Molecular Neurobiology, 56(2), 1137–1166. doi:10.100712035-018-1130-9 PMI*D:29876878*

*Optimized Deep Convoluti*onal Neural Networks for Identification of Macular Diseases from Optical Coherence Tomography Images - Scientific Figure on ResearchGate. (n.d.). Available from: https://www.researchga*te.net/figure/Left-ResNet50-architectu re-Blocks-with-dotte*d-line-represents-modules-that-might-be_ fig3_331364877

Padikkapparambil, J., Ncube, C., Singh, K. K., & Singh, A. (2020). Internet of Things technologies for elderly health-car*e applications. In Emergence of pharmaceutical industry growt*h with industrial IoT approach (pp. 217–243). Academic Press. doi:10.1016/B978-0-12-819593-2.00008-X

Park, G. M., & Kim, J. H. (2016, July). Deep adaptive resonance theory for learning biologically inspi*red episodic memory. In 2016 international joint c*onference on neural networks (IJCNN) (pp. 5174-5180). IEEE.

Park, S. A., Lee, A. Y., Park, H. G., & Lee, W. L. (2019). Benefits of gardening activities for cognitive function accordin*g to measurement of brain nerve growth factor levels. Internati*onal Journal of Environmental Research and Public Health, 16(5), 760. doi:10.3390/ijerph16050760 PMID:30832372

Park, T. J., Deng, *S., Manna, S., Islam, A. N., Yu, H., Yuan, Y., ... Ram*anathan, S. (2022). Complex oxides for brain-inspired computing: A review. Advanced Materials, 2203352.

Patel, G. H., Sestieri, *C., & Corbett*a, M. (2019). The evolution of the temporoparietal junction and posterior superior temporal *sulcus. Cortex, 118, 38–50. doi:10.1016/j.cort*ex.2019.01.026 PMID:30808550

Payne, H. E., Jedrzejewski, R. I., & Hook, R. N. (2003). Astronomical Data Analysis Software and Systems XII. Astronomical Data Analysis Software and Syst*ems, 12, 295.*

Peeters, R. R., Kornprobst, P., Nikolova, M., Sunaert, S., Vieville, T., Malandain, G., Deriche, R., Faugeras, O., Ng, M., & Van Hecke, P. (2004). The use of super-resolution techniques to reduce slice thickness in functional MRI. International Journal of Imaging Systems and Technology, 14(3), 131–138. doi:10.1002/ima.20016

Pena, D., Suescun, J., Schiess, M., Ellmore, T. M., & Giancardo, L.Alzheimer's Disease Neuroimaging Initiative. (2022, January 3). Toward a Multimodal Computer-Aided Diagnostic Tool for Alzheimer's Disease Conversion. Frontiers in Neuroscience, 15, 744190. doi:10.3389/fnins.2021.744190 PMID:35046766

Pernet C, (2018). Brain Morphometry: Methods and Clinical Applications. The General Linear Model: Theory and Practicalities.

Phillips, J., Buckwalter, W., Cushman, F., Friedman, O., Martin, A., Turri, J., ... Knobe, J. (2021). Knowledge before belief. Behavioral and Brain Sciences, 44. PMID:32895070

Pini, L., Pievani, M., Bocchetta, M., Altomare, D., Bosco, P., Cavedo, E., Galluzzi, S., Marizzoni, M., & Frisoni, G. B. (2016). Brain atrophy in Alzheimer's Disease and aging. Ageing Research Reviews, 30, 25–48. doi:10.1016/j.arr.2016.01.002 PMID:26827786

Pollack, M. E., Brown, L., Colbry, D., McCarthy, C. E., Orosz, C., Peintner, B., ... Tsamardinos, I. (2003). Autominder: An intelligent cognitive orthotic system for people with memory impairment. Robotics and Autonomous Systems, 44(3-4), 273–282.

Ponce, H., Moya-Albor, E., & Brieva, J. (2018). A novel artificial organic control system for mobile robot navigation in assisted living using vision-and neural-based strategies. Computational Intelligence and Neuroscience.

Popov, A., Miller, A., Miller, B., & Stepanyan, K. (2017, February). Estimation of velocities via optical flow. In 2016 International Conference on Robotics and Machine Vision (Vol. 10253, pp. 6-10). SPIE.

Pouyanfar. (2018). A survey on deep learning: Algorithms techniques and applications. ACM Comput. Survey, 51(5), 92.

Qassim, H., Verma, A., & Feinzimer, D. (2018, January). Compressed residual-VGG16 CNN model for big data places image recognition. In 2018 IEEE 8th annual computing and communication workshop and conference (CCWC) (pp. 169-175). IEEE. 10.1109/CCWC.2018.8301729

Radford, Metz, & Chintala. (2015). Unsupervised representation learning with deep convolutional generative adversarial networks. Academic Press.

Ramezanpour, H., Görner, M., & Thier, P. (2021). Variability of neuronal responses in the posterior superior temporal sulcus predicts choice behavior during social interactions. Journal of Neurophysiology, 126(6), 1925–1933. doi:10.1152/jn.00194.2021 PMID:34705592

Rangel, J. C., Cruz, E., Escalona, F., Bauer, Z., Cazorla, M., García Rodríguez, J., ... Gomez Donoso, F. (2018). Geoffrey: An Automated Schedule System on a Social Robot for the Intellectually Challenged. Academic Press.

Rawat, P., Singh, K. D., Chaouchi, H., & Bonnin, J. M. (2014). Wireless sensor networks: A survey on recent developments and potential synergies. The Journal of Supercomputing, 68(1), 1–48. doi:10.100711227-013-1021-9

Razali, N. M., & Geraghty, J. (2010). Genetic algorithm performance with different selection strategies in solving TSP. Proc. world Congr. Eng., 1-6.

Reinares-Lara, E., Olarte-Pascual, C., & Pelegrín-Borondo, J. (2018). Do you want to be a cyborg? The moderating effect of ethics on neural implant acceptance. Computers in Human Behavior, 85, 43–53. doi:10.1016/j.chb.2018.03.032

Rezende, E., Ruppert, G., Carvalho, T., Ramos, F., & De Geus, P. (2017, December). Ma-licious software classification using transfer learning of resnet-50 deep neural network. In 2017 16th IEEE International Conference on Machine Learning and Applications (ICMLA) (pp. 1011-1014). IEEE.

Robinson, M. D. (2017). New applications of super-resolution in medical imaging. In Super-resolution imaging. CRC Press.

Rosenblatt, F. (1958). The perceptron: A probabilistic model for information storage and organization in the brain. Psychological Review, 65(6), 386–408. doi:10.1037/h0042519 PMID:13602029

Roy, M. K., Aggarwal, G., Bansal, A., & Juneja, D. (2022, January). Open domain Conversational Model using transfer learning. In 2022 12th International Conference on Cloud Computing, Data Science & Engineering (Confluence) (pp. 280-284). IEEE. 10.1109/Confluence52989.2022.9734155

Sable & Gaikwad. (2012). A Novel Approach for Super Resolution in Medical Imaging. International Journal of Emerging Technology and Advanced Engineering, 2(11).

Saez-Pons, J., Syrdal, D. S., & Dautenhahn, K. (2015). What has happened today? Memory visualisation of a robot companion to assist user's memory. Journal of Assistive Technologies.

Sahu, A. K., Padhy, R. K., & Dhir, A. (2020). Envisioning the future of behavioral decision-making: A systematic literature review of behavioral reasoning theory. Australasian Marketing Journal, 28(4), 145–159. doi:10.1016/j.ausmj.2020.05.001

Salakhutdinov, R., & Hinton, G. (2009). Deep Boltzmann machines. Proc. 12th Int. Conf. Artif. Intell. Statist., 448-455.

Salvatore, C., Cerasa, A., Battista, P., Gilardi, M. C., Quattrone, A., & Castiglioni, I. (2015). Magnetic resonance imaging biomarkers for the early diagnosis of Alzheimer's disease: A machine learning approach. Frontiers in Molecular Neuroscience, 9, 270. doi:10.3389/fnins.2015.00307 PMID:26388719

Samma, H., & Suandi, S. A. (2020). Transfer Learning of Pre-Trained CNN Models for Fingerprint Liveness Detection. In Biometric Systems. IntechOpen. doi:10.5772/intechopen.93473

Sampson, J. R. (1976). Adaptation in Natural and Artificial Systems. SIAM, 18, 529-530.

Sanchez, L., Muñoz, L., Galache, J. A., Sotres, P., Santana, J. R., Gutierrez, V., Ramdhany, R., Gluhak, A., Krco, S., Theodoridis, E., & Pfisterer, D. (2014, March). SmartSantander: IoT experimentation over a smart city testbed. Computer Networks, 61, 217–238. doi:10.1016/j. bjp.2013.12.020

Sant'Anna, A. (2018). Episodic memory as a propositional attitude: A critical perspective. Frontiers in Psychology, 9, 1220. doi:10.3389/fpsyg.2018.01220 PMID:30072933

Sarica, S., & Luo, J. (2021). Design knowledge representation with technology semantic network. Proceedings of the Design Society, 1, 1043–1052. doi:10.1017/pds.2021.104

Sastry, Goldberg, & Kendall. (2005). Genetic Algorithms. Academic Press.

Sayyaparaju, S., Amer, S., & Rose, G. S. (2018). A bi-memristor synapse with spike-timing-dependent plasticity for on-chip learning in memristive neuromorphic systems. 19th International Symposium on Quality Electronic Design (ISQED), 69-74. 10.1109/ISQED.2018.8357267

Scataglini, S., & Imbesi, S. (2021). Human-centered design smart clothing for ambient assisted living of elderly users: considerations in the COVID-19 pandemic perspective. In IoT in Healthcare and Ambient Assisted Living (pp. 311–324). Springer. doi:10.1007/978-981-15-9897-5_15

Schuecker, J., Schmidt, M., van Albada, S. J., Diesmann, M., & Helias, M. (2017). Fundamental activity constraints lead to specific interpretations of the connectome. PLoS Computational Biology, 13(2), e1005179. doi:10.1371/journal.pcbi.1005179 PMID:28146554

Schuler, C. J., Burger, H. C., Harmeling, S., & Scholkopf, B. (2013). A machine learning approach for non-blind image deconvolution. Proc. IEEE Conf. Comput. Vis. Pattern Recognit., 1067-1074. 10.1109/CVPR.2013.142

Seetha, J., & Raja, S. S. (2018). Brain tumor classification using convolutional neural networks. Biomedical & Pharmacology Journal, 11(3), 1457–1461. doi:10.13005/bpj/1511

Sengupta, A., Ye, Y., Wang, R., Liu, C., & Roy, K. (2019). Going deeper in spiking neural networks: VGG and residual architectures. Frontiers in Neuroscience, 13, 95.

Shahraray, B., & Brown, M. K. (1988, January). Robust depth estimation from optical flow. In 1988 Second International Conference on Computer Vision (pp. 641-642). IEEE Computer Society.

Shamsi, J., Shokouhi, S. B., & Mohammadi, K. (2018). On the capacity of Columnar Organized Memory (COM). IEEE 61st International Midwest Symposium on Circuits and Systems (MWSCAS), 65-68.

Sharma, S., Sharma, S., &Athaiya, A. (2017). Activation functions in neural networks. Towards Data Science, 6(12), 310-316.]

Sheth, A. (2016, March). Internet of Things to smart IoT through semantic, cognitive, and perceptual computing. IEEE Intelligent Systems, 31(2), 108–112. doi:10.1109/MIS.2016.34

Shon, D., Im, K., Park, J. H., Lim, D. S., Jang, B., & Kim, J. M. (2018). *Emotional stress state detection using genetic algorithm-based feature selection on EEG signals*. International Journal of Environmental Research and Public Health, 15(11), 2461.

Shrestha & Mahmood. *(2016). Improving genetic algorithm with fine-tuned crossover and scaled architecture. J. Math.*, 10.

Shrestha, A., & Mahmood, A. (2019). Enhancing siamese networks training with importance sampling. Proc. 11th Int. Conf. Agents Artif. Intell., 610-615. *10.5220/0007371706100615*

Siebner, H. R., Funke, K., Aberra, A. S., Antal, A., Bestmann, S., Chen, R., Classen, J., Davare, M., Di Lazzaro, V., Fox, P. T., Hallett, M., Karabanov, A. N., Kessel*heim, J., Beck, M. M.*, Koch, G., Liebetanz, D., Meunier, S., Miniussi, C., Paulus, W., ... Ugawa, Y. (2022). Transcranial magnetic stimulation of the brain: What is stimulated? A consensus and critical position *paper. Clinical Neurophysiology, 140, 59–97. doi:10.1016/j.clinph.2022.04.022*

Siew, C. S., Wulff, D. U., Beckage, N. M., Kenett, Y. N., & Meštrović, A. (2019). Cognitive network science: A review of research on cognition th*rough the lens of ne*twork representations, processes, and dynamics. Complexity, 2019, 2019. doi:10.1155/2019/2108423

Silver, D., Huang, A., Maddison, C. J., Guez, A., Sifre, L., van den Driessche, G., S*chrittwieser, J., Antonoglou, I., Panneershelvam, V., Lanctot, M., Dieleman, S., Grewe, D., Nh*am, J., Kalchbrenner, N., Sutskever, I., Lillicrap, T., Leach, M., Kavukcuoglu, K., Graepel, T., & Hassabis, D. (2016). Mastering the game of go with deep neural networks and tree search. Nature, 529(7587), *484–489. doi:10.1038/nature16961* PMID:26819042

Silver. (2016). Mastering the game of go with deep neural networks and tree search. Nature, 529(7587), 484.

Simpson, (2015). Uniform learning in a dee*p neural network via 'oddball' st*ochastic gradient descent. Academic Press.

Sipper, M., & Moore, J. H. (2021). Conservation machine learning: a *case study of random forests. Sci Rep., 11(1),* 3629. doi:10.103841598-021-83247-4 PMID:33574563

Smirniotopoulos, J. G. (1999). The new WHO classification of brain tumors. Neuroimaging Clinics of North America, 9(4), 595–613. PMID:10517936

Smith, S. M., Vidaurre, D., Al*faro-Almagro, F., Nichols, T. E.*, & Miller, K. L. (2019). Estimation of brain age delta from brain imaging. NeuroImage, 200, 528–539. doi:10.1016/j.neuroimage.2019.06.017 PMID:31201988

Soh, P. J., Vandenbosch, G. A., Mercuri, M., & Schreurs, D. M. P. (2015). Wearable wireless health monitoring: Current developments, challenges, and future trends. IEEE Microwave Magazine, 16(4), 55–70. doi:10.1109/MMM.2015.2394021

Song, C., Liu, B., Liu, C., Li, H., & Chen, Y. (2016). Design techniques of eNVM-enabled neuromorphic computing systems. 2016 IEEE 34th International Conference on Comp*uter Design (ICCD), 674*-677. 10.1109/ICCD.2016.7753356

Song, L., Li, Y., & Lu, N. (2022). ProfileSR-GAN: A GAN based Super-Resolution Method for Generating *High-Resolution Load* Profiles. IEEE Transactions on Smart Grid, 13(4), 3278–3289. doi:10.1109/TSG.2022.3158235

Song, M., Zhang, Y., Cui, Y., Yang, Y., & Jiang, T. (2018). *Brain network studies in chronic disorders of consciousness: Advances and perspectives.* Neuroscience Bulletin, *34(4), 592–604. do*i:10.100712264-018-0243-5 PMID:29916113

Srivastava, N., Hinton, G., Krizhevsky, A., Sutskever, I., & Salakhutdinov, R. (2014). Dropout: A simple way to prevent neural networks from overfitting. *Journal of Machine Learning Research, 15, 1929*–1958.

Stucki, R. A., Urwyler, P., Rampa, L., Müri, R., Mosimann, U. P., & Nef, T. (2014). A web-based non-intrusive ambient system to measure and classify activities of daily living. Journal *of Medical Internet Research, 16(7), e3465. do*i:10.2196/jmir.3465 PMID:25048461

Su, K., Li, J., & Fu, H. (2011). Smart city and the applications. Proc. IEEE Int. Conf. Electron., *Commun. Control (ICECC). 10.1109/ICECC.*2011.6066743

Sukanya, C. M., Gokul, R., & Paul, V. (2016). A survey on object recognition methods. International Journal of Science. Engineering and Computer Technology, *6(1), 48.*

Sun, N., & Li, H. (2019). Super resolution reconstruction of images based on interpolation and full convolutional ne*ural network and application in medical fields. IEEE Ac*cess: Practical Innovations, Open Solutions, 7, 186470–186479. doi:10.1109/ACCESS.2019.2960828

Sun, Y., Xu, H., Liu, S., Song, *B., Liu, H., Liu, Q.,* & Li, Q. (2018). Short-term and long-term plasticity mimicked in low-voltage Ag/GeSe/TiN electronic synapse. IEEE Electron Devic*e Letters, 39(4), 492–495. do*i:10.1109/LED.2018.2809784

Szegedy, C., Liu, W., Jia, Y., Sermanet, P., Reed, S., Anguelov, D., ... Rabinovich, A. (2015). Going deeper with convolutions. In Proceedings of the IEEE conference on com-puter vi*sion and pattern recognition (pp. 1-9). IEEE.*

Szegedy, C., Vanhoucke, V., Ioffe, S., Shlens, J., & Wojna, Z. (2016). Rethinking the in-ception architecture for computer vision. In Proceedi*ngs of the I*EEE conference on computer vision and pattern recognition (pp. 2818-2826). IEEE.

Tadić, B., Andjelković, *M., & Melnik, R. (2019, August 19). fu*nctional Geometry of Human connectomes. Scientific Reports, 9(1), 1–2. doi:10.103841598-019-48568-5 PMID:31427676

Tan, A. H., Carpenter, G. A., & Grossberg, S. (2007, June). Intelligence through interaction: Towards a unified theory for learning. In International Symposium on Neural Networks (pp. 1094-1103). Springer.

Tan, M., & Le, Q. (2019, May). Efficientnet: Rethinking model scaling for convolutional neural netwo*rks. In International co*nference on machine learning (pp. 6105-6114). PMLR.

Tang, J., Deng, C., & Huang, G.-B. (2015). Extreme learning machine for multilayer perceptron. IEEE Transactions on Neural Networks and Learning Systems, 27(4), 809–821. doi:10.1109/TNNLS.2015.2424995 PMID:25966483

Taylor, G. W., Fergus, R., LeCun, Y., & Bregler, C. (2010). Convolutional learning of spatio-temporal features in Computer Vision. Springer.

Teh, Y. W., & Hinton, G. E. (2001). Adv. Neural Inf. Process. Syst.: Vol. 908-914. Rate-coded restricted Boltzmann machines for face recognition. Academic Press.

Ten Kate, M., Ingala, S., Schwarz, A. J., Fox, N. C., Chételat, G., van Berckel, B. N. M., Ewers, M., Foley, C., Gispert, J. D., Hill, D., Irizarry, M. C., Lammertsma, A. A., Molinuevo, J. L., Ritchie, C., Scheltens, P., Schmidt, M. E., Visser, P. J., Waldman, A., Wardlaw, J., ... Barkhof, F. (2018). Secondary prevention of Alzheimer's dementia: Neuroimaging contributions. Alzheimer's Research & Therapy, 10(1), 112. doi:10.118613195-018-0438-z PMID:30376881

Theckedath, D., & Sedamkar, R. R. (2020). Detecting affect states using VGG16, ResNet50 and SE-ResNet50 networks. SN Computer Science, 1(2), 1–7. doi:10.100742979-020-0114-9

Thiebaut de Schotten, M., & Beckmann, C. F. (2021). Asymmetry of brain structure and function: 40 years after Sperry's Nobel Prize. Brain Structure & Function, 1–4. PMID:34779912

Thomas, N. W., Beattie, Z., Riley, T., Hofer, S., & Kaye, J. (2021). Home-based assessment of cognition and health measures: The collaborative aging research using technology (CART) initiative and international collaborations. IEEE Instrumentation & Measurement Magazine, 24(6), 68–78. doi:10.1109/MIM.2021.9513638

Tian, D., Zhou, J., & Sheng, Z. (2017, May). An adaptive fusion strategy for distributed information estimation over cooperative multi-agent networks. IEEE Transactions on Information Theory, 63(5), 1. doi:10.1109/TIT.2017.2674678

Tian, D., Zhou, J., Sheng, Z., & Leung, V. (2016, June). Robust energy-efficient Mimo transmission for cognitive vehicular networks. IEEE Transactions on Vehicular Technology, 65(6), 3845–3859. doi:10.1109/TVT.2016.2567062

Toepper, M. (2017). Dissociating Normal Aging from Alzheimer's Disease: A View from Cognitive Neuroscience. Journal of Alzheimer's Disease, 57(2), 331–352. doi:10.3233/JAD-161099 PMID:28269778

Tresp, V., Esteban, C., Yang, Y., Baier, S., & Krompaß, D. (2015). Learning with memory embeddings. arXiv preprint arXiv:1511.07972.

Trébuchon, A., Liégeois-Chauvel, C., Gonzalez-Martinez, J. A., & Alario, F. X. (2020). Contributions of electrophysiology for identifying cortical language systems in patients with epilepsy. Epilepsy & Behavior, 112, 107407. doi:10.1016/j.yebeh.2020.107407 PMID:33181892

Tsai, R. Y. (1989). Multiple frame image restoration and registration. Advances in Computer Vision and Image Processing, 1, 1715–1989.

Vandewalle, P., Süsstrunk, S., & Vetterli, M. (2004). A frequency domain approach to super-resolution imaging from aliased low-resolution images. Technical Journal.

VandeWeerd, C., Yalcin, A., Aden-Buie, G., Wang, Y., Roberts, M., Mahser, N., Fnu, C., & Fabiano, D. (2020). HomeSense: Design of an ambient home health and wellness monitoring platform *for older adults. Health and Technology, 10(5), 1291–1309. do*i:10.100712553-019-00404-6

Vargas, Mosavi, & Ruiz. (2017). Deep learning: A review. Proc. Adv. Intell. Syst. Comput., 1-*11.*

Verburgt, L. M. (2020). The history of knowledge and the future history of ignorance. KNOW: A Journal on the Formation of Knowledge, 4(1), 1-24.

Wang, B., Zhang, X., Xing, S., Sun, C., & Chen, X. (2021). Sparse representation theory for support vector machine kernel function selection and its application in high-speed bearing fault diagnosis. ISA Transactions, 118, 207–218. doi:10.1016/j.isatra.2021.01.060 PMID:33583570

Wang, L., & Alexander, C. A. (2019). Brain science and brain-inspired artificial intelligence: Advances and trends. Journal of Computer Sciences and Applications, 7(1), 56–61.

Wang, M., Li, *H.-X., Chen, X., & Chen, Y. (2016).* Deep learning-based model reduction for distributed parameter systems. IEEE Transactions on Systems, Man, and Cybernetics. Systems, 46(12), 1664–1674. doi:10.1109/*TSMC.2016.2605159*

Wang, P., Kong, R., Kong, X., Liégeois, R., Orban, C., Deco, G., ... Thomas Yeo, B. T. (2019). Inversion of a large-scale circuit model reveals a cortical hierarchy in the dy*namic resting human brain.* Science Advances, 5(1), eaat7854.

Wang, W., Pedretti, G., Milo, V., Carboni, R., Calderoni, A., Ramaswamy, N., ... Ielmini, D. (2018). Learning of spatiotemporal patterns in a spiking neural network with resistive switching synapses. Science Advan*ces, 4(9), eaat4752.*

Wang, W., Subagdja, B., Tan, A. H., & Starzyk, J. A. (2010, July). A self-organizing approach to episodic memory modeling. In The 2010 International Joint Conference on Neural Networks (IJCNN) (pp. 1-8). IEEE.

Wang, Y., *Zhan, G., Cai, Z., Jiao, B., Zhao, Y.,* Li, S., & Luo, A. (2021). Vagus nerve stimulation in brain diseases: Therapeutic applications and biological mechanisms. Neuroscience and Biobehavioral Reviews, 127, 37–53. *doi:10.1016/j.neubiorev.2021.04.018 PMID:*33894241

Wang, Z., Wu, H., Burr, G. W., Hwang, C. S., Wang, K. L., Xia, Q., & Yang, J. J. (2020). Resistive switching materials for information processing. *Nature Reviews. Materials, 5(3), 173*–195.

Wang. (2022). Single Image Super-Resolution Reconstruction Using Deep Residual Networks with Non-decimated Wavelet Edge Learning. ACTA ELECTONICA SINICA.

Wei, F., Yin, C., Zheng, J., Zhan, Z., & Yao, L. (2019). Rise of cyborg micro*robot: Different stor*y *for* different configuration. IET Nanobiotechnology / IET, 13(7), 651–664. doi:10.1049/iet-nbt.2018.5374 PMID:31573533

Werbos. *(1975). Beyond Regression: New t*ools for prediction and analysis in the behavioral sciences. Academic Press.

Whitley, D. (1994). A genetic algorithm tutorial. Statistics and Computing, 4(2), 65–85. doi:10.1007/BF00175354

Wieser, I., Toprak, S., Grenzing, A., Hinz, T., *Auddy, S., Karaoğuz, E. C.,* . . . Wermter, S. (2016, September). A robotic home assistant with memory aid functionality. In Join*t German/Austrian Conference on* Artificial Intelligence (Künstliche Intelligenz) (pp. 102-115). Springer.

Wu, C., Zhang, J., S*elman, B., Savarese, S., & Saxena, A. (2016, May).* Watch-bot: Unsupervised learning for reminding humans of forgotten actions. In 2016 IEEE International Conference on Robotics and Autom*ation (ICRA) (pp. 2479-2486). IEEE.*

*Wu, Y., Zhang, G., Gao, Y., D*eng, X., Gong, K., Liang, X., & Lin, L. (2020). Bidirectional graph reasoning network for panoptic segmentation. In Proceedings of the IEEE/CVF Conference on Computer Vision and Pattern Recognition (pp. 9080-9089). 10.1*109/CVPR42600.2020.00*910

Xia, Q., & Yang, J. J. (2019). Memristive crossbar arrays for brain-inspired computing. Nature Materials, 18(4), 309–323.

Xiong, Z., Sheng, H., Rong, W. G., & Cooper, D. *E. (2012). Intelligent transportation systems f*or smart cities: A progress review. Science China, 55(12), 2908–2914. doi:10.100711432-012-4725-1

Xu, H., Zhai, G., & Yang, X. (2013). *Single image super-resolution with detail enhancement bas*ed *o*n local fractal analysis of gradient. IEEE Transactions on Circuits and Systems for Video Technology, 23(10), 1740–1754. doi:10.1109/TCSVT.2013.2248305

Yang, C.-Y., Ma, C., & Yang, M.-H. (2014). Single-image super-resolution: A benchmark. In Europe*an conference on* computer vision. Springer.

Yang, S., Hao, X., Deng, B., Wei, X., Li, H., & Wang, J. (2018). A survey of brain-inspired artificial intelligence and its engineering. Life Research, 1(1), 23–29. doi:10.53388/life2018-071*1-005*

Yin, D., Chen, X., Zeljic, K., Zhan, Y., Shen, X., Yan, G., & Wang, Z. (2019). A graph representation of functional diversity of brain regions. Brain and Behavior, 9(9). Advance online publication. *doi:10.1002/brb3.1358 PMID:31350830*

Yin, Y., Wang, F., Yang, Y., Tian, M., Gao, L., & Liu, H. (2022). Abnormalities of hemispheric specialization in drug-naïve and drug-receiving self-limited epilepsy with centrotemporal spikes. Epilepsy & Behavior, *136, 108940. doi:10.1016/*j.yebeh.2022.108940 PMID:36228484

You, K., Liu, Y., Wang, J., & Long, M. (2021, July). Logme: Practical assessment of pre-trained models for transfer learning. In International Confere*nce on Machine Learning* (pp. 12133-12143). PMLR.

Yu, D., & Deng, L. (2015). Automatic Speech Recognition: A Deep Learning Approach. Springer. doi:10.1007/978-1-4471-5779-3

Zagzebski, L. (2017). What is knowledge? The Blackwell guide *to epistemology, 92-116.*

Zeng, H. M., Han, H. B., Zhang, Q. F., & Bai, H. (2021). Application of modern neuroimaging technology in the diagnosis and study of Alzheimer's disease. Neural Regeneration Research, 16(1), 73–79. doi:10.4103/1673-5374.286957 PMID:32788450

Zeng, K., Zheng, H., Cai, C., Yang, Y., Zhang, K., & Chen, Z. (2018). Simultaneous single-and multi-contrast super-resolution for brain MRI images based on a convolutional neural network. Computers in Biology and Medicine, 99, 133–*141. doi:10.1016/j.compbiomed.2018.06.010 PMID:29929052*

Zhang, H., Yang, Z., Zhang, L., & Shen, H. (2014). Super-resolution reconstruction for multi-angle remote sensing images considering resolution differences. Rem*ote Sensing, 6(1)*, 637–657. doi:10.3390/rs6010637

Zhang, J., Shao, M., Yu, L., & Li, Y. (2020). Image super-resolution reconstruction based on sparse representation *and deep lear*ning. Signal Processing Image Communication, 87, 115925. doi:10.1016/j.image.2020.115925

Zhang, L., & Wu, X. (2006). An edge-guided image interpolation algorithm via directional filtering *and data fu*sion. IEEE Transactions on Image Processing, 15(8), 2226–2238. doi:10.1109/TIP.2006.877407 PMID:16900678

Zhang, X., Zhuo, Y., Luo, Q., Wu, Z., Midya, R., Wang, Z., ... Yang, J. J. (2020). An artificial spiking afferent nerve based on Mott *memristors for neur*orobotics. Nature Communications, 11(1), 1–9.

Zhang, X. Y., Zhang, X. Z., Lu, F. Y., Zhang, Q., Chen, W., Ma, T., ... Liang, T. B. (2020). Factors associated with failure of enhanced recovery *after surgery program in patients undergoi*ng pancreaticoduodenectomy. Hepatobiliary & Pancreatic *Diseases International, 19(1), 51–57.*

Zhang, Y., Chen, M., Guizani, N., Wu, D., & Leung, V. C. (2017). SOVCAN: Safety-oriented vehicular *controller area network. IEEE Comm*unications Magazine, 55(8), 94–99. doi:10.1109/MCOM.2017.1601185

Zhang, Y., Qiu, M., Tsai, C.-W., Hassan, M. M., & Alamri, A. (2017, March). HealthCPS: Healthcare c*yber-physical system assiste*d *by* cloud and big data. IEEE Systems Journal, 11(1), 88–95. doi:10.1109/JSYST.2015.2460747

Zhang, Z. (2016). Naïve Bayes Classification in R. Annals of Translational Medicine, 4(12), 241. doi:10.21037/atm.2016.03.38 PMID:27429967

Zhang, Z., & Jung, C. (2021). GBDT-MO: Grad*ient-Boosted Decision Trees for Multiple Outputs.* IE*E*E Transactions on Neural Networks and Learning Systems, 32(7), 3156–3167. doi:10.1109/TNNLS.2020.3009776 PMID:32749969

Zheng, W., Liu, X., Ni, X., Yin, L., & Yang, B. (2021). I*mproving visual reaso*ning through semantic representation. IEEE Access: Practical Innovations, Open Solutions, 9, 91476–91486. doi:10.1109/ACCESS.2021.3074937

Zhong, N., Yau, S. S., Ma, J., Shimojo, S., Just, M., Hu, B., Wang, G., Oiwa, K., & Anzai, Y. (2015). Brain informatics-based big data and the wisdom web of things. IEEE Intelligent Systems, 30(5), 2–7. doi:10.1109/MIS.2015.83

Zhou, B., Wu, K., Lv, P., Wang, J., Chen, G., Ji, B., & Liu, S. (2018). A new remote healthcare system based on moving *robot intended for the elderly at* home. Journal of Healthcare Engineering, ●●●, 2018.

Zhou, L. (2016, May). On data-driven delay estimation for media cloud. IEEE Transactions on M*ultimedia, 18(5), 905–915. doi:10.1109/TMM.2016.2537782*

Zh*ou.* (n.d.). QoE-driven delay announcement for cloud mobile media. IEEE Trans. Circuits Syst. Video Technol., 27(1).

Zülch, K. J. (2013). Brain tumors: Their biology and pathology. *Springer-Verlag.*

Özyurt, F., Sert, E., & Avcı, D. (2020). An expert system for brain tumor detection: Fuzzy C-means with super resolution and convolutional neural netw*ork with extreme learning machine. Medical H*ypotheses, 134, 109433. doi:10.1016/j.mehy.2019.109433 PMID:31634769

Fang, L., Monroe, F., Novak, S. W., Kirk, L., Schiavon, C. R., Yu, S. B., Zhang, T., Wu, M., Kast*ner, K., Latif, A. A., Lin, Z., Shaw,* A., Kubota, Y., Mendenhall, J., Zhang, Z., Pekkurnaz, G., Harris, K., Howard, J*., & Manor, U. (2021). Deep learning*-based point-scanning super-resolution imaging. Nature Methods, 1*8(4), 406–416. doi:10.103841592-021-01080-z* PMID:33686300

About the Contributors

Tanupriya Choudhury is a highly accomplished individual with an impressive academic and professional background. He holds a bachelor's degree in CSE from West Bengal University of Technology, Kolkata, India; a master's Degree in CSE from Dr. MGR University, Chennai, India; and a Ph.D. degree, which he received in 2016. In addition to his educational qualifications, Dr. Choudhury has fourteen years of experience teaching and conducting research related to Human computing, Soft computing, Cloud Computing Data Mining, etc., making him an ideal candidate for the Senior Associate Professor position at UPES Dehradun's School CS Cluster of Informatics. Recently Dr. Tanupriya was honored with the Global Outreach Education Award for Excellence best young researcher award 2018 (GOECA). This prestigious award recognizes his contribution towards advancing knowledge within this field through various domestically and internationally conferences, resulting in over 250 published papers since then! Furthermore, he has filed 25 patents to date and received 26 copyrights from MHRD due to the development of his own software programs. His achievements speak volumes about his dedication to furthering technology-related research while inspiring others around him by demonstrating that hard work leads to success! He has been associated with many conferences throughout India as a TPC member, session chair, etc. He is a lifetime member of IETA, a senior member of IEEE, and a member of IET(UK) and other renowned technical societies. He is associated with Corporate and a Technical Adviser of Deetya Soft Pvt. Ltd. Noida, IVRGURU, Mydigital360, etc. He holds the post of Honorary Secretary in IETA (Indian Engineering Teacher's Association-India), He is also holding the Senior Advisor Position in INDO-UK Confederation of Science, Technology and Research Ltd., London, UK, and International Association of Professional and Fellow Engineers-Delaware-USA.

Bhupesh Kumar Dewangan completed Ph.D. in computer science and engineering and working as an Associate Professor in the Department of Computer Science and Engineering, at the OP Jindal University Raigarh, India, Bachelor of Technology from Pandit Ravi Shankar Shukla University (State University), Raipur and Master of Technology from Chhattisgarh Swami Vivekananda Technical University (State Technical University), Bhilai in computer science and engineering. He has more than 40 research publications in various international journals and conferences with SCI/SCOPUS/UGC indexing. He has three Indian patents on Cloud computing and resource scheduling. His research interests are in Autonomic Cloud Computing, Resource Scheduling, Software Engineering, and Testing, Image processing, and Object detection. He is a member of various organizations like ISTE, IAPFE, etc. Currently, he is editor in special issue journals of Inderscience & IGI publication house, and editor/author of two books of Springer & Taylor and Francis publication house.

* * *

Garima Aggarwal is currently working as an Associate Professor in Department of Computer Science and Engineering Amity University, Noida. She received her B. Tech degree in Electronics Engineering from Kurukshetra University, Kurukshetra in 2005. She has completed her M.Tech Degree from Ch. Devi Lal University in Computer Science in 2007. She has completed her PhD from Amity University in Computer Science & Engineering in 2018. Her area of interest Includes Digital Data Security, Steganography, Cryptography, Artificial Intelligence, Machine Learning, and Image Processing. She has authored and coauthored 20+ peer-reviewed research papers in international journals and conferences.

Rishabh Chauhan is currently pursuing his B. Tech degree in Computer Science with a specialization in Data Science from Amity University, Noida.

Omprakash Dewangan has more than 17 years of academic and administrative experience. He holds M.Tech. Degree in Computer Science Engineering. He has published more than 43 research papers in reputed national and international journals including UGC Care and Scopus. He is also guiding M.Tech. Students. His area of research includes Machine Learning, Sentiment Analysis, Digital Image Processing, Data Mining etc. She has 6 patents in his credit. He has also published more than 2 books, 2 books by lambert publication and 5 book chapters by national publications. She has received more than 1 awards for lifetime achievement, outstanding teacher's award and many more.

Sara Karami is a Master graduated from New York Institute of Technology. She is interested to the projects in the field of Artificial Intelligence (AI) and data science.

Vania Karami is a researcher with a special interest in multidisciplinary research projects in Biomedical Engineering, Computer Science, and dementia due to the Alzheimer's disease. She has several publications in the reputed journals. She obtained her BSC and MSC in Biomedical Engineering. She is Ph.D graduate of one health and Life Science in 2020. Following her Ph.D, she started her Postdoctoral research fellow in Montreal Neurological Institute (MNI). She is currently working on integration of behavioral- and neuroimaging-based markers for early detection of Alzheimer's disease.

Madhu Khurana is currently working as Lecturer in Cyber Security in the Department of Cyber & Technical Computing, University of Gloucestershire, United Kingdom. She has earlier worked as a Lecturer- Computer Programming at Northern Regional College, Belfast from 2019-2020. Earlier she worked as an Assistant Professor at Amity University Uttar Pradesh, India from 2009-2018 and 2000-2006. She has worked as Training In charge at NIIT Ltd., India. She received the MSc.in Applied Cyber Security from Queens University Belfast, UK and M.S. (Cyber Laws and Cyber Security) degree from National Law University, Jodhpur, India and MCA from Indira Gandhi National Open University, Delhi, India. She is pursuing PhD in Cybersecurity from University of Gloucestershire, UK. Her research interests include Malware analysis, Malware Image visualisation, machine learning algorithms, IoTs.

Rita Komalasari is a lecturer at YARSI University. Her current work is focused on Ambient Assisted Living (AAL) systems to help older people.

Hussain Mahdi is a lecturer at Computer and Software, College of Engineering, University of Diyala, Iraq. He has a great background of Electrical & Electronics with an experience of nearly two decades. He received the PhD from university of Kebangsaan Malaysia and Master of Science from University of Technology, Bagdad, Iraq. He is IEEE Region 10 Young Professional Committee South-East Asia coordinator (2017-2019), IEEE Region 10 Humanitarian activities committee (2017-2021), IEEE PES Young Professional Committee academic lead (2017-2021), IEEE IAS Chapters Area Chair, R10 Southeast Asia, Australia and Pacific (2018-2019), and IEEE Region 10 PES students Chapters Chair (2019-2020), IEEE PES Day 2019 Global Chair, IEEE HAC Event committee member (2019-2020), IEEE PES Chapter Students Activities committee Awards and recognition Chair (2021-2022), and IEEE PES HAC Committee (2021-2022). During serving under IEEE he won the Student Leadership Award 2014 & 2015 from UKM, IEEE Malaysia student leadership award 2015, Best Social Activity Award 2015, IEEE Malaysia Section Outstanding Student Volunteer Award 2015, 2016 Darrel Chong Award winner Silver category for project entitled Asian School on Renewable Energy, and winner Bronze category for project entitled Flood Relief Missions, IEEE MGA Young Professional Achievement Award 2017, and 2018 Young Professionals Hall of fame Award for IEEE PES Young Professionals committee.

Princy Mishra is working as an Assistant Professor in OP Jindal University, India.

Giulio Nittari received his degree in Chemistry and Pharmaceutical Technologies at the Sapienza University in Rome. From 2015 to 2018 he obtained a PhD in Tele-medicine and Tele-pharmacy at the Centre of Tele-medicine and Tele-pharmacy at the University of Camerino. Since 2018 he has been working on a Post-Doctoral research at the University of Camerino on the development of a project to identify and define the operative protocols of tele-medicine and tele-pharmacy in remote areas. From 2013 to 2015 he was pharmaceutical consultant at the "Botero" Specialized Clinic in Rome. His work consisted in the preparation of e-prescriptions, the publication of scientific brochures for pharmaceutical companies, tele-consultation and monitorisation of pharmacological therapies of a selected group of patients using electronic devices of tele-consultation. Since 2015 he is a pharmaceutical consultant at the head of the "Centro Internazionale Radio Medico", (CIRM) Foundation, of great importance in Italian tele-medicine history since 1935, offering no-profit medical assistance to ships and aeroplanes with no doctors on board. Since 2018 is co-founder of "Telepharmatec s.r.l", innovative University of Camerino spin-off. Since 2019 is co-founder of the European University Academy of Aesthetic Medicine (EURICAM), spin-off of the University of Camerino. EURICAM originates from the University's long experience in organizing successful internationally acclaimed Level 2 Masters in Aesthetic Medicine and Therapy. EURICAM is an innovative and highly scientific organisation focused on promoting high quality standards among professionals operating in the field of aesthetic medicine and research, a strong reference for both doctors and patients. Since January 2021, is professor in "Health Technology and Management" and "Health Protection Through Tele-medicine" in the training course of "Managerial in Health Law and Management of HealthCare Organizations Research of Osimo and the Univerity of Camerino". From 2021 to 2022 is to be Guest Editor for the special issue on "Telemedicine in the Era of CO-VID-19" for the "Journal of Environmental Research and Public Health", (IJERPH) ISSN 1660-4601 IF. 3.40. Dr Nittari's scientific activity is based on the following: - UV-Vis spectroscopy, Fluorimetry, Calorimetry - Production Techniques of recombinant proteins in prokaryotic cells - Extraction and Purification techniques of proteins, DNA and RNA - Semi quantitative and quantitative PCR - SDS-PAGE; Western blotting - Gel filtration chromatography - Cell Culture Technique - Flow Cytometry - Microcalorimetry. Among his literary production: Scopo: HI: 7 Cit.

N.: 279 (in the last 5 years). Google Scholar: All Citation Indexes: 431, Since 2016: 430, Total H Index: 8, since 2016: 8; i-10-index total: 7, from 2016: 7. Other themes treated as Post-Doctoral Researcher is over-weight and obesity epidemiology, a global 21st century emergency and challenge in public health. These experiences have been collected into the chapter, "Epidemiology of Obesity in Children and Adolescents", published in the volume "Teamwork in Healthcare", published by Intech Open, London. As praiseworthy consultant in the field of pharmacy and pharmaceuticals at the presidency of C.I.R.M., Dr Nittari has dealt with maritime tele-medicine and tele-pharmacy, a field which has spent a great amount of energy in research focusing on new frontiers. For his scientific commitment, he is member of the National Register of Scientific Research (art. 64, comma 1, DPR 11.07.1980, n.382). His work has been used to improve the quality of assistance that C.I.R.M. offers its users. Dr Nittari's recent scientific research involves the application of I.C.T. methodologies and machine learning to the field of tele-medicine and tele-pharmacy to improve standards of medical assistance towards remote patients. This approach, also oriented to the study of the Covid-19 pandemic, has produced six articles published in peer-reviewed international magazines in 2020.

Rashmi Sharma, Ph.D. (Computer Science), M. Tech (CSE), MCA, Sun certified java 2 programmers (SCJP2), is working as an Assistant Professor in the Department of Information Technology of Ajay Kumar Garg Engineering College, Ghaziabad. Research and interest area are but are not limited to Machine Learning, Sensor Networks, the Internet of Things (IoT), Soft Computing, Artificial Intelligence, Machine/Computer Vision, Data sciences, and mining. She has published 3 patents and approx. 35 papers in Scopus indexed international journals, international conferences, etc.

Shiddarth Srivastava is a fourth-year student at AKGEC Ghaziabad majoring in Bachelor of Technology in Computer Science and Information Technology. He has published two research papers and has filed two patents. One of his patents is related to the development of a system and method for preventing reckless driving. The model can detect dangerous vehicles and excessive speeding and can notify drivers to take necessary actions. It also enables emergency vehicles to exit traffic if needed and can identify accidents, notify the nearest tollbooth, and fine vehicles that overspeed after warnings. This patent is a unique and authentic model that has been approved by the Indian Patent Office. The second patent that Shiddarth has filed is related to the development of a system to avoid the black marketing of drugs. Unfortunately, there is a significant problem with the black marketing of drugs, particularly during the ongoing COVID-19 pandemic. Shiddarth's patent aims to prevent the black marketing of drugs by developing a system that can track the distribution of drugs, ensuring they reach their intended destinations. In addition to filing patents, Shiddarth has also published two research papers. One of his research papers examined different cybersecurity algorithms, which he presented at ICEBEC-2022. The other research paper that he worked on is related to Blockchain in Healthcare Data Safety and Privacy, which is focused mainly on Indian healthcare data and systems. The study aims to develop a data monitoring and verification design that can lead to faster insurance settlements, less corruption, and better decision-making. Overall, Shiddarth's research and patent work demonstrate his commitment to solving critical societal problems and developing innovative solutions using cutting-edge technologies like blockchain and machine learning.

Index

A

Alzheimer's Disease 67-68, 79-83
Ambient Assisted Living (AAL) 6, 84-85, 93-94, 99
Analytics 43, 104, 111, 134, 139, 141, 143, 145, 149-150, 152, 154
Applications 1-2, 6, 11, 18, 26, 28, 37, 42-43, 47-48, 50-51, 53, 56-57, 62-63, 65, 77, 79, 81-82, 89, 91, 95, 100-101, 103, 109-110, 130, 136, 138-140, 146-147, 149, 152-155, 157-159, 163, 169, 179
Artificial Intelligence 1-2, 14-19, 21-29, 40, 42-43, 67, 81, 87, 91, 96, 100, 102, 116, 135, 143-145, 148, 179

B

Big Data 41, 43, 103, 111, 115, 134, 139-143, 152-154, 156, 178-179
Brain Association Graph 100, 105
Brain Mapping 133
Brain MRI 46, 57, 62, 64, 66, 77-78, 158, 161
Brain Tumor Classification 157, 159-161, 170, 178-180
Brain-Computer Interface 4-5, 100, 109
Brain-Inspired AI 100
Brain-Inspired Artificial Intelligence 100, 102
Brain-Inspired Computing 1-2, 13-14, 100, 102-103, 108, 111-112
Brain-Inspired Robot 102
Brainnetome 100, 105, 111

C

Challenges 1-2, 25, 43, 46, 48, 60, 68, 93, 95-96, 98, 140, 148, 153, 178
Cognitive Computing 1-2, 101, 103, 139-143, 145-150, 152, 154-155
Connectome 100, 105-106, 113-114
Convolutional Neural Networks (CNNs) 20, 27

D

Data Handling 22
Deep Learning 9, 16-17, 20, 23, 25, 27-30, 33, 35, 39-46, 48, 59-60, 66, 69, 78-81, 103, 135-136, 157-159, 161, 168, 172, 177-179
Dementia 67-68, 70, 80-83, 88-89, 94

E

Early Detection 67, 69, 71, 75, 77-78
Efficientnet 165, 180
Electroencephalography (EEG) 8, 27, 106

F

Functional MRI 18, 23, 27, 57, 65

G

Graph Theory 105

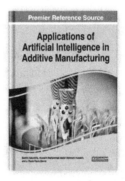
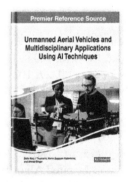

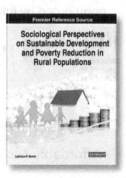

Printed in the United States
by Baker & Taylor Publisher Services